TABOO:
SACRED, DON'T TOUCH

An Autobiographical Journey Spanning Six Thousand Years

Kay Taylor Parker

Published by
Kay Taylor Parker
4872 Topanga Canyon Blvd., Suite 126.
Woodland Hills, CA 91040

Copyright 2000 by Kay Taylor Parker

Dedicated to -
The more than seven million "Star Beings" on Earth today
whose soul mission is to participate in Earth Ascension –
the great dimensional shift.

I feel you, I hear you and I join with you
in holding a love of all ages
for our Planet and its Peoples.

Cover photo: *Alisha Tamburri*
Back cover photo: *Steve Zambrano*
Graphics: *Melissa Reischman*

Copyright 2001 by Kay Taylor Parker

All rights reserved. This book may not be reproduced in whole or in part, without written permission from the publisher, except by a reviewer who may quote brief passages in a review, nor may any part of this book be reproduced, stored in a retreival syatem, or transmitted in any form or by any eans electronic, mechanical, photocopying, recording, or other, without permission from the author.
First printing, March 2001, Second printing June 2016

ISBN 13 - 9780971368408

Contents

Foreword: The Soul's Journey 1

Chapter One: Chosen 5

Chapter Two: Echoes of Atlantis 21

Chapter Three: Mother Superior, Mother Bearer 31

My Journey To Self Discovery

Chapter Four: America 47

Chapter Five: Why Porno? 67

Chapter Six: The First Time - On Film! 93

Chapter Seven: Orgasm 113

Chapter Eight: The Princess's Tears 133

Chapter Nine: Merlin 155

Chapter Ten: The Gay Italian Lifetime 175

Manifesting My Authentic Self

Chapter Eleven: New Beginnings 193

Chapter Twelve: Channeling 213

Chapter Thirteen: Knodessi's Story: The Codes 253

Chapter Fourteen: Full Circle 275

Foreword: The Soul's Journey...

Whether a person is a believer in past lives or not, it cannot be denied that each soul has a journey of growing and evolving. Each must endure the tragedies, the dramas, pain and separation…eventually arriving on the other side of those experiences, to hopefully appreciate and manifest the wisdom in what they have learned and ultimately to move into gratitude, peace and bliss.

As humans living a third dimensional existence, our brains are unfortunately—or fortunately — not sophisticated enough to remember all of the lifetimes, all of the journeys, wherever they were, and in whatever body they took place. There is however, a mysterious record of all this data in our DNA which, if necessary and with guidance by a qualified practitioner, may be carefully accessed to provide us clarity and understanding and to assist in our healing process.

More people than ever are remembering and attuning to those hidden truths within the unconscious and super conscious minds; awakening to their true identities as souls and realizing that they have a specific and profound mission. And the world at large mirrors these changes in one way or another, revealing those areas of our collective consciousness still in resistance to the Light and needing to shift out of darkness—aggression, violence, greed and avarice into compassion, grace and love.

I wrote this book initially at the urging of others who knew of my career in the adult film genre during its "Golden Age," during the 1970's and 1980's, and who also knew of my spiritual approach to integrating my experiences. And while I understood that there was a purpose to my adventures, I couldn't put the pieces together at the time. What was clear to me was that it had to do with becoming free and stepping into my full power as a woman, of knowing who I was and relinquishing who I was not. One might say that it was a strange avenue to take to acquire this self-knowing—and many have said that, but therein is the difference between a left brain and a right brain response. The right brain, unimpeded by the logic and conditioning of the left hemisphere, recognizes a bigger picture—one of the soul's journey through lifetimes and of its eternality and divinity.

So why did I take such a dramatic and controversial path? The answer requires introducing the concept of Karma–the law of balancing experiences and actions, in this life and in past incarnations. So, what actions in my past could possibly have motivated me to abandon all reasoning and logic at the moment of decision-making of whether to be or not to be a porno actress and perform sex on screen? For years, in my personal dark moments—my dark nights of the soul—while struggling to move beyond my conditioning and fear, I have addressed an inner persona I sometimes call my Mother Superior. This aspect of my ego self is, to a large degree, a "bleed-through" from a pivotal past life where I, in fact, reached mother superior status. I played the part well; I was a strict-disciplinarian and there was hell to pay if my novices didn't perform to my standards. Despite whatever vows of love and humility I had taken, I was fire and brimstone draped in a habit. I am sure that I thought I was serving God by performing this way, but it is clear that I had a lot to learn in terms of universal, unconditional love-ing.

How better to balance my ledger then, than to go to the other extreme, so to speak: to strip down naked and perform in a profoundly overtly sexual manner, for the whole world to see! I often speculate how I, in my nun's habit, would respond to the me in present times, who bared all for the camera.

Could I not have balanced out my spiritual ledger in a less controversial way, one might ask? Probably, but we live in a time of great flux and change, of the great shift from the Piscean to the Aquarian paradigm of which prophets, old and new, have spoken. The human race must change and grow –we must realize who we really are, return to our hearts and restore harmony to our planet. Time is of the essence.

So, I believe that my soul chose a way to be visible and effective, and since I am recognized by the men across the world, I chose a way to impact collective global male consciousness.

Through my perusals of dozens of my lifetimes and, with a specific focus on one in particular, I arrived at the unmistakable fact of my Soul Mission being to assist in the evolution of human consciousness. My work is to assist others to wake up to a greater realization of who they are and why they are here. And from the point of view of my most significant lifetime, six thousand years ago in Egypt, where I served as a high priestess named Knodessi, where I actually foresaw the profound planetary changes occurring in modern times, my soul calls out,

"This is an important story I must tell. It is for my great love of humanity that I must tell it. Please do not turn from me, there is much to be done and we are all needed."

Chapter One: Chosen

There was a voice I heard now and again as a child that whispered to me,
"You are one of the chosen."
I had no idea whose voice it was or from whence it came. It was a total mystery.

Growing up was a struggle for me, as it was for so many of my generation, in particular those I have come to know as "star children" or "star beings," These are individuals who have lived before on another world prior to embarking upon their wheel of incarnation on Earth, and who have chosen to play a role in planetary evolution, and are often called old souls.

My early childhood memories of post-World War II England are of frustration and a deep sense of not belonging. I felt like a stranger in the sad gray world in which I found myself, trapped somewhere between space and time, in fact I had a closer relationship to the world of non-matter than the physical reality. Perhaps this was due for the most part, to the fact that I was frequently sick. My "British lungs," as an American doctor called them many years later, labored with colds, infection and bouts with asthma. (The number of "star children" I have met or have heard of who also suffered with asthma is uncanny, but the fact seems logical to me since, on a consciousness level, the lungs harbor grief.) The hours ticked by as I painfully and desperately held on to life, the sound of my own little lungs wheezing and fighting for each breath was deafening. Lying down constricted my breathing even more and so, propped up in my chair, infirm and helpless I prayed to God in my young innocent way for freedom and for the asthma attacks to end.

Our doctor prescribed little yellow pills for my condition which I hated because they made me feel strange, light-headed and nauseous. My dear Mum, at a loss as to the appropriate course of action, would insist that I take them anyway. Inevitably they made me vomit, after which typically I would fall asleep out of sheer exhaustion. Later on I was prescribed one of the first ever asthmatic inhalers, a contraption consisting of a glass chamber and a black rubber bulb. It reminded me too much of the scary dentist's gas mask and I refused to use it. But perhaps this was for the best since I learned not to be dependant on the drugs it administered.

Even then, in moments when I was gasping for air, the voice was there assuring me,

"You are one of the chosen."

Curiously, as I was growing up, along with the voice was a knowing, a deep sense that somehow I was different, yet deeply immersed in unworthiness, I could not integrate such feelings. Besides, one wasn't supposed to feel they were special. Such indulgences went against the grain of the prideful British conditioning, which already held me captive.

Adding to my feelings of alienation and displacement I felt confused about the place I called "home." It didn't feel like home to me. I sensed even then that I was connected to something far greater than what my little mind could fathom. So had God, in fact, made a terrible mistake and set me down where I didn't belong, I used to wonder? In moments of stillness in those early years, as my young consciousness came awake, an awesome sense of a greater reality, sometimes accompanied by an image of a vast expanse of barren terrain, rose up inside me. When I closed my eyes, the panorama I saw seemed identical to footage we have since witnessed from Mars, smooth and lifeless, but in my next breath the surface became distorted, pocked, dark and threatening as if a huge explosion had taken place. Occasionally as an adult I have experienced the same unnerving vision and sensation. Was I in fact tuning into a far distant memory of another lifetime or existence on another world, or was it a premonition of some future event? It seemed far too real, too specific an image to be the random ramblings of a child's subconscious mind. I've wondered ever since what significance it holds to my present reality. Perhaps the answer is close at hand.

I joined the thousands of kids of my generation who rushed to Saturday morning children's matinees at our local theater where we were introduced to "Flash Gordon" movies. We ooed and aahed at the dashing hero's daring exploits and we booed and hissed at the bad guys, the scary aliens. And our imagination ran wild. Yet on one of those Saturday mornings (I was around eleven years old,) as the handsome space traveler battled strange-looking space beings, an all-consuming energy came over me propelling my spirit out of my body, lifting me high above everyone else in the theater. I was held suspended for a few moments and then returned to my body and into my seat. This was the earliest out-of-body experience I can recall, which I remained too scared to ever mention until well over 30 years later when OBEs were generally accepted as common place among New-Agers. So, even that early on, I had a sense of multi-dimensional reality, something that had to do with the stars, far beyond what I could physically see and touch.

How can we deny the existence of a greater power? Are we really willing to turn a blind eye to the many synchronicities that happen in our lives day in and day out--those wonderful "coinky-dinks" as I call them: events that demonstrate a higher order or wisdom to the course of our lives?

As I've recapped my own life, I have seen distinct aspects of the blueprint of my life, like a treasure map if you will, complete with signs, people, events and circumstances all aligning to bring me to this current point of my journey. It is dramatically clear that even the "bad stuff," the painful memories of relationships and experiences which were challenging and bleak at the time, were absolutely perfect and timely as part of the bigger picture.

I have heard that Astronaut Edgar Mitchell, while circling Earth in the Apollo space capsule, caught a glimpse of that higher reality from his unique point of view. He observed planets and constellations all hurtling through space at unbelievable speeds and yet there seemed to be perfect order. As he looked at that extraordinary expanse from another angle, there was our little blue planet, about the size of a quarter from his vantage point; Earth, with its seven billion plus incarnated souls, their collective missions, challenges and baggage—or Karmic Density—as I like to call it; the DNA encoding anchoring a person in their third dimensional existence. What an unbelievable and revelatory experience that must have been for Mitchell and others who have witnessed Earth from such a lofty place. How could anyone not be changed forever by such an experience?!

What is mind boggling for me is the idea of all that energy—the combined negative emotional frequency of Earth's inhabitants, of what could be accomplished if that energy were transformed. Wow! But that is the task at hand—to balance collective consciousness so that Mother Earth may make her transition gracefully through what many elders are calling Ascension, the shift from third to fourth dimensional reality and beyond which was signified by the end of the Mayan Calendar and its December 2012 timeline.

Undeniably there are significant events in all of our lives that prove to be turning points, whether we're consciously aware or spiritually motivated or not. A person will enter our reality and suddenly our path is redirected. Is this divine intervention? What if we had stayed where we were or taken a different path? Would we still have aligned with the experiences and persons we needed to fulfill our "cosmic contracts" or karma? I believe that we each have an invisible "cosmic team" of guides and higher selves gently nudging us towards making pivotal decisions. But Earth is the free-will zone, so in fact, it is our given right to choose as we see fit. Does our destiny become fulfilled, regardless of what choices we make? And what if we do opt to go against the grain of what our soul needs for its growth?

The questions continued ad infinitum although, as I have matured in my own spiritual awareness, answers to many of these quandaries have been answered.

For me personally, it was the time when I decided to choose back to Spirit, to acknowledge my own multi-dimensionality and the fact that I am a co-creator in my life, that my human experience became so much richer and more deeply purposeful. Choosing back consciously and thereby accepting responsibility for every aspect of our life's experiences is one of the most freeing and empowering steps a person can take. To choose to recognize the supreme intelligence, the thread running through all of our experiences is to live consciously. I couldn't live my life any other way.

As I've deepened my own levels of accountability to all things, persons and events around me, my own life experiences have taken on substance and dimension beyond what I'd ever imagined to be possible. By asking myself why I created a so-called negative or challenging experience, and by recognizing the gift in each situation, I may expedite my healing and resolve my past. And, as I do that I may evolve out of the traps of limiting behavior, patterns and conditioning. To recognize the *higher purpose* of the intricacies of my life's path, takes me to a deeply fulfilling place where I know that I am actively co-creating with God.

In the mid 1970's, a dear friend who lived and studied with a spiritual group in Mount Shasta in Northern California for several years gave me a manuscript. It was written by Willard Wannall who was stationed in the military in Hawaii in 1955 and who was assigned by his superiors to produce a report on UFO sightings. There had been a preponderance of strange activity in the night skies over the Hawaiian Islands around that time and countless witnessing of objects other than regular airplanes. Willard's research led him to a group of people who had been observing flying saucers for years and through their influence and friendship a whole new level of reality opened up to him.

But Willard's life changed dramatically when he was introduced to his personal extraterrestrial guide who began to teach him about the journey through "the seven veils of consciousness." Then, abruptly, Willard's research was canceled, and his material was confiscated by the military authorities. Too deeply immersed into his experiences to quit, he committed himself to the local military hospital for psychiatric evaluation and there, right under the noses of the hospital personnel, he continued his studies with his extra-terrestrial guide, learned the art of teleportation and began his inter-dimensional space-ship travels.

I admit that at the time, although I was not consciously ready for all the information contained in the manuscript, receiving it was a turning point for me. Obviously, on an unconscious level I had called for a trigger to unlock a door within my unconscious mind to propel me forward in my quest for deeper understanding and soul connection. The way I see it, my friend's high self and my own were collaborators and chose the book as the means by which to accomplish the deed. Perhaps there was a kind of "spiritual promise" from a past life that Ted, my friend, would facilitate me in this way.

My girlfriend Linda and I had taken a weekend trip to Stewart Mineral Springs near magical Mt. Shasta in Northern California. It was once a place where Native Americans returned time and again to rest and renew their energies and has remained an idyllic spa of rejuvenation and healing. During the weekend, I met with Ted for lunch in the little town of Shasta. As we were leaving the cafe, he told me that there was something he wanted to give me and requested that we stop by the residence where his group lived and worked. Linda agreed to make the detour on our way back home to Mill Valley, however the following day we were late getting underway for our return drive, and I could sense my friend's growing reluctance to get going. Never the less, I insisted. My intuition told me this was important and that the extra time it would take for the detour was insignificant.

We found the location easily and announced at the gate that we were there for Ted. Minutes later, my friend appeared and without any explanation or introduction handed me the simply bound manuscript called "Wheels within Wheels." As I took the book into my hands I felt a jolt of energy, a deep connection to the message being delivered to me. I began to cry spontaneously, although I had no idea why. These were not normal tears such as those triggered by emotional reaction, rather they were the kind I experience as a result of a deep soul connection (the difference being the size of the tears, which indicates to me a far more profound bio-chemical reaction has occurred).

I was unable to speak as I hugged Ted good-bye. And, as we drove away Linda apologized for doubting my need to make the stop. She sensed that something beyond what we could see and understand in that moment had occurred for which she automatically felt reverence. Although we had never discussed it, clearly the thread that drew us together as friends in the first place was a spiritual connection and, as with so many friends, we came into each other's lives to facilitate part of our life's journey. By being each other's mirror for a while we grew and learned. Then, having bridged the way for other members of our spiritual family to arrive, we went in separate directions. Maybe our paths would meet again, perhaps not.

Books were to play a major role as spiritual turning points for me. Again my friend Ted was an agent of inspiration when, in the late 1970s, he suggested that I read Paramahansa Yogananda's "Autobiography of a Yogi." A remarkable book that has been translated into many languages has moved and inspired millions of people the World over. For me personally, as is often the case, it is less about the words and stories written on the page but more to do with the frequency contained therein. Without doubt, Master Yogananda's own journey inspired me to a deeper relationship with my own soul.

One only has to visit any of the Self-Realization Centers established by Yogananda in Southern California to understand what I am talking about. Each of the centers, but specifically the unique Lake Shrine at the end of Sunset Boulevard in Pacific Palisades, mere blocks from the Pacific Ocean, are beautiful sanctuaries which embrace all religions and provide a glorious respite from the frantic pace of the outside world. There seem to be invisible codes within the energies of such books as "Autobiography of a Yogi" that trigger soul awakening. I certainly believe that, in some rare cases, it's not even necessary to actually read a literary work of such spiritual potency. Just to have a book of such significance in one's possession can bring about a degree of self-realization. The soul knows what it senses!

Most significantly, in the early 1980s, while he was on a trip to Los Angeles, where I had relocated, my friend introduced me to yet another amazing publication, "Initiation." The author, Elisabeth Haich, a beloved yoga and spiritual teacher in Zurich, wrote the book at the urging of her students. Haich describes feelings she had even as a child, about her awareness of a greater reality and a higher truth. In the early chapters, she writes that even though she experienced her parents as basically very loving individuals, there were times when she had questions about her existence which they could not answer to her satisfaction. She interpreted this as a lack of true loving and, at a very young age, she felt driven to run away from home. She composed a letter to her parents telling them of her plan to run away, insisting that she wanted to know where and who her "real" parents were. Her spiritual cognizance of a heavenly parent was amazingly intact for someone so young, as she reckoned that real parents would not do and say some of the things hers did. I deeply connected to her sentiments regarding her Earth home and her Mother and Father. Many of the feelings she felt as a child were parallel to my own feelings of life growing up in England.

"Initiation" proved to be another major turning point for me, because Elisabeth's life story in the 20th century is related in juxtaposition to her amazing and profoundly intricate recall of a previous lifetime as a young priestess in ancient Egypt. Apparently, her yoga students finally convinced her to write the book since they had often been privy to her stories of her clear and detailed memories about the lifetime, and of the profound wisdom she imparted from that ancient civilization. She weaves the two lifetimes together explaining events and identifying individuals who were with her then and in modern times, thus presenting an inspiring overview of her personal destiny.

After I read the book I suddenly realized that I was not alone. At that time, I had no idea that my own ancient life experiences held equal significance to me, particularly those in Egypt centuries before the time of Christ and probably not too distant from the timing of Elisabeth's pivotal lifetime. Clearly though, as I later discovered, one lifetime in particular also held major keys for me, in relationship to my current destiny.

It seems to hold true that when we discover that others have similar experiences to ours, it becomes easier to accept our own challenges, to rise to the task of healing and learning the lessons that are present. Through others' inspiration we find the courage to remain on our path. Perhaps it is because we realize that we are involved in a collective process and therefore we *are* not alone. Never the less, the true spiritual journey inevitably remains a lonely one, for each of us must endure our own unique experiences. No man is an island, yet it is our unworthiness of being supported or loved that anchors us in the "lone ranger" syndrome within our life struggles. I've heard it said often that not all those who wanted to be here now at this amazing time of change, were chosen. This is a profound truth to remember at times when life is challenging and hope seems lost.

Since the 1970's, a timeline when many Indigo children began to incarnate, we have witnessed a profound and exponential growth in collective consciousness and spiritual awakening. Self-awareness and the human potential movement has long gone mainstream, providing larger numbers of people access to information that can help them not only to heal and to evolve, but to understand the true purpose of their lives. The support of which so many have dreamed is becoming increasingly accessible.

As I became firmly ensconced in my work as a counselor and spiritual mentor, it became clearer and clearer to me that the voice I heard as a child proclaiming me to be special, whether it was my own Soul, High Self, guide, or God Him/Herself talking to me, it was reminding me that what made me special was that *I* had chosen. Ultimately *what* I had chosen, and the reason *why* I had chosen to be here now, was to play my part in the quantum leap in consciousness transpiring upon our little Planet. How I would play my role would be one and the same as my personal unique journey of self-discovery, one that would take me down some very interesting roads, each with its definitive higher purpose.

To try to be normal or live a normal life proved to be futile for me, as I believe it may be for many Star Children. Because we are here as way-showers, much of what we have to share--our gifts and talents-- involves setting a precedent, and constructing the foundation for the new paradigm; the Aquarian model for living in our culture.

For each person, this new paradigm would require the deepest level of responsibility with the creative process, absolute trust in the perfection of all things and unconditional loving of self and others. In doing this, our priorities automatically change and we break away from our materialistic greed and fear driven realities, and begin to experience a broader and more spiritually based reality, one of abundance and harmony for all.

To exemplify this new way of being and living, first and foremost, I had to feel safe--not to mention worthy and deserving, of moving into total expression of my authentic self—of being all that I am. The significant lifetimes where I had been disgraced or even killed for speaking my truth and asserting my power had been surfacing from my cellular memory, illuminating areas within my consciousness that had blocked or sabotaged me in the past.

But there was more, much more to this process, pivotal in establishing a totally cohesive relationship to the Divine. I had to search for and heal anything from my past that would have given me cause to separate from my high power. To accomplish this I was guided to take a long and fascinating journey, backtracking through my Soul's path multi-dimensionally to search for the highest truth about my human existence.

Often, just when I thought I had surely exhausted all the information I needed to further bridge the gap, an inner wisdom would urge me to go deeper, my High Self would once again crank open the vaults to the library of my past life history and more would be revealed.

In August 1987, at the time of the "Harmonic Convergence," so named by the very brilliant Jose Arguelles, famous for decoding the Mayan calendar in his book "The Mayan Factor," the New Age took on new deeper meaning. Many thousands of people simultaneously gathered at special places all around the World, responding to and honoring similar messages recorded in their own mythology and folklore. A resonant, collective agreement emerged that the event heralded a turning of the evolutionary tides, that a grand celestial and cosmic event was occurring, and it was a time for celebration.

According to Mayan mythology this was the time when the tomb of Quetzalcoatl, the horned serpent, would burst open spilling forth 144,000 seeds which would spread out into the World heralding the new paradigm and a new spiritual consciousness. Dr. Arguelles, in a book called "Surfers of the Zuvuya," would further speculate on the origin of the magical Maya, their abilities, and whether they were in fact less calendar makers, rather extra-terrestrial "synchronic engineers."

As my own inner movement took me through experiences both exhilarating and scary at the same time, I began to finally understand the meaning of those words I had so often heard in my head growing up. It was becoming clear as to what chosen meant, as I simultaneously recognized more and more of my spiritual family of chosen ones. The New tribes were gathering, drawn together by a magical invisible magnetic force and recognition of the bigger picture of which we were all part.

Some months after the "Harmonic Convergence," I was at a book signing of the "Mayan Factor" in Santa Monica. A line of people stood patiently waiting for Arguelles to sign copies of his book they had just purchased. The friend I had accompanied also waited for an autograph. Being the quintessential people-watcher, I stood to one side of the crowd rather than wait in line with my friend Diana. Suddenly, as if tired by the process of signing, Arguelles stood up and began to speak to the crowd huddled together in the small bookshop. He spoke gently and reverently about his personal experiences and shared his thoughts about our collective evolutionary progress. His deep connection to the subject matter was evident, his passion inspirational. The issue he had touched upon then seemed to hit a deep core within him, and he became choked up with emotion, and was unable to continue speaking. His wife, who was standing close-by, stepped forward to his side, fluidly picking up where he had left off.

"What I think Jose was saying is..." she continued, perfectly completing his thought process. Their apparent bond was deeply moving and I silently offered up a prayer for such a communion with a spiritual life-partner.

Jose disappeared for a few minutes while his wife continued to express their mutual sentiments, and then he reappeared, playing a large bamboo flute. The tones of the instrument were deep and resonant, and quite hypnotic. He moved to the front of the crowd, by that time silent and still, mesmerized by the heavenly sounds permeating the room. Jose had chosen to continue his communication non-verbally in a universal language none could mistake and one that, if the audience was willing, could transport them into an altered state, if only for a few minutes.

As I looked over the small group of people, I saw an energy configuration of the subtlest purple in the shape of a perfect heart over the crowd. I thought my eyes were playing tricks on me. No doubt though, moved as I was, I had slipped into a state of consciousness where my eyes could see beyond our limited third-dimensional reality. The sight amazed me. It was a physical manifestation of the energy we were collectively experiencing: balance, harmony and perfect blending of male and female energy. Love!

I have sought that kind of love all of my life. Perhaps each of us secretly and, in some cases, desperately yearns for that depth of feeling and relationship with another. And maybe it is that search that motivates and propels us forward for I believe we have known it before. It is the kind of love I know I came to embody, to demonstrate and to exemplify-- to be! That was the path I chose, that has been and continues to be my journey--the search for and the demonstration of absolute love, divine unity and at-one-ment with the creator; the energy from whence we all came. I suppose that this has been my quest since the very first time I set foot on this planet 48,000 years ago in ancient Atlantis. My lifetimes of experience might well be called a totally comprehensive study course in "Unconditional Love 101"!

When I first sat down to tell my story in the early 1980's, it was a very different book. Indeed I was a very different person. I had reached a milestone, a precarious turning point with an unknown future. What I did know is that I had to journey deeper into my relationship with God and with my purpose for being here, now. I was just completing a career spanning the better part of a decade as an actress in the adult film industry and, subsequent to my retirement, as public relations director for a company that was one of, if not the largest producer and distributor of X-rated films at that time. In addition to my work in front of the camera, I chose to share what I had learned through my experiences in X-rated films by examining my relationship to my own sexuality. I frequently lectured, wrote articles, and fraternized with members of the Academic community in pursuit of deeper fulfillment of my purpose within the realm of Human Sexuality.

Although privately my lifestyle was very low-key, I had reached celebrity status in the "adult entertainment arena," a somewhat quirky honor garnering ongoing attention and recognition. (With the advent of the Internet, this acknowledgment would continue to accelerate and grow beyond what I could possibly ever have imagined.) At that time I felt that my relationship to my Adult Film career had run its course and that I would better serve my purpose by concentrating on my other work. And even after I closed the door on the last incarnation of my fan club at the end of the millennium, which I thought was a most apt time to do so, the irony of my continuing and ever growing popularity seemed more profound.

To many individuals I encountered along the way, the obvious route was for me to continue to capitalize on my film career, to fill my book with erotic anecdotes and exposés of life in porn. I went along with this theory for a while by blending energies with a co-writer and producing a completed proposal package for a publishing deal. Around the same time I signed a contract with a now defunct agency in Los Angeles to produce my story as a made-for-television movie. This came so close to reality that, as they say, I could taste it. But it was not to be. The time wasn't right.

Since then, these many years later, I realize that I played a big part in sabotaging the projects. My layers of unworthiness were still prevalent, preventing both the book and film projects from manifesting. I believe that the rest was in Spirit's hands because

I know that when something is right, it moves forward. Divine intervention will play its part. In retrospect, the earlier manuscript of what was to be my autobiography was flat and uninteresting, a one-dimensional story the likes of which has probably been told dozens of times before. And the problem with finalizing a story for the film deal was that each time I met with potential producers, I couldn't identify the conflict in my life and without conflict there is no story. I consistently played down every challenge and hardship I'd experienced, minimizing their relevance to the plot of my life. Consequently I talked myself out of deal after deal.

"Well," I contended repeatedly, "I was never abused or raped or held at gun-point. I had no children out of wedlock and I wasn't alienated from my family or in trouble with the law. My lot in life just wasn't so tough – compared to others."

And therein lay another way in which I repeatedly denied my own pain and undermined the true significance of my life drama by comparing myself with others. The truth was and is that there were considerable traumas, not the least of which was an incident a few days before my 21st birthday when, for all I know, I saved my Mother's life. There was abuse-- we didn't call it that then-- and there was a gun incident where I ran out of my home in the line of fire and miraculously was unharmed. And, it remains that I have spent a lifetime realizing that my pain was real and relevant.

Long before I even aspired to write a book, I recall blurting out to a friend, "Sometimes we have to go back to where we came from to remember what we came to get!"

It was one of those statements that just popped out of my mouth out of the blue. I wrote it down because it seemed that it could be used in many different contexts. In the simplest of situations, we recall our steps when we misplace an object, tracing back until we realize where we left it. We forget because all the clutter in our minds gets in the way of remembering our original action. Ultimately we are lead back to the item still exactly where it was the whole time we searched.

It became clear then that for me to tell my story the way I wanted, to deliver the message I desired and to share in the most honest way I knew, I had to "go back to where I came from to remember," but that wasn't just about retracing my steps to Birmingham, England where I was born, or Kent where I grew up in my current lifetime. It would require looking way beyond the time I spent in Germany before my journey to America in 1965 and the early years of sex, drugs and rock 'n roll in Northern California. And, in the end, my days in porno, though not insignificant, would provide little more than anecdote to the total picture.

I believe that for me, the story ultimately began on my home planet far, far away in our Milky Way Galaxy and with an agreement I made to participate in a huge project and grandest of experiments. Since life in the Pleiades was vastly different from the dense existence on Earth, part of that agreement would involve gradually powering-down into the third dimensional human frequency. My memory banks have revealed information to the effect that I came originally to Earth from my home planet in the Pleiades System, to mate with another from my own home planet and then to return. Perhaps this was for the purpose of infusing data into my DNA for later and the reason why I chose to first visit and procreate with a soul family member already on Earth after which we returned together to the Pleiades. Subsequent to this, along with other members of my soul family, I began my wheel of incarnation, culminating now, here in the third millennium to complete the task we had collectively chosen. The same Soul Family members and I would accompany each other for lifetimes and eons to come. Many are here today.

Chapter Two: Echoes of Atlantis

Many Star Beings remember Atlantis. Perhaps this is in large part because, as a civilization, it was most reminiscent of life on our home planets.

In recent years, much information about the lost continents of both Atlantis and Lemuria(also known as Mu) has been channeled, and it is certainly difficult to reach a final determination as to the exact dates of these ancient worlds. One school of thought is that Atlantis existed between 75,000BC to 10,500BC, yet another suggests dates of roughly 20,000 years after the first settlement on Lemuria (Mu) at around 89,000 BC. There seems to be a consensus of opinion that places the Atlantian Continent off the east coast of North America, reaching as far south as the northern tip of South America and spanning much of what we know today as the Atlantic Ocean. The much larger continent of Lemuria is said to have been located in the middle of the Pacific Ocean.

In his trilogy called "Exploring Atlantis," Dr. Frank Alpers alludes to the massive construction of a subterranean civilization beginning around 78,000 BC by visitors from other galaxies and distant universes taking hundreds of years to complete. There is also mention of a war between the two civilizations lasting five thousand years and of a series of tunnels joining the two massive continents. Considering the fact that recorded history, as we know it, spans a mere six to seven thousand years, and that changes to planetary land masses have been relatively imperceptible (until very recently,) it's difficult to fathom a picture of life in a culture reputed to be far more advanced spiritually, scientifically and technologically than ours. But when the idea of Extraterrestrial intervention is introduced, the whole picture becomes more palatable and we begin to see a certain congruency with our present history and the true significance of this third millennium into which we have just transitioned.

It's necessary to consider how different the karmic density or resonant harmony was on the planet during those far distant times compared to present times — some millennia down the proverbial road. The vibratory frequency of Earth at that time was certainly more fourth dimensional than third — in other words, more ethereal — which may explain why, when we think of Atlantis in general, we imagine a Paradise on Earth, where people lived in harmony with the Earth and each other, and where environmental and healing technology was far more highly evolved than what we know today. For those of us who recognize the profound significance of our current life mission, and who engage in past life recall as a means to self-actualization, reconnecting to Atlantinian lifetimes is crucial and, to a large extent, bittersweet.

Advanced and powerful crystal technology is synonymous with Atlantis. For most people who have taken a more than passive interest in its history, there is a reminder of the abominable and tragic results from its abuse. Ultimately these misdeeds, it is said, caused massive explosions of unthinkable proportions, breaking up landmasses and finally even sinking a huge part of the great continent. We also hear or read of the misuse of power and knowledge in the area of genetic engineering and the creation of horrific mutations and monsters.

Ironically, over the last two or more decades, the commercial gift market place has provided the opportunity for many of us to purchase raw quartz crystal and other precious and semi-precious stones to use as divining tools to connect us to the earth energies. In particular, a group of privately owned crystal skulls are said to be profound storehouses of information and wisdom for these times. Many individuals are awakening to their inner shaman as they remember how, in the distant past we utilized the innate vibratory qualities of the stones for healing and energy modulation. Certainly modern technology has recognized the qualities in quartz crystals as reliable frequency conductors. And now, as the computer age takes center stage, science and genetic engineering makes quantum leaps, leading us to believe that we are capable of just about anything. This is most assuredly reminiscent of Atlantis

and we are reminded—warned even—that history has a tendency to repeat itself.
...to a large degree it was repeated in ancient Egypt...

At this most amazing time in history, I often wonder if one of the reasons many star beings still resist awakening to their true power, the power of the divine consciousness within, is because that truth is overshadowed by memories of Atlantis. One Austrian seminar leader specifically focuses on the scars from Atlantis, claiming that therein indeed lies significant answers to why many of us continue to hold ourselves back in our present life experiences. I am inclined to agree. These were our earliest lifetimes of course where many of us were still adapting to our human being-ness. Even though I believe that for many, their destiny was to apply their innate talents and power and establish extraterrestrial technology on Earth, free will and ego ran rampant, power was abused and eventually all hell broke loose. That memory, still woven into our DNA, would then have a twofold purpose: to remind us of who we are in our authentic natures, and secondly, that in human form, we are subject to the willfulness of the lower ego in this three-dimensional free-will zone.

With this in mind, I wonder are we collectively willing to rewrite history for the sake of all life everywhere, in this Galaxy and beyond.

Over the years of personal past life work, I have come across a number of Atlantian incarnations from which I had scars. Several of the events I discovered might well be soul-overlays or past life imprints. This occurs where a collective resonance, along with images and other data, is woven into the DNA encoding, so an incarnated individual may have certain human experiences. This is a phenomenon found predominantly in new souls, individuals who have no history of lifetimes on other planets, and who incarnate directly on Earth. According to the specific agreed upon destiny of the individual, memory is downloaded into the DNA to be activated at the appropriate time for that soul's evolution. In this way, when certain issues show up in a person's present life journey, the memory data is accessed so as to give the individual greater insights and depth of experience.

I must trust though, that in my own case, these lives were very real experiences with which I now poignantly resonate as I further explore our species' origins.

One specific lifetime, prior to my significant Egyptian incarnations, is one I refer to as my "Atlantian Priest Gardener" lifetime, where I fell from grace in a big way. Even though I knew that as I explored these far distant events, my karma from those experiences and actions had long since been balanced—in other words, I *had* paid for my errors, **I had however not forgiven myself.**

The date I am given for this particular life experience is 23,100BC and relatively late in the Atlantian culture. This was my third Earth lifetime and my name was Durnael. As a boy of age 18, I chose to commit myself to temple life. Prior to the most significant events of that lifetime, I loved two women, one as an adolescent, and the other during my thirties—a priestess who had crossed my path and whose presence was powerful and intoxicating. These were, for the most part, passing fancies, mere opportunities to tune into and to relish the female frequency. Years passed, and I applied myself to my duties religiously and with a pure heart and focus.

In my early forties I was awarded the honor of presiding over the temple gardens, a position I had long desired. The gardens were every bit as sacred as the temple itself, where every stone, bush, pond and flower was integral to its energy matrix. Designed with great precision, each plot of garden calculated into one or another ritual or celebration, since many a ceremonial procession passed through the grounds en route to the main temple structure. Yet many rituals and blessings were also performed solely in the gardens and so a requisite spiritual integrity existed throughout the entire complex.

I was serene, contented and harmony prevailed over my life until...One day, a young woman, nay a girl indeed, appeared in the garden. She was a vision to be sure, the epitome of innocence and naiveté, a precious diamond in the rough. The instant I laid eyes upon her, my fate was sealed. It might be said that she was my ultimate temptation for, from that moment on, my life was turned upside down. From whence my beautiful seductress came I did not discover. Suffice it to say, she simply wandered into the garden that fateful day, lured by the beauty, fragrance and sacred ambiance. Her eyes shone with fascination for all she saw and she exuded a deep passion for life and for learning. It was unusual for anyone without specific purpose in alignment with temple proceedings and protocol, or seeking sanction in some way, to enter the grounds. Yet it might be said, a profound synchronization of energies had occurred and, in a single moment, our lives came together for a reason, broader and more complex than what our minds could possibly have imagined.

From that day on, the young woman became the focus of my thoughts and emotions. For all my training and unity with the creator, my human emotions began to take me on a strange and all-consuming journey. I anticipated her daily visits with a strange longing, and hunger for the enormous pleasure her presence brought me, and for the bedazzlement I felt by her innocence and Light. We behaved as friends, although I became her confidante, father confessor and teacher. She danced around me, plying me with questions, listening eagerly to my answers and observations, and hanging on my every word. Never had I felt such joy, but it was to be short-lived.

A strange interval in my young amour's visits to the sacred garden occurred. Two, three, four days—a lifetime to me—passed without a trace of her enormous presence. I was concerned at first, but on the fifth day my heart lightened as I caught a glimpse of her familiar gait as she entered the gates of the sacred compound. She glided towards me exuberantly as if bursting with something she wanted to share. This demeanor delighted me yet, at the same time, strangely unnerved me. Whatever had happened that had so profoundly thrilled her I instinctively knew that I would not feel the same.

As she poured out her news to me of a young man she had met and under whose love-spell she had immediately fallen, my heart sank. She gushed and chattered on about her amour, describing every moment they had spent together in flowery detail, and how she knew they were soul-mated. This was clear. A harsh reality set in as emotions began to rise inside of me I had never entertained, feelings which were as alien as they were all-consuming. At first she hardly noticed the radical change in my demeanor, but just as on the day we first met, in an instant, my life changed.

She finally noticed the shift in my energy and was confused and saddened by my lack of enthusiasm and joy for her news. Inexperienced as I was in the realms of such emotions, I internalized my own confusion and incapacity to integrate these new realities before me. The door to my heart slammed shut and I retreated into a darker place than I had known existed. That was just the beginning. I had fallen prey to every conceivable negative and spite-filled emotion in the book. It was as if a demon took over and launched me on a journey into hell on Earth. One might say that within a very short time, I experienced and mastered the worst of humanity—inside myself.

Externally I maintained a form of congeniality with my young female friend, but I quickly conferred with the appropriate officials and devised a way to send her lover on a mission abroad. After her lover was gone, I watched as her buoyancy disappeared and her spirit dimmed, as she retreated into a deep sadness. Naturally, not knowing that I was responsible for her paramour's departure, she questioned me as to the ways of life and why the fates had chosen to disrupt her happiness. My answers, though disguised as wise adages and spiritual precepts, were sickeningly self-serving. Worse yet, I intuitively knew that the young man would not return.

Before too much longer, compounded by the weight of my guilt, the distress of seeing the maiden pining for her departed love further manipulated my emotions. In an angry outburst and profoundly out of character, I banished her from the sacred garden, placing the blame for the decision outside of myself rather than admitting to my own lower ego motivation. By sending her away I would at least be spared the agony of seeing her despair and the reminder of my own sins. She did not go willingly and repeatedly agonized over why and who had seen fit to exile her, thus denying her the other joy in life, me. My reasoning with her was only met with further questions as to what it was she had done wrong and why it couldn't be rectified. The distraught girl pleaded, offering to do penance for her non-existent errors or whatever atonement the elders saw fit. The more she pressed me, the harsher my own reaction became. There was little or no hint remaining of our loving and beautiful friendship that once was. Despite my training and spiritual backbone, I had acted like a spurned and vengeful lover.

The pains of these events tortured my beloved young amour for the rest of her life, causing her great emotional imbalance and eventually resulting in her death. It might be said that she died of a broken heart, securing in place definitive DNA programming for her future lives.

I, on the other hand, continued my life in service to the temple and sacred gardens, burying myself in my duties so as not to have to confront my remorse, but my life was long and lonely. There is a great irony in the fact that the insignia woven into my tunic during my life as the priest Durnael symbolized Honesty—The Balance Of Polarities, a fact my friend Dianna and I discovered as we worked together to channel information for her book Meditative Magic, which is a compilation of Pleiadian glyphs and sacred symbolism.

I have identified both the young woman I so desperately loved and her sweetheart as playing significant roles in my current lifetime. Others who were there in ancient Atlantis I also recognize today as part of my incarnate soul family members, yet the significant bleed-through traits associated with the circumstances from that lifetime are seen primarily in the two major characters. The girl was my friend Charles who was in my life for a decade during the 1980's and 1990's, struggled with emotional and deep abandonment issues during his lifetime. I believe I was able to assist him in a degree of healing in current times, through our purely platonic relationship. In the case of the lover, it was as if the tables were turned in our current lifetime. This was someone I deeply loved and desired to be with for a long time, yet circumstances continuously relocated him. In retrospect, an ongoing relationship clearly was not meant to be; we both had too many other roads to travel.

My personal scars from that particular set of circumstances in Atlantis have manifested in some of the ways I have judged and excommunicated myself from God from time to time, like an inner judge and jury making sure that I stay on track. The good news is that I have a fool-proof system for self-monitoring, on the other hand, to say that I have been hard on myself is a radical understatement. But aren't we all harder on ourselves, than others? This is certainly consistent with what I experience in my work. Forgiving *oneself* remains the biggest struggle for most people. Forgiving *myself* for the hardships I perpetrated on Charles took many sessions of inner work for me. Ultimately, I had to realize that not only had I already paid for my transgressions over many lifetimes, but that those experiences were pivotal to the vast plot of his/her journey. On the Cosmic level, it had been set up that way.

Perhaps the fact that was a male lifetime has contributed much to my specific focus in current times on the balance of the inner male and female (or yin/yang.) Ultimately this translates to the balance of the brain hemispheres—the creative and the logical.

Another popular adage proclaims that, "We teach best what we most need to learn." If this is so, I may finally reach a level of mastery in Inner Harmony before I leave this lifetime – maybe!

Ultimately dear Durnael set in place a strong male priest frequency in my DNA which, over my many lifetimes, served as an anchor for my spiritual leaning. The "sensitive priest" resonance is one I frequently recognize in men I encounter, especially those who are star beings. I call them "priests in civilian clothing," and I am moved and compassionate towards their challenges in these transitional times. Overcoming the stereotypical male conditioning is no easy task; the ego must be tamed, the libido checked and their greatest power, their ability to love, must be realized. Finally, fear must be relinquished and replaced by trust in the Divine and perfect plan unfolding—in other words, the reliance upon spiritual wisdom and not the logical mind must take precedence.

Time and time again we see demonstrations of the power of love that reach the media and into the homes of millions, warming the collective cockles of our soul, yet when push comes to shove in personal confrontational situations, most will forget these examples of higher truth and strike out reactively. For the most part, this knee-jerk responsiveness stems from our many scars—from our past lives and present life—still needing to be healed. These areas which are still unresolved overshadow the memory of yet other incarnations where the power of the mind and will, applied intelligently and with spiritual integrity, resulted in harmony and peace.

This is why I say to those men I encounter, those priests in civilian clothing, "Dare to wake up and heal, dare to be truly great, dare to dynamically love, dare to move past all conditioning and step into the new paradigm—come on in, the water's fine!"

Chapter Three:
Mother Superior, Mother Bearer

Ageless and Bronzed
Nursing suckling child to whom
She whispered sweet love whispers –
Like a Greek Goddess yet A Dream child,
Freckled and hung with Motherhood –
She spoke of breast-feeding and wishing
By the stream that flowed by the cabin
On the clouds.
Hawaii, 1976

It is strangely ironic that I have not experienced Motherhood this time around. But I know well of being a Mother figure. Friends over the years have commented that I do have children: I just didn't give birth to them. It's their way of acknowledging my nurturing tendencies.

During the 1970s in Northern California, there were several individuals who dubbed me "Mama Kay," a nickname remaining with me until I left for Los Angeles. Earlier on I imagined myself a sure candidate for childbearing, yet as the years marched on it seemed less and less likely to happen. Even as more and more women were having babies well into their forties, blatantly challenging the biological clock theory, my desire waned. Finally I released the idea once and for all as I aligned with what I believed to be my higher destiny.

In my examination of so many past lives, I've discovered that my experiences as a female parent have been as diverse as they have been pivotal to the "bigger picture" – to my overall karma.

To begin with, there was a lifetime in ancient Egypt where I, together with my five children, worked as slaves on the construction of a pyramid. It was a life of great hardship and labor yet, along the way, I began to receive messages from a higher power. I concluded then that in fact it was our extraterrestrial ancestors making contact and availing themselves to assist us. Naturally, receiving their help required our combined receptivity and willingness to fearlessly and quietly align with a far greater reality than our circumstances. Beyond that, my children and I would have to relinquish our human egos sufficiently to receive the alien communications.

Two of my four sons, too attached to their macho ways and their rage towards their oppressors to even imagine a life as a co-creator, rather than martyr and victim, resisted and refused. They even unwittingly played their part in exposing me for my unconventional beliefs and practices. Ultimately their fear and ignorance brought me to scrutiny by those on all levels, including the Pharaoh. Eventually I was killed, stoned to death by other hysterical slaves.

History indeed repeats itself. Those challenges are not unlike those we confront now at the beginning of the 21st century. A new paradigm, crucial to our survival, requires us to part with the old ways and our limited concepts. Despite the awesome technology that prevails and dominates our lives, many still doubt and deny their innate spirituality. Programming from our past still limits, sabotages and disempowers even those who are aware and even embrace a yet greater reality. What's wrong with this picture?

In my early thirties I discovered painful memories from another major childbearing lifetime as the wife of a powerful Chinese warlord. In that particular life I brought thirteen children into the world and died giving birth to the last. This was a situation where my husband was absent most of the time. His warring antics perpetually took him away from home. In between battles he would return, impregnate me, and then leave again. Despite living in great wealth and luxury, mine was a lonely existence, one in which my husband was a literal stranger to me.

This individual, whom I'll refer to as TM, was in fact the same young man from the Atlantinian lifetime who aroused my jealousy and the one I sent away. In current times, TM was a long-time love with whom I had hoped for a more conventional relationship. We first met in Northern California in 1968 through a mutual friend and immediately felt the deep karmic connection of our previous lives, that "soul-mate" magnetic pull that indicates there is unfinished business. I rarely had any warning before TM's visits which, although brief and unscheduled, sustained and nurtured me. They were brief windows of joyful and potent dreamtime, after which he was gone again.

Unworthy as I was in those days of having what I wanted, I accepted the situation, never asking for more. Although there were times when I truly felt that he and I were destined to be together and I yearned to have a child with him, it did not come to pass. He did however conceive children with other women, proving indisputably that it was not in the cards for us. I guess one might say, I'd been there, done that, literally to death!

TM had often expressed his desire for many children. He often mentioned that he dreamed of thirteen. Thirteen? It seemed an idealistically high number and an odd one at that.

In fact, I discovered the Chinese lifetime several years later in the aftermath of having been sideswiped in a car accident. No amount of therapy or chiropractic adjustments seemed to alleviate the pain I had sustained in my back as a result of the impact of the accident. In my usual way of applying myself to personal issues and challenges, I searched using Applied Kinesiology to determine if there were any levels of consciousness causing my pain. In one deeply concentrated session I found a "past life energy bleed-through" that was anchored in my back. It was related to childbearing, and being left alone, and was associated with the Chinese life.

I immediately felt a degree of relief from my back pain as I began to process the issues from that lifetime. The first step in fully releasing the energies was one of understanding the lessons I learned from those experiences. This involved bringing in my High

Self to explain the higher purpose to my lower selves (my ego,) in other words, allowing my innate wisdom to access and to integrate the truth of why I created the experiences. Secondly, I needed to feel compassion for myself (and for others if necessary) for the travails and burden from the years of lonely childbearing. Finally, and perhaps most importantly, forgiveness of the situation and any individuals involved had to be applied to seal and permanently lift the karma of that lifetime.

I use this particular process frequently, both for myself and in my work with others, to resolve both past life and present life issues.

Believing that this was valuable information also for TM, I went out of my way to share the discovery with him, stressing the point that I felt he also had serious karmic "bleed-through" from that particular life together. He had since relocated to another state for his work requirements on a well-known TV series but, in perfect synchronicity, Spirit intervened and sent me to his location for a weekend on business. During my time there, he and I met briefly and I shared what I had discovered although I'm not sure what impact, if any, it made on him. Subsequently our life paths took off in opposite directions and we have only seen each other once since that time.

When I returned to Los Angeles from the weekend trip my back pain was gone!

TM was also my twin son in a life of nobility in ancient England. Recall of the grief I still harbored from this lifetime emerged when my friend Diana and I were deeply ensconced in researching our past lives together. She had been TM's twin sister. Tragically my children, when still quite young, took it upon themselves to go for a carriage ride without supervision. It was a cold winter's day when they decided to embark upon their adventure. The ground was covered with snow and ice, providing the worst conditions for anyone to travel in a horse-drawn carriage. But the little daredevils were restless and determined to have some fun.

Then tragedy struck, the vehicle slid out of control as they rounded a curve in the roadway and overturned. In an instant both children were mortally wounded and my world turned upside down.

My husband then (in current time another person with whom I had a brief but primary relationship) and Father of the twins had been away on business when the accident happened. Rather than trust me in recounting what had taken place, he opted to listen to others' accounts of the event, including a vicious fabrication from a revengeful manservant who had begun a rumor accusing me of an adulterous affair. In fact, my husband was the one guilty of extra-marital activities. But in his grief, guilt and shame, he blamed me for the tragedy and punished me relentlessly. Ultimately I died from physical and emotional malnutrition.

As Diana and I sat in her living room uncovering facts from this lifetime, I felt overwhelming waves of grief surfacing and I fell to the ground on my hands and knees sobbing,

"My babies, my babies!"

I screamed as I saw them lying in the snow, their blood red and warm as their little lives ebbed away. The helplessness I felt was unbearable and my heart heaved. Simultaneously Diana experienced a sharp stabbing pain in her kidneys indicating the dynamics of the injuries she had sustained. The question for both of us was how to heal the memory of such a painful trauma – fast! I opted to rewrite the script, in other words, to change what I had remembered and transform the energy, and how and with whom it manifested in my present life. The loss of the children and my own guilt that I hadn't prevented the accident was the worst of my pain. I therefore chose to imagine myself kneeling in the snow with Diana in my arms. To diffuse intensity of mortality and finality of death through the destruction of her young body, I imagined her looking up at me, winking and, drawing from her innate ageless wisdom saying,

"See you next time around Ma!"

That imagery worked for me – it broke the spell, my pain lifted and I was able to file the experience away under "M" for Motherhood and all the emotions associated with that expression and those circumstances. Dianna likewise chose a similar technique to alleviate her discomfort. It took me a while longer and more inner work to forgive my husband for his mistreatment of me. Appropriately, I was able to work this issue out in my relationship with him in current times, thus empowering myself and healing my relationships with men in general.

Of the many incarnations I have discovered where my matriarchal duties carved out the primary lessons and challenges of my lives, second only to my most memorable Egyptian lifetime, which I will talk about later, none left a greater impact on my current lifetime than those spent in the convent. In particular, in eighth century Germany, I began my cloistered life as a young girl and rose to the position of mother superior. The patterns lingering in my cellular memory from this spartan and disciplined existence in dedicated service to God, have resonated through and significantly challenged me in present times and throughout my life (and perhaps all the lives in between). Regardless of the events of that lifetime, the lessons delivered proved invaluable and fundamental to my personal evolution. So it is with the mystical patterns running through *all* of our earthly experiences.

As a child growing up in Twentieth Century England, the chill and sparseness of the post-war era and my Father's disciplinarian ways compounded the existing tendency I had towards self-denigration and self-admonishment. To say that I've been hard on myself is a gross understatement! Over the years I have peeled off multiple layers from what often felt like a curse from my role as Mother Superior, where the martyr-like resonance of, *damned if I do and damned if I don't*, is a central theme. Several of the young novices from that lifetime, who were pivotal to my journey then in the Cloister, have reappeared in my current lifetime.

One young female in particular took center stage for a while. Not only did I hold myself especially responsible for her, I performed over and above the call of duty on her behalf. She had been perhaps the most reluctant novice of all those I oversaw, bitterly unhappy and resentful of her fate. Over-bearing parents (the same individuals who parented her in current times) had coerced her into entering the order. She consequently disobeyed the rules, resisting both her studies and duties, while at the same time exhibiting a fierce passion for closeness with God. Any efforts on my part to assist her were met with staunch defiance (a quality I recognized in present times,) requiring me to reprimand and apply further disciplinary actions. It was after all, part of my responsibility as Mother Superior and therefore expected of me. But for the otherwise bright and talented young novice, punishment seemed at best futile. To add to my own frustration I secretly felt that her talents would have been best served elsewhere.

Tragically, she took her own life. I grieved her loss deeply and unconsciously punished myself in innumerable ways for not having been able to save her. Many years later, at the time of my own death, I was still unresolved with her suicide. Consequently, many of my patterns of self-chastisement were bound to be carried through to inevitably manifest at a future time to be resolved. (It's interesting to consider the fact of our much older past life history, dating all the way back to Egypt, culminating there in the eighth century, and whether or not I might have had an inkling of that at the time.)

Destiny brought the young nun and I back together in 1976 in San Francisco on the set of one of my first movies. Elizabeth replaced a script supervisor who had been fired. A short while later and mere days before I left for Los Angeles we ran into each other providing the opportunity for us to exchange phone numbers as we realized that we were mutually bound for The City of the Angels. We agreed to meet up after our arrival.

Divine synchronicity effortlessly lined up an apartment in the center of Hollywood, from an actress friend who was leaving to assume a job in New York. At the exact moment I pulled up in front of her building, after driving from San Francisco, her cab arrived to take her to the airport. Talk about timing! Within a few weeks, however, I was forced to move due to complications with the lease. Yet another friend lined me up with a vacant duplex in her split-level 50's style apartment complex in another part of town. Again the synchronicity of events was awesome although the new location was a little over my budget. I knew that Elizabeth, who had been camping out on the couch of a male friend, was also anxious to relocate and so I proposed a temporary roommate arrangement. She agreed.

One of my mentors once warned of so-called "temporary arrangements." Years prior he had reluctantly taken a "temporary" job with the US Postal Service – it lasted ten years! Perhaps hidden between the lines of such intention is resistance to consistency and commitment because it goes without saying that what we resist, persists. While Elizabeth and I repeatedly voiced our desire to have our own places, our arrangement became the longest "temporary" roommate situation I'd ever heard of, ironically also ten years!

"Why so long?" I often queried, appealing to my guides and other mentors. After all, we were very different both in character and taste and we both felt a lack of personal sovereignty within our living space. I was told that the unusually long span of time as roomies served to allow us to heal a long and dramatic past actually originating in ancient Egypt. There our experiences as Mother and daughter set the tone for challenges over many of our future lifetimes, naturally including our days in the Cloister. I did not begin to tap into my deep scars from our Egyptian life until much later, yet Elizabeth and I were mutually aware of our significant past together and did our best to deal with issues we recognized were obvious carry-overs from our past-lives.

In the way that history always repeats itself, the dynamics of our relationship in current times were eerily parallel to those lives when I was her Mother. The most obvious characteristic was that I was older, and already had a few years of deep commitment and study on my spiritual path under my proverbial belt.

It was no secret that, early on in our co-habitation, she mildly complained to her friends about her roomie who was always meditating, yet she followed my lead in many ways, and began to develop a relationship to her own higher spiritual power. Much like in other incarnations, however, it didn't come easily to her and she struggled profoundly in coming to terms with the hand she felt she had been dealt in life. To accept responsibility of having co-created her personal universe, including her choice of parents, was a truth she struggled to deeply integrate. Without the acceptance of that reality she would, as many people do, remain victim to her life circumstances. I availed myself always to assist and counsel her and she did accept my help, but only up to a point. There was, of course, as in all relationships, a definitive line not to be crossed and we honored that.

As platonic friends and room-mates for a decade we would often comment on the ironies of our relationship. Elizabeth jested that, were we both not strictly heterosexual, we would be a "common-law" couple. My sentiments ran more along the lines of,

"We either love each other a lot or we have a ton of karma together."

Both were true.

My dear sweet, talented, profoundly creative and most colorful friend passed this plane on Thanksgiving morning 1998 after an incredibly courageous battle with breast cancer.

From the onset Elizabeth had opted against allopathic medicine and committed to the teachings of Mary Baker Eddy and the Science of Mind philosophies. A week before her passing I drove her to the organization's sanitarium in South Pasadena where the angelic presence is powerful beyond words. Elizabeth still imagined a miracle healing and she asked that her friends hold that picture for her. We complied. In her last days I prayed that she would finally achieve the kind of relationship with God that had both motivated and tormented her lifetime after lifetime.

At her memorial, a beautiful celebration of her life by so many diverse friends, family, students (from her teaching role at the American Film Institute) and film work associates, I wrote a testimonial to our amazing friendship in the style of an e-mail message (she would have appreciated that) and I read it aloud. In it I recalled that she had been with me through my entire career in porno while she pursued her own distinguished vocation in the area of mainstream low-budget film production, culminating in her prestigious position at the American Film Institute.

I remembered that, had it not been for her keen eye, I would have been immortalized on the sidewalk outside the erstwhile Pussycat Theater on Santa Monica Boulevard in Hollywood as Kay Paker!

During those days, big-budget X-rated films held flashy premiers with much fanfare and paparazzi. It was July 12, 1984 and, as part of the regalia surrounding the release of a New York production called "Firestorm," Eric Edwards and I became the third and fourth actors to be inducted as super stars outside the infamous Adult Theater. In the same fashion that Hollywood acknowledged and immortalized its stars outside Grauman's Chinese Theater by imprinting their hands in cement, so the Pussycat Theater's management had begun a tradition of honoring adult stars.

Placing one's hands and feet in wet cement was no problem, although writing is somewhat challenging. The cement must be exactly the correct consistency otherwise the indentation will not hold. On that particular evening, distracted as I was by so many flashing cameras and media personnel, I dug the etching implement (the handle of a paint brush if memory serves) into the soggy wetness and scratched out the letters *Kay Paker* instead of *Kay Parker*. Thank God Elizabeth was watching. I felt my friend's elbow in my ribs as she whispered,

"You might want to re-write that!"

I disguised my embarrassment, quickly grabbed one of the attendants and asked him to smooth over my name so I might resign, this time correctly. Grateful to my friend, the evening continued with a showing of the movie, a decently produced film in which Eric Edwards gave an outstanding performance.

In my memorial to my dear friend, I also reminisced about how, one evening, we finally deduced that the drummer we had both dated. (I had actually lived with him) in Marin County was one and the same person. What are the odds of that? From time to time she had heard me comment on Joey, my "ex," but had not imagined in a thousand years that it might be the same person she had experienced long after he and I had parted company.

Following our move to Hollywood, I took a job as a waitress at a small, yet well-known kosher restaurant in Beverly Hills. I waited tables and simultaneously rose to "stardom" as an X-rated movie star. (When I received offers for films, I simply took time off.) Along the way, Elizabeth also took a part-time job in the same small eatery.

Most significantly, Elizabeth and I lived together through the years succeeding "Taboo," a low-budget film shot in 1980. The movie became a huge success ultimately triggering a long and tedious list of sequels. I also co-starred in the first two sequels and, years later, agreed to make a non-sex cameo appearance in "Taboo 9." By this time, the original movie had become a cult classic.

In a way the original "Taboo" changed my life. My role? A Mother, of course! The central theme of the film was the indulgence of my character, Barbara Scott, in an incestuous sexual relationship with her son, a conflict both scandalous yet broad in its appeal to the thriving Oedipal Complex in men of all ages.

And in the way I am compelled to relate to the events of my life by drawing parallels and examining synchronicities, "Taboo," by definition, would stand as a metaphor for my personal destiny and life challenges.

In bespeaking the role of Motherhood in all of my lifetimes I cannot overlook the intricate dynamics of perhaps the most significant lifetime with TM where I was his wife and Mother to his children. I felt the resonance of this incarnation heightened during a time when I was researching information about the Shroud of Turin. During the time of my studies with my spiritual teacher, a team had formed to work on a project involving the history of the ancient relic it is said wrapped Jesus' body after His crucifixion. The controversy surrounding the holy cloth continues. Regardless of the findings of countless carbon dating tests and other examination, its status as a sacred relic remains intact as if a testament to the power of collective belief.

During this period of time I had a dream where I was with Jesus and we walked and talked like Brother and Sister. I felt a love like no other I have ever experienced; it filled me to overflowing like being caressed with a million kisses. It was indescribable. I knew that I had witnessed Him, and beyond that I had experienced the complete and unconditional love He exemplified and that I could never again settle for less than that.

Some years later, after my retirement from films, I began to deeply heal my relationship with my Father. A significant part of this process involved finding resolution to my relationship with TM since, as is the case for most of us, issues in our primary emotional relationships are usually in fact about one or another parent, or both. I tapped into the other lifetime as TM's wife and discovered it was during the life of Christ. TM was a rabbi and as his wife, I was sworn to obey and love only him. We had three children of whom two were Diana and Elizabeth, whose major life challenges were similar to those in current time and space. My personal pains and areas of unresolved issues stemmed from the fact of having witnessed the Master and His teachings and loving him completely – certainly more deeply than I loved my husband. Secretly I desired to leave my life and follow Him. For all these thoughts I had to forgive myself. I believed I had sinned deeply and broken my marriage vows by entertaining such notions, thereby deeming myself unworthy. Despite the undeniable truth I had discovered, I felt deeply shameful and judged myself relentlessly.

Aaron, my friend, mentor and partner in cosmic endeavors, who has been at my side in many lives, remembered me there and how, after the crucifixion and the personal guilt I felt for my passivity towards my husband and family, I made a vow that I would sacrifice anything to fulfill the promise Jesus revealed of the transformation of the human race. My dear mentor reminded me, that during that lifetime two thousand years ago, he told me that in a future life, I would become a representative and example of that unconditional infinite love, (in essence the Mother Goddess energy.) It is my primary intention.

My Journey to
Self Discovery

Chapter Four: America

America! It really did exist.

In the wee hours on November 12, 1965, I landed in New York.

How quickly it had all transpired. It had never been a conscious desire of mine to come to the United States, this land of milk and honey. Up until that point the massive continent of which I knew relatively little had never entered into my dreams; I certainly had no obvious motivation to visit. Unless--the fact that when I was growing up I was an avid movie watcher had anything to do with this monumental step I had taken. During the years my family and I spent overseas in Malta, the major social activity for kids was a trip to the naval base to see movies. Pictures, we called them.

I had a particular passion for the Hollywood musicals. The singing and dancing lifted my spirits and brought me much joy. In fact, these fantastic illusions which were a primary lifeline for me at that time and perhaps provided the fuel for the adventures I would manifest in the future.

After our return from the Mediterranean, back in soggy, cold olde England, listening to the episodic radio sagas or "serials" as they were called was our evening ritual. We huddled around the only heat source in our house, the coal burning fire in the living room, until Mum called for us to go to bed. Since we didn't have television in our home until I was sixteen, I would save my pennies and make the outing to the pictures in the next town. We dressed to the nines for our forays to the theater in the nearby town. (The building remains intact today, having evolved from movie house to bowling alley and presently, a supermarket.) I remember one occasion, dressed in a posh new tweed suit, taking the double-decker bus to see "A Summer Place" and becoming infatuated with the tall, gangly, bronzed Troy Donahue. In my wildest dreams I couldn't have ever imagined that, many years later, not only would I meet him and he would acknowledge *my* film career, even more outrageously, we would appear in a film together.

During my adolescent period, I occasionally came across a movie magazine and I spent hours meticulously cutting and pasting pictures of movie stars into a series of scrapbooks. After I left England the scrap-books were stored in the attic and later, in the mid-eighties, my parents burned them in a spring cleaning effort (I was miffed that they hadn't asked me if I wanted them.) However, in the realms where thoughts become dreams I wondered if my hobby had been a way of unconsciously creating my future.

Yet even though the world I found in movies was a marvelous escape for me, the farthest I fancied myself actually moving from England at that time, was to the (European) Continent. In fact, whenever I would try to imagine where I would spend my adulthood, the very idea of remaining in England always seemed unthinkable, oppressive and full of constriction to me. Consciously I had no other aspirations except leaving home.

Now, a few years hence, destiny had prevailed and due to a strange series of events, I found myself on the other side of the Atlantic. I was sick and weak and everything around me seemed fuzzy and out of focus. Due to an overbooking on my original Icelandic flight from Frankfurt, several other passengers and I had been bumped up to a direct and much shorter flight to New York. Although I appreciated the reduction in flying time we landed at John F. Kennedy airport in the early morning hours long before our original scheduled arrival time.

The plan had been for my Sponsor's brother to meet me around ten o'clock. We would then drive to New Jersey to join the rest of the family who were arriving on a military flight a short while later. Together we would all head for Virginia to stay at their family home for a few days before embarking upon a long road trip winding up in Santa Fe, New Mexico, where the Everett family had decided to retire from military life.

CHAPTER FOUR: AMERICA

Since my schedule had been thrown way off, it seemed apparent that I was stranded, alone for the night, in the deserted airport in the new land I would never have dreamed would become my permanent home.

All the passengers from my flight had dispersed and it seemed I was the only person in the airport. I glanced around me, feeling quite bewildered by my circumstances. Banks upon banks of blindingly bright fluorescent lights stretched as far as the eyes could see draining the life out of everything around. Desolate didn't even begin to describe how it felt, but with my old trusty trunk and a couple of other bags by my side, there was naught else to do but wait.

Indeed, until that very moment, America had existed only in my imagination. It had been a mere six weeks prior to that day that my American friends who were stationed in Germany had offered me the opportunity to re-locate to the United States. I was, after all, at a crossroads in my life with little or no apparent direction. This transition had come about after I had returned to Germany following a three-month stay in England due to my Father's serious illness. My parents had moved into a new home that needed a lot of work and I had remained to help out since Dad was still too weak to do much except delegate chores. My brother John and I had labored hard and long, digging and organizing the large overgrown garden, in addition to laying cement around the bungalow's perimeter to minimize mildew and invasive weed growth.

The year prior to the time of Dad's illness, I had spent a year living and working in Munich as an "au pair" for a highly respected theatrical family. It had been a wonderful time of growth and exposure to a new and exciting culture. My employer's husband was a director of theater and opera in Germany. Frau Rennert was a retired opera singer who had given up her career to raise her three children, which she did with amazing dedication and style. For as long as I was there, I was considered one of the family and shared in the fun and laughter which dear Frau Doktor constantly evoked. When I announced that I was to return to England due to my Father's circumstances, their disappointment was evident. We mutually loved and cared for each other and although I experienced great happiness there, I knew it was time to move on. I had met my goal of learning to speak another language and a future as a domestic was not in the cards. Once again my Father had been the catalyst for change.

My parents planned to take a few days vacation and visit some friends in Wales before returning home to Kent for my twenty-first birthday. The day before their departure, out of the blue my Father flew into one of his rages. I had suggested to my Mother that they use one of my suitcases, considerably newer and lighter in weight than their old mildewed navy surplus models, which were stored in the attic. My gesture pushed my Father's pride button and he lashed out at me—as if for no apparent reason. I stood by horrified and helpless as Dad transformed before my eyes, his eyes glaring and his body shaking in uncontrollable rage. Once again, as so many times in the past, I was the trigger for his outburst. Back then, my logical mind strained to understand what I had done wrong. But this was illogical behavior, fueled by deep pain and frustration and, my Aunt Mary enlightened me years later at Dad's funeral, his undisputable envy of my youth and freedom. I was used to his outbursts in childhood and adolescence but this time it was different. This time he also struck out at my beloved Mummy.

What ensued was termed a "primary trauma" by a body worker, who over a period of time in 1992 assisted me to release my rage towards my Father. At that time I was struggling to heal some relatively serious physical conditions and the suitcase incident surfaced. What I had never fully acknowledged were the deeper dynamics involved and that it had been a life-threatening situation where I had intervened, perhaps to save my Mother's life.

Mum had accepted my invitation to borrow my suitcases causing Dad to lash out at me, only this time, he turned on her also. He pushed her into their bedroom and slammed the door shut. Then, silence--a silence both ominous and unnatural considering the preceding outburst. Moments later, a slight whimper resonated from the quietness, a sound that chilled me to my bones and compelled me to take action. I was propelled forward and into their room, where my Mother was lying helpless on their bed. My Father's hands were around her throat.

I flung myself at him, placing myself between the two of them, pounding on him with my fists and yelling at him to release her. He reciprocated and began to wrestle with me. As I felt the force of my own rage erupting I didn't recognize myself. My head and heart pounded almost unbearably. For the first time in my life, I was fighting back. I screamed at him,

"Don't you ever lay hands on my Mother again or I'll call the police!"

As our mutual rage intensified, Dad knocked me to the ground and repeatedly kicked me until Mum's pleading brought him back to a degree of sanity. I slid into numbness and a kind of time warp.

When I finally gathered my senses a short while later, I announced to my parents that I would pack my bags and leave immediately, since my presence seemed to create such disharmony. Upon hearing this, his wrath still simmering, my Father hissed back,

"You're not going anywhere. You're still under-age and you'll do what I say!"

I wasn't about to argue with him and possibly refuel the previous scenario. So, I stayed in house-arrest, a quasi-prisoner until the day after my birthday.

My Father's intentions were certainly never to harm my Mother or myself, of this I became absolutely clear during the time I was healing years later, but the truth was that his rage had spun out of control and my Mother's life had, in that moment, been in jeopardy. To finally recognize and acknowledge the seriousness of the situation was not only a breakthrough for me, but was of tremendous assistance in my healing process. I had always down-played the incident with rationalizations such as, "there are always others worse off than me" and typically, I made others' pain — in this case my Mum's — bigger and more important than my own.

Needless to say, following that event in 1965, my birthday was not a happy occasion. Traditionally, twenty-one marks the graduation from adolescent to adult, a date to be celebrated, but I was hardly in a jolly mood. My parents returned from their brief holiday the day prior and Mum tearfully appealed to me to forgive Dad. *She* obviously had.

"Dear, your Father is so sorry for what happened," she insisted tearfully.

For her sake I wanted to be able to move beyond my shock of the event and let bygones be bygones, but it was more than I was capable of at the time. I needed to hear from *him* that he was sorry. At that time, I neither had the courage nor the ability to confront him. Of course, Dad didn't say a word to me either and the incident was never mentioned again during his lifetime. The climate around the house remained strained and all unresolved feelings and emotions were, as usual, swept under the rug.

Ultimately my birthday was a somber one. I couldn't have felt less like celebrating. A small group of friends and family had been invited to the house, but it was all I could do to muster up enough enthusiasm to express my gratitude to each of them for their best wishes and gifts, each of which was accompanied with the traditional cardboard key, signifying the key to the door of adulthood.

During the afternoon, with my imminent departure in mind, I negotiated the sale of a pair of pretty purple suede shoes I'd purchased in Germany to my friend Loraine (the friend with whom I had taken my original trip to the Continent.) The money provided the funds for a train ticket back to Germany. There was no doubt in my mind that I had to leave — as soon as possible!

Later that day I packed my trunk and, early the next morning,

CHAPTER FOUR: AMERICA

I left my parents' British country bungalow. Mum was heartbroken. It was clear, I told her, that my presence was disruptive and that the only solution for everyone's sake was for me to go. She knew it was true, after all I was the one, it was said, who was so much like Dad. He and I could not live under the same roof any more.

Mum stood by my side as I went into my parents' bedroom for the second time within that period and kissed my Father good-bye on the cheek. Huge tears flowed down my Mother's face but Dad and I proudly held our emotions in check. Had circumstances been different I might have thrown my arms around him and told him I loved him. He might even have reciprocated, but not then. (In fact, I do not recall my Father ever telling me he loved me.) Choking back my sentiments, I was unable to utter any words of farewell at all. My Mother saw me to the door in silence for fear of breaking down again. She squeezed me quickly, told me to take care of myself and waved good-bye. I was off again on the next leg of my destiny. My beloved Father as always had played his part well.

It was about a mile to the bus stop from my parent's bungalow. My heart was heavy as I stoically carried my trusty trunk—no easy load, down the lane to catch the bus to the local train station. My destination was Victoria Station in London and the ferry train back to the Continent. At that point it seemed that there was no other place to go except back to Germany, and so Wurtzburg once again became my destination. I was still very much in shock from the preceding events and I have no memory whatsoever of the train ride. I felt comforted however to know that my American friends were there.

Mrs. Everett and I had become close during the nine or so months I worked for her and her family prior to my move to Munich. Not one to socialize with the other American wives, she chose to live off the military base and interact with the local gentry rather than her peers. I admired her for that. She and her husband had rented a small house-- which was actually the guesthouse--belonging to a local doctor. Their three boys slept in the basement. It was far from luxurious, but offered more colorful advantages over the alternative. (My own parents had likewise opted for civilian housing when we were stationed in Malta.) Frequently, I would finish off my duties and Mrs. E. and I would go into town to shop and explore. In that way I became more of a companion for her than domestic help.

The Everetts introduced me to certain staples of American life such as football and hamburgers, and eventually to a young military guy I dated for a while. My friends came to know me well and cared about my welfare. When they offered me the opportunity to come to the United States, it became clear that their caring went deeper than I had imagined. At the time I returned to Wurtzburg, the conclusion of their tour of duty in Germany was only a couple of months away, a fact that obviously precipitated their offer to me. They sensed that I could use the opportunity to make a quantum leap myself. Since by that point my German was very good (the children of the family in Munich had taken me in hand and taught me well), I had taken a job at the local department store Kaufhof. In a few short weeks of working in the haberdashery department at the men's sock counter, I became a reluctant expert but I derived little pleasure from tales of foot problems of the local male gentry. Clearly there was no future there for me.

I therefore seriously contemplated my friends' generous offer, which would not only provide me with a green card and a loan for a plane ticket, but assurance that they would also be there to assist me to get on my feet in the U.S. All things considered, my decision came relatively easily.

Whatever red tape it took to prepare my papers, Major Everett was able to pull strings to expedite the process. I was required to undergo a physical that I failed the first time. The doctors were concerned with a spot that had shown up on my chest x-ray. However the problem simply turned out to be a shadow, perhaps a scar; the manifestation of a lung infection I had battled that winter. My second x-ray showed improvement and I was given a clean bill of health. The paperwork went through expeditiously and within a very short time I was proud recipient of a brand new green card.

Then, America!

The reality that I had actually landed on American soil hit me square between the eyes. I tried to imagine what was outside the airport. My body was weak and feverish and cried out to lie down. There was little else I could do for a few hours but rest anyway. I pulled my luggage close to me, bundled myself up in my coat and attempted to create a little nest for myself.

I was about to surrender to my exhaustion when I saw them—an group of strange men clad in black from head to toe with long beards and ringlets falling down the sides of their faces from beneath their tall hats. Their demeanor was intense and somber and frankly, terrified me. Although they seemed to be immersed in a world of their own as they shuffled along in small rapid steps, I imagined that they were making a beeline for me! Visions of being kidnapped by these sinister looking beings flooded my mind. At that moment, to my immense relief, a person I recognized from my flight appeared from the rest room. I fled toward her, camouflaging my panic as best I could to ask her if she could keep an eye on my bags while I went to relieve myself.

In retrospect, I realized how profoundly symbolic this event was. Of course, at that time I had no idea who the men were. But the fact that the first people I would encounter upon my arrival in this new land would be a religious group, let alone Hassidic Jews, seems to me now an omen of sorts, a dramatic metaphor for the thread running through my life. Perhaps it was their intensity, or their odd appearance, or the ancient resonance encoded in my DNA-- memories of my own Jewish past lifetimes, which so frightened me. Many years later one of these lifetimes would surface from my unconscious mind as part of my process of healing and personal transformation.

I washed my face and freshened up a bit, stalling my

re-emergence from the restroom until I felt that enough time had passed for the strange individuals to be gone. All I wanted to do was lie down, preferably in a warm bed, recover from whatever ailed me, and let reality sink in. Normally I considered myself to be a fairly courageous individual, yet, in that moment, my bravado was sadly lacking. The coast was clear, the men in black were gone and I cautiously left the restroom. I thanked my fellow traveler for watching over my bags and assured her that I was fine. The stark whiteness of the empty airport corridor engulfed me once more. I sank back down into my heap of belongings and surrendered to the fatigue and infection in my body.

As I allowed myself to relax, impressions of the scheduled events to follow occurred to me. The thought of driving to Virginia and spending a whole week with the entire Everett family became unthinkable. We were apparently going to be staying with Mrs. Everett's elderly, though adorable Grandfather, whose house they had mentioned was quite small. Three growing boys, their parents who--it had become increasingly clear to me--both had drinking problems, the Grandfather, their highly strung dog Heidi, and me, all under one roof! I couldn't imagine my energy holding up enough to get there, let alone the few days to follow. I also contemplated the schedule beyond the respite in Virginia; a long car ride with the same group of characters, through the South to our final destination of Santa Fe.

What to do? I felt desperate. In a moment, a solution occurred to me; I would call Jay's parents. Maybe I could stay with them for a couple of days to recover. Jay was the military guy the Everetts had introduced me to, and who I had consequently dated back in Wurtzburg. His parents lived in upstate New York. Upon our introduction I had become immediately infatuated with Jay although, in retrospect, it seemed that I had been more attracted to the illusion of who he was, rather than the reality. Nonetheless, Jay was a lovely person with a most mischievous way about him, a great sense of humor and an air of daring and adventure. He was US Army, but not regular Army. "Intelligence," he told me, and that was all I knew as he flew hither and thither on matters he could not or would not discuss with me. I could not contact *him*; only he could contact me, a pattern which recurred in several of my relationships later on, one which was frustrating and emotionally painful.

After I took the job and moved to Munich in 1963, Jay often drove down from Wurtzburg in his Mercedes sports car, his pride and joy, and we would take off for weekends in the Alps. We especially loved Berchtesgarten, a picturesque ski resort, best known as one of Hitler's favorite winter homes.

Crazy as it seemed after the fact, Christmas of 1964 we decided to get engaged and drove to England to announce our intentions to my family. En route we argued--about what I have no recollection--and in a defiant act of immaturity, I chug-a-lugged a bottle of screwdrivers he had fixed for our road trip. Disgusted with me, Jay dumped me into the bathtub in our hotel room in Boulogne, and put me to bed. The next day we realized that our decision to be engaged was grossly premature and, by the time we arrived at my parent's home in Kent, we had abandoned the idea completely. By the time I left for the United States, Jay and I had drifted apart considerably. Besides, I was totally pre-occupied with my impending journey, the dimensions of which boggled my mind.

Jay's Mother and I originally met on a trip she had made to Germany to visit her son, and so we had already established a rapport. She fully expected me to make contact when I arrived in the United States, Jay had insisted. Because of the prevailing circumstances however, I felt obliged to go along with my Sponsor's family plans, and so it was uncertain as to whether I would have the opportunity to visit upstate New York. Yet, as I sat in that deserted airport, I realized that here was a perfect answer to my dilemma. After all, Jay's Father was a doctor. I was weak and feverish and a little medical attention would be perfectly in order!

I waited for nine o'clock, which I felt was a respectable hour, and then phoned Jay's parents' home. His Mother answered and my prayers were promptly fulfilled as she invited me to come and stay with them for a few days. It was easy to reach them, she insisted, and instructed me to take a bus right outside the terminal to deliver me to a location close to their New York home where she and her husband would be waiting for me. Their offer was an incredible relief.

Mrs. Everett's brother arrived at the original scheduled time to pick me up. I explained what I had decided and, several phone calls later, all parties agreed upon my plan and I was on my way to Tuxedo Park and hopefully, recuperation.

My new life outside the airport terminal began with an ice-cream soda at a Howard Johnson's.

"One of America's great institutions," declared my hosts who, true to their word, were at the assigned destination to meet me. I was way too out of it to appreciate their gesture, not to mention that it was inconceivable to me that anyone would eat ice cream in the dead of winter. I took a couple of bites and declined the rest.

My host's home was beautiful, as flawlessly decorated as a magazine lay-out and for me it was the lap of luxury. I was weaker than I had thought and nestled in the comfort of the queen sized bed in their guest room as Jay's Mother generously tended to my every need. A couple of days later his Father, concerned by my condition, took me into Manhattan for an examination by a colleague, a lung specialist. I was amused that the doctor ruled out any serious problem with his diagnosis of "British lungs." I wondered what he meant by that. That something about being British determined the condition of my lungs? Strange, except if one considers the extreme ramifications of the fossil fuel burning era in Great Britain. In addition to being asthmatic, I had been breathing coal smoke all of my winters of my childhood. Had that been a contributing factor to my weakened lung condition? At that point in my evolution, not being one to ask questions, I simply accepted the doctor's conclusion, relieved and grateful beyond words that it was nothing more than an infection, and that basically all I needed was rest.

So, for the next few days I convalesced in my host's beautiful home while my sponsors visited with their family. Then it was time to head Southward. Major and Mrs. Everett and I rendezvoused in New York and, stopping en route to gather up the rest of the clan, we began the long drive to Florida, through Louisiana to our final destination of Santa Fe.

In retrospect, I find it fascinating that I began my American life in the Southwest, in New Mexico, the Land Of Enchantment, with its adobe structures, red soil and rich Native American history. Curiously, although I didn't stay long in Santa Fe, I felt quite at home and nurtured by the energy of the land. The Native Indian culture immediately enveloped me and I eagerly soaked up it up. Yet many of the white Americans I met there seemed out of place, as if in hiding--but from what--the fangs of society? I had heard that there was an abundance of old money there. The amazing elegance I witnessed in several of the homes I visited during my year's stay there was proof of that.

Almost immediately upon my arrival in Santa Fe, I found work in a small French boutique in the central courtyard of La Fonda Hotel right off the Plaza in the center of town. Owned and operated by a remarkable French woman, Suzette International was far more than it appeared to be, as was Suzette herself! It was not the frou-frou boutique it seemed to be at first glance, in fact, it served as a major fashion resource for the wealthy locals, as well as hotel patrons. The few clothing items, accessories and quality gift items displayed inside the doors of the gift shop lured unsuspecting customers into the thriving inner sanctum, where the rest of the merchandise was obscured in a back room.

When patrons arrived, they described what they were looking to buy and were then invited to sip demitasse coffee while items were selected from the racks in the back room and brought out onto the shop floor for perusal by the customer. The dynamic Parisienne had loyal, long-standing clients who came from far and wide to be clothed exclusively by her. She personally designed clothing for them and, at least several times a year, flew to Paris to oversee the construction and production of her line as well as shopping for other merchandise for the store.

Suzette's client list was star-studded. Some of these celebrities would make special trips to Santa Fe to buy their seasonal wardrobes while others had second homes there. Among the most auspicious of these were members of the wealthy King family from Texas who inspired the TV series, "The Beverly Hillbillies," and the elegant British actress Greer Garson.

In general, my role was of a kind of general assistant. I performed menial tasks as well as occasionally waiting on clients. My uniform consisted of outfits from Suzette's junior lines and I was called upon to model clothes for clients who were shopping for their daughters. Suzette, who had a daughter roughly my age living in Europe at boarding school, generously took me under her wing. I was honored that she invited me stay at her home, a onetime residence of the Archbishop of Santa Fe, when she was away on business trips to Paris. I cared for her dogs and relished my time in her tastefully decorated all-white home environment.

Naturally I had shared my background with my employer, including my year as an au pair for a distinguished theater and opera family in Munich, where I had cultivated a great love of the music. Hearing this, Suzette used her clout to enroll me in the prestigious Santa Fe Opera Usher Corps, positions I understood were normally reserved for the elite daughters of the town. Once a week I gratefully donned my long skirt and colorful serape and headed for the beautiful open-air Santa Fe Opera House where the natural surroundings were incorporated into the backdrop of the season's productions. Of the many productions I saw, I distinctly remember a production of "Tosca" with the lights of Los Alamos twinkling in the background. What a magical beginning to my new life!

After living with my sponsors for three months, I had repaid them for the ticket they had so generously produced for my flight to the US. It was time for independence, as a funny little trailer, stuck away in a corner of town, was offered as a domicile. Humble though it was, my green trailer became my home for the remainder of my stay in New Mexico and, it served me well.

Shortly after my arrival Suzette introduced me to the son of a client. Gary seemed every bit the rich kid to me, defiant and restless, yet I felt a strange sense of compassion for him. He attracted a very diverse set of friends and when we were together I felt danger ever present. It wasn't that comfortable to be around him, but the truth of the matter was that I hadn't met any others of my own age group. He was all I had! This was the mid-sixties and there was a conspicuous lack of young people of my own age group around town. Most of the sons and daughters of Santa Fe's permanent residents attended college out of state, the majority were students at the University of Colorado in Boulder.

One weekend Gary and I took a water-skiing trip with a friend of his who was from a distinctly more working-class family than his own. His friend's father owned a boat supply company and so, towing a brand new speedboat behind his friend's truck, we set off for a lake north of Santa Fe. I was excited to learn to water-ski.

Gary and I were riding in the back of the truck loaded with all kinds of equipment, including naturally, as boys will be boys, an ample supply of beer. Suddenly, within any warning at all, pandemonium broke loose; the truck whip-lashed around like a toy car, jerking violently and sending gas cans and other gear flying through the air. A loud cracking noise ensued; the boat was wrenched loose from the tow bar and disappeared into the gulch alongside the road. For a moment, it looked as if we were going with it. The brakes screeched and we came to a halt, miraculously still intact on the road. The boat however now lay, smashed to pieces, at the bottom of the arroyo.

Gary's friend's cab door swung open, and he came rushing around to the back of the truck to see if we were hurt. For the most part we were fine although in shock. But one of the flying gas cans had hit Gary and there was an ugly gash in his forehead. He stoically brushed it off as nothing. Although I felt badly shaken up, I had not sustained any injuries. There was no doubt at all that our guardian angels had been present and we had been protected. At that point my choice would have been to turn around and return to town but the boys were determined to continue on, relatively undeterred. There was a boat rental company at the lake and a magical thing called insurance would solve the issue of the demolished vehicle lying at the side of the road. I couldn't believe that the boys seemed relatively unfazed by the incident - almost as if this kind of thing was normal to them. So, we continued on, and in fact, did enjoy a weekend of fun during which I received a crash course in water skiing - no pun intended.

In the fall of 1966 I decided that I would follow the boys of Santa Fe to Boulder, Colorado where they all attended the University of Colorado. I fancied that perhaps I too could go to college. At least I should try. Once college vacations were over Santa Fe would once again be lonely without friends of my own age. I had certainly been enchanted by New Mexico in countless ways, yet destiny seemed to be beckoning me to move on once again. It took no time to put my affairs in order, pack my dear old trunk again, and prepare for the next leg of my journey.

Gary and a friend of his allowed me to ride north with them. They agreed that I would be able to stay a few nights with them in a house they and others rented off campus. In exchange for bed and board I agreed to cook for them. But the question was whose bed? By this time Gary and I had cooled towards each other and I was infatuated with a friend of his. I'm sure "Topher" was attractive to me because of his defiance and irreverent mannerism. My penchant for dating men who were non-conformist in some way prevailed even then. Once we arrived in the bustling college town I was unsure that I had done the right thing by leaving New Mexico. I felt out of place and intimidated by the academic atmosphere and its definitive lifestyle. As it turned out, I slept on the couch at the boys' house until one of them, a compassionate type, mentioned that a female classmate of his was looking for a roommate. He promptly set up a meeting for me with Helga, a Viennese woman and language student studying for her doctorate, who wished to minimize her living costs to pay for her tuition. Helga and I hit it off immediately and I moved into her one-bedroom apartment.

It was tight quarters. Once again my bed was the couch but for the few months I was in Boulder, it worked out. I took a job in a woman's dress shop right off campus and tried to settle into a dramatically different lifestyle. A Virgo like me, Helga was strictly a no-nonsense person. She was very practical and neat, kept things simple and studied constantly. A close friend and lover of hers, a doctor in psychology, spent a night at the apartment now and again. Through my conversations with him I began to observe areas of my own psyche in need of growth, particularly in terms of my relationships with men and my own sexuality. He became somewhat of a sexual mentor for me, coaxing me to let down my armor and open up to a more expansive awareness of my body and receiving love. But I was confused and awkward — he and Helga were so much more advanced than I, sexually speaking.

A short time later I discovered I was pregnant, by which of my Santa Fe boyfriends I was unsure. I was scared, confused and felt ashamed as I realized I had been naïve and gullible. Worse yet, I had neglected to use birth control. Abortion seemed to be my only choice. In those days the procedure was still illegal and costly yet magically, my friends came to my rescue, providing the funds and contacts for me to resolve my situation. Helga's psychologist friend knew a doctor who was willing to perform the procedure and set up the appointment for me. The whole process was quick and relatively painless although I did not fully process the emotions connected to the whole experience for years. Clearly, once again I had been well protected and I was grateful.

Later the same night, back at the apartment, I began to assess my life's situation. I had not been able to produce sufficient documents to gain eligibility for college and continuing to work in the dress shop held no appeal. Beyond that, I spent much of my free time hanging out with the boys, drinking beer and generally feeling very out of place. Suddenly Boulder didn't make any sense to me. But where would I go now -- back to Santa Fe? My intuition ruled against it.

San Francisco! It hit me in a moment of clarity. I had always wanted to visit the great city by the bay. Before her enrollment at Colorado University Helga had spent several years there and was emphatic about how much she had loved the city.

"*You'll* love it," she insisted, urging me to go, and, in the way that I had made my decisions up until that point, since no other options had become apparent; it seemed like a good idea. I decided to go for it.

Suddenly another striking synchronicity occurred. On my second to last day of work at the dress shop, I met a girl named Diana who shared that she was flying to San Francisco herself the following day to begin a new life. Likewise she had no friends or contacts there. Sight unseen, Diana agreed to share the apartment that she had prearranged there. I was now assured of a place to stay upon my arrival. Since funds were short, I opted to drive, rather than fly West. Several days later, I boarded a Greyhound Bus bound for California to begin the next phase of my life.

CHAPTER FOUR: AMERICA

The "flower child" era was in full bloom and the City by the Bay promised to be colorful. Just *how* colorful, I had no idea! Back in Santa Fe I had witnessed the influx of colorful young people arriving from San Francisco, refugees of the backlash of the counter culture of the war in Vietnam who had dropped out and entered into an alternative lifestyle, only to discover that an aspect of its so-called freedom was, in and of itself, somewhat out of control. I can only guess that these individuals were perhaps some of the most deeply affected by the insanity of the era, and the profound ironies of a movement, for all its good intentions, which became indifferent to its original purpose.

As for myself, I was yet to begin my foray into hippie-dom and the free-love movement. Upon arrival at the Greyhound bus terminal in San Francisco, I caught a cab to the address where my new roommate awaited me. Our apartment was high in the Twin Peaks area with a panoramic view of the city--an apt beginning to my new life. San Francisco was to become the most fascinating and diverse classroom I had entered to date. Diana and I soon moved to the foot of Twin Peaks to a less expensive apartment but within three months she met a young man whom she promptly married.

Within the next two years I moved so many times I lost count, but finally, an offer to rent a charming Victorian cottage in the little town of Sausalito, across the Golden Gate Bridge in Marin County propelled me into a new phase and a lifestyle that was curiously diverse, wonderfully exotic and full of self-exploration.

Chapter Five: Why Porno?

"Our Kay was always acting it up!"

What? My Father's words took me totally by surprise. My Mother nodded in agreement as my mouth fell open. The friends and family members standing close by pricked up their ears and listened for Dad to elaborate, most likely it would be in his typical sarcastic manner. I wasn't sure I wanted to hear this…

His uncharacteristic comment came as a response to a vague question by my Aunt Mary, who was actually interested in my acting career. Inquiries about my life in America were rare, perhaps a result of typical English reserve? I've never been sure of this. Certainly at the root of this trait is the cultural and formative training of which the rule about "…not speaking unless spoken to" was a significant part. Beyond that there was the typical inhibition about expressing oneself and, in the case of my immediate family members, an even more overt self-consciousness in the presence of my Father. I had occasionally suspected that there was also a subtle, albeit unconscious, umbrage taken that I escaped the confines of family life and flew the coup.

So I downplayed my part and, not wanting to appear too much the prodigal daughter, I understated my comments and shared minimally about my life in California. The truth told, my personal self-consciousness about expounding too much upon my adventures overseas stemmed from a fear of evoking Dad's sarcasm. After all the years it still had a vicious sting and I avoided it at all costs.

It was the same dear inquiring Aunt, who, four years later in 1989 at my Father's funeral enlightened me,

"Your Dad was very proud of you but he was envious of your freedom." Apparently he had made known his feelings to all but me. My Aunt's words reduced me to tears and I broke down and sobbed. Mary was married to my Father's younger brother Derek and, unlike the rest of the family, has never been one to mince words or to hold back her truth,

"You know how the Taylor boys are…" she added at the reception after the funeral, emphasizing the family trait towards emotional suppression.

We were gathered in the garden of my parents' home in Kent on that typical English autumn day. The event had a deeply surrealistic overtone, as do perhaps most funerals. An overcast moody gray sky seemed to intensify the rich copper and brown tones of the thick carpet of leaves upon the ground. The navy and black clothing of the family members present added a dramatic contrast, while I, in my usual unconventional manner, had opted instead to wear a beautiful silk rust-copper outfit. Even in school I felt compelled to break convention whenever I could get away with it. If the rule dictated sleeves, I went sleeveless, if a collar was standard, I opted against one. After all, I figured, I sewed most of my own clothes, so I found at least one way to be creative and express myself. As shy and introverted as I was, I opted to be different, even then.

As she spoke, Mary threw a sidelong glance to her husband who was standing silently close by,

"It's hard to get them to talk about anything!"

She was right of course. Everyone nodded in agreement. The men in our family had set the precedent; verbal communication was difficult at best and old patterns die hard.

Strangely, the conversation between Dad's older brother, my Uncle Jack (who passed away in 2005,) and I after the funeral was the most lengthy we ever had. It was true that I hadn't seen many of my relatives since the early seventies and, for the most part, we were strangers. I had left England in my teens and my sporadic trips back were brief and rarely permitted contact with the entire clan. Jack initiated the conversation with a question,

"How do you do it?"

"Do what Uncle Jack?"

"Well, you have to be…"

It was then obvious then that he had begun to tally the years since we had last seen each other and was attempting to compute my age. I supplied the answer to his equation,

"I'm forty five," I shook my head, not quite believing it myself. I neither felt my age nor, as I had been told often, did I look it.

"So how do you do it?" again the question came with sincere curiosity,

"How do you look so young?"

I was very flattered and surprised at my uncle's intention to extend our exchange.

"Well, I suppose I would have to say, clean living. I don't drink or smoke. I meditate every day, I exercise and do yoga. My focus is my spirituality. I accept responsibility for my thoughts and deeds. That's it in a nutshell I suppose."

This was the best answer I could come up with on the spot and strangely, one I felt shy delivering, after all this was my Father's brother—Dad and I would never have had this kind of conversation.

Uncle Jack digested my response to the best of his ability, but his mannerism indicated that his interest ran deeper than I had thought and I felt deeply grateful that this event opened up the lines for future communication between us. Perhaps part of the reason for our connection was that fact that Uncle Jack's own wife was a devout churchgoer who spoke freely of her relationship to God. Aunty Amy was too sick to attend Dad's funeral and eventually passed this Earthly plain in 1994. Although she had always impressed me with her faith, for as long as I can remember, she was burdened with physical suffering. Amy had longed for a child and was unsuccessful in her attempts at conceiving for many years. But finally, at an age considered to be quite late in life, she was successful, and gave birth to a daughter, my cousin Joyce whom I've never met.

I loved my Aunt dearly. The earliest memories I have, dating back to late 1940's, just prior to our first trip to Malta, are of her and Uncle Jack's home in Birmingham. After all the years, I still recall their living room and a magical machine called a gramophone. For most of my childhood I carried the guilt of having accidentally broken a couple of their records, the old brittle 78s, and out of fear of punishment, hiding them in the back of the cabinet. After Aunt Amy's passing, Uncle Jack and I corresponded and, at least for a moment in time, I felt that I was sharing with him in a way I had longed to do with my Father.

For Dad though, it had always been a struggle to understand and accept me as I am, not to mention explaining me to others. So his comment about, "Our Kay always acting it up" at that particular family reunion, while at least an attempt to interact with everyone, still bore hints of his acerbic nature. It was a given that I was the odd one of the family, the black sheep, the one who didn't belong, at least I felt that way. And the fact was that I had been gone so long that I felt much like a foreigner when I came back to visit.

Without doubt I had lost much of my English accent and I'd adopted a primarily American way of speaking so to my dear Mother I sounded quite alien. She expressed her confusion remarking,

"You do sound funny Dear!"

Following her comment, I made a concerted effort to re-adjust my speech patterns, to eliminate American colloquialisms and replace them with whatever British jargon I could remember. But it felt unnatural and apologetic. Naturally, as is always the case, the old expressions and British cadence returned naturally after a few days. In more recent years I have become less inclined to be so concerned about how I sound.

Back in childhood and throughout my adolescence, despite what we were or weren't supposed to say, I dared to question and attempted to do things differently with a kind of silent determination. I was the middle child and even at a young age I tried to be the peacemaker, to initiate more logical responses in dealing with family matters, even those not directly involving me. The constant disharmony just didn't make sense and the fighting seemed completely unnecessary. I knew even then, there were much more rational and intelligent ways of resolving things. My efforts, however, only served to further irritate my Father. When issues directly involved me and Dad's anger would once again erupt, my dear Mummy would inevitably move to my defense. Naturally this would provoke him even more and his anger would turn to a full-on rage. At this point the familiar feeling of dread would envelope the whole family, a feeling so oppressive that we feared any movement would spark an outburst and someone would "get it"! We tiptoed cautiously around as if walking on proverbial eggshells, avoiding confrontation or contact with him at all costs, until his mood shifted.

The scars from those early years ever present, I had therefore humbled myself at this family reunion. Unaware that Dad was listening to the exchange between Aunt Mary and me, I had offered one of a series of rote answers I gave to my family—or to anyone unaware of what a channeled guide, with whom I frequently consulted, once referred to as my "unusual career on the visual arts!" In such situations, I spoke truthfully of my Hollywood experiences; I simply omitted any reference to the fact that I was not primarily involved in mainstream films. Instead I would elaborate upon the small roles I had procured in "legitimate" movies.

During part of my X-rated film career I was listed with a Hollywood agency specializing in supplying talent for minor parts requiring full or semi-nudity in mainstream films. This also included body doubling for major stars in provocative or sexually explicit scenes. In those days, since it could ruin a star's career to bare all, or even some, their agents strongly advised against it. How times have changed! Certain risqué scenes were purposefully shot two ways with the more liberal European and overseas markets in mind. Just as the Adult Film Industry would shoot hard "X" rated and "soft-X" rated scenes for different markets, so Hollywood filmmakers would shoot two versions with the second allowing nudity above the waist.

Europe was still considered much more tolerant of semi-nudity, whereas the American market still clung to its puritanical ethics and double standards.

My brief appearance in "Best Little Whorehouse in Texas" was originally to have been shot in semi-nudity, at least that's what I was told at the initial meeting with the director. However, the creative minds on the production decided instead to reproduce a famous Rita Hayworth photograph as part of the opening montage of the film. The montage traces the "whorehouse" over more than half a century to the present day. In the shot, I appear in a lacy slip (duplicating the one worn by Ms. Hayworth,) kneeling on a bed and casting a lustful glance towards a young service man standing in the foreground. It was exciting to be on the Hollywood set although, sadly, I didn't get to see either Dolly Parton or Burt Reynolds, the two stars of the film. Time slipped by as the many technicians worked away recreating my scene to perfectly match the Hayworth pin-up, and what everyone thought would only take a few minutes, ran into hours. This is typical in the movie-making process.

The part of this story I omitted for my family was the very ironic twist that on the same day that I shot my scene for "Whorehouse..." at Universal studios, I was contracted to fly to San Francisco to film an X-rated version of the same story called "Memphis Cathouse Blues." It was therefore crucial, that I made my flight to San Francisco that afternoon and I was compelled to apply pressure to the Universal production team to complete my scene in a timely fashion. I couldn't help but feel really important that day.

As it turned out, a couple of family members had indeed seen "Best Little Whorehouse," and spotted me. This was most surprising, if not uncanny, since I often joked that if a person sneezed, they would miss me.

Another call I received from the same agency was for a role in "Masada," a TV mini-series starring Peter O'Toole and Peter

Strauss. It depicts the story of the ancient Israeli mesa fortress on the shores of the Dead Sea, where a religious Jewish sect (the Essenes) sought refuge to escape enslavement by the Romans and who there committed mass suicide.

This became another favorite story of mine about my film experiences, although what I couldn't share was the fact that I had actually appeared topless for the studio's European version. However, I felt confident that even if the mini-series was shown on British television, which it inevitably would be, it was unlikely I would be recognized in my role as one of the Moabite whores who serviced the Roman soldiers. The story alone was rich enough as I described the thrill of being on a huge Hollywood sound stage, which had been transformed into a Moabite desert camp complete with animals and all the accouterments of nomadic life, plus hundreds of extras and technicians. Add to this the fact that the women who were chosen were coached by Marge Gower of the famous Marge and Gower Champion dance duo from Hollywood musicals.

In the scene, I and other "whores" were displayed on a small platform, twirling seductively before the Romans legions queuing up for sexual favors. After being selected, each woman disappeared into a tent where her turbaned "pimp" sat sentry to collect the payment from the sex-starved soldier. What I couldn't share with my family was the feeling I experienced when the European version was filmed. The other women and I were asked to remove the tops of our costumes. Breasts were bared and all eyes were upon them! It was truly one of the most challenging moments in my entire career. Baring all in front of a camera on a closed porno set was one thing, but this experience was profoundly different.

One story I couldn't relate at all to my family was the fact that I was the body stand-in for Barbara Felden in The Nude Bomb, a silly movie based on the popular Television series, Get Smart, starring Don Adams as secret agent Maxwell Smart. As the title implies, this story was about the agents retrieving a bomb which, when detonated, renders everyone nude. Naturally, at the conclusion of the film, the bomb goes off and all clothing is vaporized. The last shot of the movie shows Barbara Felden as Agent 99, in the buff, fleeing, away from the camera. Upon closer inspection of the derriere however, one might determine that it is in fact, not Barbara's, but mine! I believe that the film also bombed at the box office – pun intended!

My adventures on "Best Little Whorehouse" and "Masada" consequently became my conversational saving graces. If I embellished upon them in any way, it would be to recount meetings with famous people, and life as a struggling actress working as a waitress in Beverly Hills at a little kosher restaurant, owned by Steven Spielberg's amazing Mother, Leah Adler.

Dad's comment about me "acting it up" echoed in my ears.

I closed my eyes — as I do when I am mentally examining something deeply — to attempt to decode my Father's tone. Was he making a rare attempt to deliver an honest statement? And did it just sound like one of his back-handed comments because he lacked conversational panache? I was confused, for a comment like this pertaining to my childhood was way out of character for him. My first impulse was to protest and somehow defend myself. How, when all of my memories of childhood were of deep repression and discipline, had I ever on earth been allowed the space to "act it up," for God's sake? And why now would he make such a comment?

My left hand automatically dropped to my abdomen, a technique I use for consoling my *inner-child*, to calm my emotions which had instantaneously reconnected me with my old childhood scars. My rational self knew better than to say anything; my parents and I had always been on different wavelengths. Besides, it was also true that I had been away from England for so long that I had forgotten many British idioms.

I waited for Mum or Dad to expound upon the statement but the conversation took other turns.

CHAPTER FIVE: WHY PORNO?

I was visiting my parents in their English countryside home and a small group of friends and relatives were gathered to pay their respects to me. This was one of my rare visits back to the country where, as I usually reply when asked, I was "hatched." I had been gone for over twenty years and, over the last decade, my return visits had become far less frequent. The long plane ride to London was none too appealing or the flood of resurging emotions I inevitably would have to confront.

I love my family very dearly. Back then I also yearned for a deep connection and emotional intimacy with my Father I would not achieve while he was still alive. And so each time I planned a trip back to the UK to visit, the reality was that to some extent, I would be stepping back into the pain of my childhood–one more time. For this reason my trips seemed less a vacation, rather more of a challenge. I therefore negotiated with my inner selves to a modicum of enjoyment by planning one or multiple side trips.

These side trips were naturally met with protest and questions that I could not answer completely or truthfully. I was deeply and painfully aware that my parents' feelings were hurt because I didn't want to visit exclusively with them, but my scars were deep - I hadn't healed yet. In addition to that was the reality that I typically became sick and asthmatic while I was back in England. The old resonance of Dad's tyrannical behavior and the familiar oppression would sweep over me like a black cloud and my breathing would become constricted. On two separate visits in fact, I had to be rushed to the hospital in the middle of the night to receive oxygen. My lungs had constricted to the point where I truly felt I was dying. I believe that in his way, Dad knew my condition was psychosomatic; along the way he had intuited that my reaction to wind triggered my asthma. It was windy the night he arrived back in England and we met for the first time when I was just two years old!

I turned from the family group, unable to get Dad's comment out of my mind. The conclusion I reached was that it was an inference that I was overly emotional, a product of a collective belief-system relating to overtly expressing oneself. It remained that no matter who you were or the prevailing circumstances, expressing oneself in such a manner was a no-no, a frivolous indulgence, narcissistic behavior which only weak people were afforded.

But so it was in post-war England! I have marveled ever since at the way in which such pain and suffering was so stoically buried. "The War" was so rarely mentioned. You just didn't talk about it, at least not in our house. I only ever heard about those memories at gatherings, where they were recounted like party favors in a humorous anecdotal way. Of course, the beer and sherry would already be flowing and alcohol became the buffer to prevent the mood from becoming too serious.

Questions in general were hushed and seriously discouraged in our house, particularly if the subject matter did not directly apply to, or involve oneself. "Children should be seen and not heard," was taken very seriously. When we went out I was repeatedly warned not to ask for anything. Oh, if only they knew that even as a babe their command had been imprinted and re-imprinted countless times into my computer, programming me with an almost paralytic inability to ask for what I wanted way into my adulthood.

It wasn't until I was firmly ensconced in my role as a counselor that I was introduced to the concept of "Psychic Contracts;" promises children make to their parents out of a plea for love during traumatic and painful events in childhood or adolescence. What I have come to see is that this is how shame is passed from parent to child. These contracts, or promises, are the means by which shame – whether sexual, emotional, intellectual or otherwise — are passed from one generation to the next, like deadly viruses. It is this particular dynamic that sheds the light on why, children of abusers will, despite their awareness of their sickness, become abusers themselves and why other addictions are perpetuated. The patterns would seem near impossible to break due to their complex dynamic,

for in shame we render ourselves unworthy. Despite our conscious awareness of the pattern itself, we continue to sabotage our success and happiness and perpetuate the destructiveness.

It is my experience that the only way to break these "Psychic Contracts" is deep inner work using specific techniques to clearly identify the shame and to explore its dynamics and root system. It is important to trace back to the time of the inception of the shame, followed by a process of releasing or handing it back from whence it came. Finally, techniques to restore the specific worthiness issue must be applied as guided by a wise and compassionate counselor. Shame requires what would be perhaps the equivalent of a "root canal" of the consciousness.

Like all children, I remained loyal to the psychic promises I made to my parents, particularly my Father. After all, regardless of his behavior, he was my Daddy and I adored him. He was as handsome as can be with his black wavy hair and startlingly blue eyes (in later years, his looks were reminiscent of the late actor Peter Finch). He wore his naval uniform proudly and I couldn't have been more proud of him

His ship, the H.M.S. Intrepid, had been destroyed off the coast of Greece and he had been one of only a handful who survived. Years after World War II, one of his shipmates wrote a book describing the tragic circumstances. The ship had actually been docked at a Greek port and was spotted by German bombers from the air. Without any warning, the British destroyer was targeted and destroyed. Dad and a few lucky individuals dove overboard and watched their ship's fate sealed. Many of Dad's shipmates were killed, blown to kingdom come. He spoke only of swimming to the Greek shore and arriving in the buff. He had slipped out of his boiler suit as he swam, since it weighed him down. To this day I cannot possibly conceive the horror of what he endured with which he never came to terms and from which undoubtedly he suffered Post Traumatic Stress Disorder.

In the 1980's Dad and my Mother vacationed in Greece and visited the grave site of many of his ship-mates. For the first time since the war he apparently broke down and cried like a baby – perhaps a healing of sorts for him, although he regretted the visit.

I continuously felt that I was a burden to my parents since I was the sensitive one, the sickly one who needed more medical attention than my siblings. And, in addition to being the middle child (who, according to clinical studies typically assumes the role of peacemaker in a family dynamic,) I was also the one who took after my Father in terms of academic aptitude. To my own surprise I passed the "Eleven Plus" examination, qualifying me for English grammar school, a higher-level education that prepares children for university or college. Consequently more money was spent on me for schoolbooks and uniforms than for my siblings who didn't pass the Eleven Plus. This fact I discovered later, I also held against myself.

So, silently and consistently, I promised to never ask for anything, emotionally or materially, perpetuating the Psychic Contract I made with Dad that windy night when we met for the first time when his shame was unconsciously and solemnly transferred to me. On the most basic of levels, I represented another mouth to feed, adding to the burden he already carried on his return home from his wartime experiences. So, even into my adulthood, this promise held strong; as an almost paralytic inability to ask for what I wanted or needed emotionally, until I became totally clear about the dynamics involved, and worked to free myself on the many levels necessary.

"You be good now!"

What on earth did that mean? Mum traditionally administered the classic warning with a sharp shake of the hand and since "bad" meant doing any of the things I was told not to do, I knew that I was safe if I just sat and vegetated. So I did! I was a mousy, scared, sickly little girl. Like infinite numbers of other children who promise to be good, their little spirits squashed, I remained locked up inside of myself for many, many years, unaware of exactly what I was still promising to be or not to be.

So where or how on earth did I manage to "**ACT IT UP**"?

During those formative years, food was rationed and the country struggled to rebuild itself after the ravages of war. The pain and agony of loss hung thick in the ethers; a film of ectoplasm that clung to everything that remained, to the walls, furniture and most particularly, the mandatory heavy window-drapes that blocked out the lights during the air raids. I remember very little before four years of age, and my earliest memories have no color to them, only shades of gray and shadows. There is no joy or laughter, although in the bleakness of those early years, there is a memory of the dollhouse with a flushing toilet that my Father made for me. But soon after I turned four, we received orders for a tour of duty in Malta. We were all to go and sadly, I had to leave my beautiful dollhouse behind and I never saw it again.

It is my belief that I played a substantial role in choosing my life's design, yet I have deeply pondered the question as to why on Earth I would have chosen to be born in wartime England, so dismal, so cold and to say the least, depressing. Why not somewhere warmer? Couldn't I have made it a little easier on myself? For years I joked about God having made a terrible mistake, yet I do believe that in our current lives we create a microcosm of all the issues from our past lives we need to resolve. This certainly might offer an explanation for the severity of some of the experiences we manifest. We humans are so fickle. How soon we forget the lessons we learn, over and over again. We rally and rise and then fall from grace with our God-selves in a flash. So, in this sense, I believe that no matter how painful my early years were, I needed those reference points. The extreme circumstances were designed to set me back on the road to greatest freedom and to secure my faith.

Beyond that basic spiritual concept is another understanding I've come to through my studies, which suggests that, for a period of time, roughly from 1943 through 1948, there was a very dense concentration of "Star Children" incarnating onto the Planet. Perhaps as many as one out of every two beings born in areas where the war had impacted most heavily and a severe loss of life had occurred (including Holocaust victims) were star children. This rapid influx of souls incarnating who were willing to fully wake-up spiritually, was necessary to begin the period of consciousness-awakening marked by the end of World War II, and culminating with the Planet's transition into the third millennium and ultimately, Planetary Fourth Dimensional Ascension.

Previous to my present lifetime I have memories of having been a German naval captain who participated in helping Jews to escape to safe ground, actions for which I was captured and imprisoned. I attempted to escape my captors and was shot in the back. My return to Germany in 1963, my effortless re-learning of the language, and many other details are evidence to me of this, although I had no idea at the time. And, like many other souls, there was little time for rest 'on the other side' before reincarnating to play our parts in the 'story' unfolding on our planet now in the Third Millenium.

Sitting in my parents' living room back in the mid 1980's, it suddenly dawned upon me what my Father was talking about when he accused me of "acting it up." My temper tantrums, was that it?

How I remember the pain of those intervals. It's unclear as to what triggered my emotional outbursts, although chances were that I was being told not to do something at the time. Clearly I remember the impact of being locked in a room to scream it out; this had been our doctor's prescription for my condition! Oh, what dire punishment for the frustration and need for attention of a small child!

After I had screamed myself hoarse and silence once again reigned, my Mother would scoop up my poor exhausted little body and rock me in her arms, tearfully assuring me that it hurt her just as much as me to inflict such a sentence upon me. That tired old cliché! In fact the truth was that she really didn't know what else to do. And, to add insult to injury, despite my young years, I was deeply aware of *her* pain. I even remember the salty taste of her tears as they rolled off her cheeks and plopped onto my little face as she held me. How was she to know that I would perpetuate that pattern on myself for years to come, shutting myself away in an imaginary dark room each time that familiar frustration would flare up inside? Worse still, how would she know that another pattern would be born of this dynamic, one of making her pain (or others' pain) greater than my own?

This became another contributing layer to the denial of my own need for healing for many years. So often throughout my adult life I have been shocked and even scared by my ability to block out pain, physical and mental. It is said that the human body can manufacture neuro-peptides, painkillers that are *thirty times stronger than morphine*. That's a staggering and awesome fact. It also explains why many of us manifest illness and dis-ease to assist in working out our issues. These conditions are red flags – indicators of deep seated issues that must be healed for us to come conscious and to become all we were meant to be as co-creators with God.

I don't remember how long the tantrums lasted - probably not long since to express frustration and emotion meant punishment. But the foundation was in place for the patterns and layers of suppression to begin weaving an intricate tapestry of self-sabotage. The rules were, no asking, no emoting, and no speaking unless spoken to. Life was lonely.

I withdrew more and more into my shyness and, it seemed, my eyes sank further and further into their sockets. Each year as autumn arrived and the temperature dropped, the dread of winter enveloped me and my allergies flared up, causing my beloved Mummy to march me off to the hospital for a battery of allergy tests. So dramatic were my symptoms and the nature of my appearance that the doctors inevitably also tested also me for tuberculosis. I was skin and bone and no amount of typical carbohydrate and fat-laden English food could add flesh to my bones.

Thank goodness for the years we spent in Malta!
The Royal Navy was Dad's career and we were stationed twice on the tiny island that lies a short distance off the coast of Sicily in the middle of the Mediterranean Sea. Malta, then under British rule, was a major seaport during the World War II, and was awarded the George Cross medal for its bravery in sustaining under great duress. Britain maintained its forces there until it won its independence later on in 1964. I was barely four and a half when Mummy, my sister Jean and I flew from Heathrow airport to join my Father (who had left earlier by sea) on the tiny island. Significantly I began school there and, three days after my sixth birthday, celebrated the birth of my brother John.

Dad's second tour of duty in Malta began when I was about eleven. Soon after I had begun grammar school and money had been laid out for uniforms and school supplies, the orders came. It was bad timing to say the least. I am aware that, at the time, boarding school was discussed. My parents weighed the fact that it would be better academically for me to stay in England, yet money was a factor and they concluded that it was too expensive for them. So I was off once again with the rest of the family to my Mediterranean paradise. I was thrilled, although I didn't feel so sure that my Father was so happy to have me along. My trepidation of changing schools yet again diminished as I reveled in anticipation of the sun, warmth and daily forays into the crystal clear ocean.

Life in Malta was the healthiest time of my childhood; the climate and warm waters agreed with me to no end. My usually bony little frame gained flesh and I swam fearlessly in the ocean like a little dolphin. I felt more at home there than ever in England.

My Father served for twenty-one years with Her Majesty's Royal Navy and, except for the periods of time we were in Malta, it seemed that he was never home for long. He would be called away on duty for what seemed like years at a time. During these times life was very different. Mummy was the strongest I ever knew her.

We would await Dad's return home from the sea with great anticipation, a strange mixture of excitement and trepidation. Upon his arrival, my siblings and I were allowed an initial burst of emotion as greeting. If he arrived during daylight, we would wait at the window and as the familiar uniform came into view, we would run down the path to meet the handsome stranger. If he arrived during the night, the following morning we would wait for Mummy's signal, and then run into their bedroom to greet him and claim our home-coming gifts.

The first couple of days or so after Dad's return the mood around the house would be high.

"My Daddy's home!" I would proclaim proudly to anyone who asked.

Then suddenly, it was as if the sky blackened and a wintry chill would descend. Dad's mood would change and life once again was dismal. It was as if he just couldn't adjust to shore life and the three females and my brother he came home to each time. Of course the reality was that at home he had to be with and confront himself and his pain, something that he and so many military men like him were just not emotionally equipped to handle.

One night, some years after my tantrums ceased, I woke up from a nightmare. My arm had fallen asleep and lifelessly lay across my throat, heavy like an iron bar. I thought I was being strangled by an intruder and screamed out. Daddy came running into my bedroom to see what was amiss. After assessing the situation, he sat down on the edge of my bed and stroked my head to console me in what was the tenderest moment I ever remember sharing with him. In that instant, from where I lay, I caught a glimpse of something I'd never seen before, a strange-looking body part emanating very interesting and magnetic energy. There, in plain view, Daddy's penis made its indelible impression upon me. Innocently, I was strangely and hypnotically drawn to it. He felt my gaze as it dawned upon him that he was naked. In a reflex reaction, he dashed from the room and symbolically took his love away from me. And, in that split second, his (sexual) shame was transferred to me – I took it on as children do out of their desire and, in that moment, need for love. The innocent event registered as a deep soul wound for me, resulting in a self-perpetuating pattern for many years.

This complex dynamic of how shame is transferred is one I have studied for years. That particular event, which I call my "penis du pere" incident, left me with deep unworthiness of God's love (since to the child her Father *is* God) and for years also rendered me unworthy of being loved sexually. Unmistakably this was one of the dynamics that contributed to leading me down the path to pornography.

In the same manner, another incident ranking as one of the most typical ways shame is passed on occurred when I was quite young. My Mother walked in one day as I sat on the living room rug examining my little genitals. Curious about my private parts and sensations already stirring in those areas, it was the most natural thing for me to have been doing. But caught up in her own embarrassment and shame, my Mother grabbed my little hand, slapped it and warned me harshly to,

"Never let me catch you doing that again!" And then added,

"Don't ever let a man touch you there."

Her personal fear and inability to deal emotionally with the situation spun off into a reflex reaction. I don't mean that in either an accusative or judgmental way, rather simply, she was not equipped to handle the moment in an intellectually and healthy manner.

I remember a conversation I had with a young mother during my thirties about a similar situation. Her daughter at that time was roughly the same age as I was when my Mother caught me in the act of exploring myself. The young woman shared with me that just weeks before our conversation she had experienced her own little daughter engrossed in innocent self-discovery. In her moment of embarrassment however, this young mother refrained from over-reacting, composed herself and instead, sat down with her daughter, joined her in her exploration and explained to her what her different little body parts were in a way the little girl could understand. I offered a prayer of relief that one little girl had been spared a heavy and perhaps lifelong dose of sexual shame.

So, in contemplating the mystery of, "why porno" – why I was drawn into the world of X-rated films?, I must first consider my shame, the shame I carried with me throughout most of my adult life, its origin and how I took it on. For it remains that shame is passed on, like a deadly virus, not intentionally or maliciously; on the contrary, its perpetration is, for the most part, unconscious and innocent. Never the less, shame deposits a burden of deep unworthiness and subjects its carrier to untold life challenges.

In 1986 I was commissioned to assist in creating a book entitled "The New Goddesses," whose purpose was to find common threads among the women of X-rated films. My role was to select five very different actresses (I was to be the sixth) who, for a generous, not to mention rare fee, would be willing to be interviewed at length. The project required a whole day's participation for each subject – with a break for lunch, sandwiches supplied by the author's wife. The writer had meticulously compiled a list of roughly one hundred and sixty questions for each interviewee for thorough examination. At that time, I believed that there were both common and conspicuously uncommon threads among my peers and myself. Since each of us chose the mutual experiences of making adult films, it stood to reason that there *were* common threads even though, culturally and socially, the other five women and I came from quite different backgrounds.

However, regardless of the superficial findings, I believe that on a deep psychological level, a common thread at the root of many individuals (male or female) opting for a career in X-rated films is sexual shame. Specifically what the individual issues are, or what lessons will be learned by participating in the industry, naturally is exclusive to the individual's own life pattern.

I believe that we enter our lives with a degree of unworthiness as part of our genetic encoding and our karmic density—the lessons that we are here to work out on Earth. Through our formative years we are conditioned by cultural beliefs as well as ideologies from those around us. We experience trauma, abuse and other hardships, resulting in further soul wounding and eventually bringing our unworthiness fully manifest as shame and other dis-ease, whether physical, mental or psychological. Then, we attract to ourselves the outer mirrors or representations of what we need to experience or learn so that we may evolve, heal and grow.

Most organized religion is notorious for having perpetrated sexual shame and separation of body and spirit. It is no secret that these same religious groups have used and abused their power to dominate the masses for their own devices for centuries. Perhaps some of us who have opted to actively participate in the porno industry agreed in some way to assist in the uplifting of these collective rifts in consciousness, as we journey through our own sexual issues. From a spiritual logical point of view, it makes sense.

As one who always chooses to examine the bigger picture, it occurs to me that as long as these rifts in consciousness exist—these soul-disconnections—the outer expression of shame will remain heightened and the porno industry will continue to reap billions upon billions of dollars, as individuals choose to focus on their sexuality through that lens, rather than through a deeper spiritual communion with their own souls, their partners, and ultimately, God.

Dr. Dean Dauw, a former Catholic priest, psychologist and sex therapist claims,
"There is only one drive stronger than the sex drive - man's drive towards God. And it's been this desire for unity with God, paradoxically, that's led us to make up so many rules and superstitions about sex."

But where did it all begin for me? Over the years, as I've worked with my past life issues and residual pockets of shame have surfaced, I've consistently explored the deepest layers and roots of my own imbalances. My self-exploration revealed collective consciousness, or more accurately, strains of collective unconsciousness, buried deep in my DNA, holding the clues. It's clear that I have been purposefully led on a particular path of discovery as part of my life mission. Several lifetimes have surfaced, including a specific incarnation in the Holy Land circa 600 BC, where my issues were related to the mixing of bloodlines and impurity. Each of these shame-based lifetimes was female and, each time, because of social or political status, I was not permitted to be with the one I loved. Whatever the reasons, in each case they were bogus since we all originated from the same tribe. Had we really forgotten so quickly the one-ness from whence we came? Oh yes!

Could it really be that from these roots sprang the myriad of patterns of separation dominating our world today? And perhaps the issues we so closely associate with sexuality are, at their root, not about sexuality at all, but are really fear-based issues of impurity born of myths regarding inbreeding.

I pray daily for miracles of ways to assist in the evolution of this consciousness. Elevating our collective relationship towards our sexuality to a higher vibration will, I believe, assist in the breaking of genetic encoding enslaving us to our own ignorance for so long. The AIDS epidemic may have already assisted to that end. (All sickness and disease has a consciousness and it is always profoundly revelatory to understand each specific imbalance from that angle.)

Many years ago, during a time when I was striving to understand the deeper dynamics of this heinous disease, a friend of mine--at that time a nurse serving on an AIDS ward in a San Fernando Valley hospital--phoned me. She told me about a specific patient whom she felt I could help.

"He will not help himself," she sighed, "He runs his business from his bed, he's always on the phone. He won't rest."

I wasn't sure how I could help the gentleman since his disease was quite progressed. My friend insisted that, provided her patient was willing to come to see me, he would benefit from the session. This was a challenge for me since I normally didn't work with those who were sick or under medical care. Most individuals who seek me out are those seeking deeper understanding and purpose in their lives. Some may have issues manifesting as one or another physical imbalance, yet more times than not, they have already chosen to approach their issue from a metaphysical and naturopathic point of view, and have at least a sense of *why* they have manifested their condition.

An appointment was made for the individual in question to see me within the next few days. Although he was weak, and used a walker, he arrived at my home feisty and mentally quite alert. We sat for a few moments as I tuned into his energy. In those days I used Applied Kinesiology (muscle testing) to begin a dialogue with the body consciousness and to determine where blocks were. In this way, one may bypass the mind, which has its own ideas of what's going on, and which may lead you down a path of erroneous information. In my client's case I used the technique reluctantly, not wanting to tire him. Instead, I changed my technique to facilitate his condition. Regardless, it didn't take long to determine there had been a major psychological shutdown eight years prior and so I quickly resorted to simple questions,

"What happened of significance eight years ago?"

That was easy: That was when he met his current life partner. I asked him to describe his mate to me, although I already had a pretty good picture in my mind. The person he described was someone who was very controlling and introverted, who perfectly matched the energy I already intuited.

What I look for in my counseling work are reasons and circumstances as to why a person has shut down, separated from their soul-self and higher selves and sadly therefore, to a great extent, from their essential Life Force. Many times, these significant events will mark the onset of a physical challenge and, indeed many times, by remembering and recognizing the specific course of events and emotions, sickness and even disease may be reversed in an instant. Not only have I experienced this personally, I have witnessed it many times with others. (Regardless, I always recommend ongoing work with the aspects of the self that took the tumble.)

I knew that AIDS attacks the immune system and that the seat of the immune system is the thymus gland. The application of Applied Kinesiology is directly related to the thymus gland, the reason I found the technique invaluable. In my research, I read in one medical textbook, "the thymus produces white blood cells in children and atrophies in adulthood."

That didn't make sense, until I heard my mentor Ryhen call the thymus the "Fantasy Center," suggesting that linear, adult thinking and logic shuts out childish things, the joy, and certainly the ability to dream. This would perhaps - on a metaphysical level at least - explain why the gland would atrophy. It became crucial therefore to keep the inner child alive and interactive to remain healthy.

I continued my line of questioning,

"What does your inner child like to do?"

"I don't have a child," he frowned, not fully understanding what I asking.

"You have a child living inside of you—your inner child. What does he like to do, what makes him happy?"

He still looked confused.

"OK, let me put it another way; what did you like to do as a child? What brought you joy?"

"Oh," he replied without hesitation, "music—I loved to sing!" Now it made sense to him. He came alive with the very thought of it.

"And when *was* the last time you sang?"

Sadly, I already knew the answer to that. I already recognized the classic example of role-playing in a relationship, where one partner will alter or adapt to please the other, thereby shutting down their flow or life essence, their spirit. It happens more times than not in primary relationships, whether heterosexual or homosexual.

The man sitting in front of me lowered his head slightly as he gave me the answer I already knew. It was after he entered into the relationship that he quit his involvement with the noted Gay Men's choir and shut music out of his life. I gently peered into his eyes.

I told him, "I know you came to me with the hope of finding a cure for your disease. From where I stand, *you* are the cure. My message to you is to resurrect your child self, reintegrate the wonder and innocence of that aspect of you back into your life, get those juices flowing. You have shut them out long enough. Stop your business activity, hang up the phone and revitalize the relationship with your inner child. If there's a chance to beat this illness, it's through that channel."

Stevie Wonder's "You Are the Sunshine of My Life" came to mind. I sang a few bars and invited him to sing together. But he struggled as if he had even forgotten how.

I concluded, "My prescription for you is to go home and force (not a word I normally use,) yourself to sing. Sing your guts out every day. It's your spiritual muscle. It's what you need the most now. Have music all around you to nurture your soul."

I finished our session in my usual manner, gave him notes and an audio-tape of our encounter and, in light of his condition, I offered to drive him home. As we drove into Hollywood, I chose my words carefully and deliberately to convince him of my message and guidance to him.

CHAPTER FIVE: WHY PORNO?

circa 1944, baby Kay with Mother and Sister.

Sweet sixteen, last year of school.

Five or six years old.

Sadly, he didn't make it—he died within a few months. I grieved for him, for the loss of his voice, and for the loss of all the souls who had sacrificed themselves in the search for love in all the wrong places.

It was soon after my penis-du-pere incident that I created the White Rabbit and entered into my fantasy life! I summoned my imaginary fury friend to come to me when I was snugly and warm in my little bed. He was as fictional as Harvey or the White Rabbit in "Alice in Wonderland," yet he was perfectly real to me and was there when I needed and wanted him. There, under the covers, he would touch me where it felt good. White Rabbit was my comfort. He was the first substitute for the love I felt unworthy of having with a real person, my earliest sex partner, illusional and taboo.

* Star Children or Star Beings: Individuals who have experienced other lives elsewhere before beginning their wheel of incarnation on Earth.

Chapter Six: The First Time - On Film!

A quarter of a century or so after I created my warm and fuzzy imaginary white rabbit I ventured forward into another world of illusion. One might ask, how on Earth could a nice girl like me, have ever chosen to become involved in the arena of the most controversial genre in entertainment, one where individuals lived out the sexual fantasies of millions? There were deeply unconscious reasons, even karmic ones, I realized much later, which threw the purest Light upon the answer as to why I chose such a profound detour in my life.

To this day, the memory of pondering my decision to accept the role as the housewife Millicent in the film "Sexworld" is like a split-screen image in my mind. On one side of the picture I am a prude; the good girl, conditioned and constrained with hair coiled in a bun, blouse buttoned to the throat and hands properly folded on my lap. On the other side of the screen, the "me" yearning to be free from the bonds of her conditioning, removes her hair pins and begins to unbutton her blouse, as if readying herself for the first take of an erotic scene.

And, in a flash, I found myself on the set of a movie, swept up in a bizarre new world, anticipating that once-in-a-lifetime event that was about to transpire—my first sex scene. I was in a time warp, filled with such heightened thoughts and emotions, the likes of which I had never experienced before. I lay semi-naked, poised and ready, with my legs spread wide on a large bed dressed with cold white satin sheets, surrounded by blazing lights, camera cranes, boom mikes and a dozen or more technicians.

Even by X-rated standards in 1977, "Sexworld" was an expensive and lavish production—close to a quarter million dollars it was rumored. This was the Golden Age of "X" Rated films, when adult movie theaters flourished and the demand for quality sex films was high, nationally and internationally. Shooting schedules sometimes were as long as two weeks in those days. Many scripts were sizeable with dialogue and story lines to match low-budget Hollywood "B" movies. In many cases, double footage of the sex scenes was shot to cater to both "X"-rated and "R"-rated domestic and foreign markets. The R-rated television channels also scooped up the *soft* versions and frequently an in-between version called *soft X*, exhibiting a little more than soft, but not completely hard X-rated footage. (The delineation was always vague to me.)

On the fateful day, Joey Sivera, the actor playing my robot stud, prepared himself off camera. We were ready for a take and waiting for a few technical adjustments to be made. The action leading up to the explicit sex footage had been shot successfully. Thus far, Anthony (Sam) Spinelli the director, seemed well pleased. I was also happy with my performance so far. Several other actors on the set had graciously acknowledged my professional attitude, applauding the way I prepared myself by applying techniques I had learned in the acting workshops I previously had taken. Now however, we were down to the nitty-gritty; the sex footage and the "money shots" and I had no idea what to expect. I felt like a fish out of water. Nothing could have prepared me for this! Even though I felt a hint of exhibitionism daring to rise within me, I also quietly panicked.

What I was experiencing in that moment didn't come close to resembling what I had witnessed a couple of weeks prior, when I watched a sex scene filmed for a movie called "V The Hot One," an X-rated take-off of the French classic "Belle Du Jour." Although it was only a speaking part, this had been my first film. Up until that point I had never even been on the set of a movie. I became immediately fascinated with the mechanics of film-making and I watched enthralled as the beautiful raven-haired Annette Haven performed a sex scene with John Leslie who was my "sponsor" into the business. (Usually sets were closed to all but the immediate crew during sex scenes but, since I was already there, no-one seemed to mind my presence.) Attempting to be as inconspicuous as possible, my curiosity peaking, I edged in as closely as I could. I felt a subtle sense of personal embarrassment, for in one fell swoop I had discovered the voyeur in myself, although I was honestly intrigued to watch how they went about putting "it" on film.

(It was ironic that my character in the film was the madam of a brothel in which the lead character had gone to seek work as a call girl to break free from her staid and meaningless home life. My role was very small and I cringed with embarrassment at how bad I felt my performance was. In my final scene I was to draw a champagne glass to my lips and take a sip. As the camera zoomed in on the glass, my hand shook so badly I thought I'd drop it. How I had wished for another take of that shot!)

Annette Haven's star quality was obvious and I was intrigued at how she conducted herself. She was intelligent, acted very professionally, demanded attention, and got it. Overtly, she seemed confident, which might have convinced me except for the unrelenting verbalizations that told a different story. I saw a sensitive, vulnerable little girl craving attention. This little child and her pain were profoundly evident when, a couple of years later in 1983, Annette and I, together with a contingency from the Adult Film Association, were invited to Washington DC to attend the "Sixth World Congress of Sexuality." It was quite a historic occasion, where, as part of a week-long conference dealing with the theme "Emerging Dimensions of Sexology," the AFA gave a film presentation, following which we participated in a panel discussion with sexologists from more than thirty-three countries. Many noted members of the scientific community were present including such academic luminaries as Shere Hite, William Masters and Virginia Johnson and many others. Annette and I, along with our fellow actors Seka and Richard Pacheco, spoke convincingly I thought, of our attempts to influence producers and maintain quality and sensuality in the films, to cater to the emerging market place in which women viewers were very much a part.

On the last day of our stay in Washington, the organizer of the trip, then president of the erstwhile Pussycat Theater chain and the AFA Jimmie Johnson, arranged for a sightseeing tour around the nation's capital that included a stop at the Jefferson Memorial. The inscription of Jefferson's powerful proclamation etched on the great monument moved me on a deeply emotional level.

"...INSTITUTIONS MUST ADVANCE ALSO TO KEEP PACE WITH THE TIMES. WE MIGHT AS WELL REQUIRE A MAN TO WEAR STILL THE COAT WHICH FITTED HIM AS A BOY AS CIVILIZED SOCIETY TO REMAIN EVER UNDER THE REGIMEN OF THEIR BARBAROUS ANCESTORS."

The significance and purpose of the trip and my own cause for personal freedom somehow were voiced in those potent words triggering my reaction. I sensed another person standing close by. It was Annette, and the tears streaming down her cheeks reflected her own identification with the profound message from Mr. Jefferson. I instinctively moved closer and felt compelled to hug her. She had also been deeply moved by the words written on the great plaque and yet I sensed that it had triggered something deeper within her. My mothering instincts emerged in an instant and I felt compelled to whisper to the little child within her,

"It's OK baby, it's OK."

She was overcome by my gesture and tried to speak. Her huge dark eyes glistened as she finally uttered,

"Gosh Kay, my Mother never held me that way!"

Somehow I knew that. I too choked up for a moment, feeling the powerful truth behind her words. We stood there for a few minutes just holding each other and finally returned to the rest of the group.

Annette was profoundly and uncharacteristically quiet for the rest of the trip, and sat by herself in deep thought on the bus. I would not soon forget such a poignant moment.

On the set of the movie "Sexworld" my emotions teetered between panic and exuberance. Could I really bite the bullet and surrender to the moment? I imagined myself getting up, leaving the set and dramatically announcing that I just couldn't do it. Inside my head, someone assured me frantically,

"It *is* an option!" while another voice countered with, "You signed the contract, you committed, and you *can't* walk off now!"

Spinelli's own words echoed in my mind, he had urged me to think long and hard about my decision.

"Honey," he had delivered with a theatrical flair, "You have to be sure you can live with it. Once it's on film, it's irreversible!"

I had read for the part of Millicent in an audition arranged by John Leslie, one of the top actors in the business. John's assurance that this director was one of the best in the business was a strong factor in agreeing to meet with him.

Sam was right out of a movie himself, the Adult Film Industry's answer to Hitchcock, if there was one, with a profile every bit as distinctive as the famous British director's and a personality to match.

He loved my reading for the Millicent role and felt I was perfect. Up until that point there had been a question as to whether this part required sex or not. John assured me that it could go either way or, I later wondered, had he used that ruse just to get me there? Regardless, Sam had insisted that it indeed had to be a sex role while proclaiming how perfect he thought I was for the part. I have come to realize that the moment I received Sam's approval was the defining point in my decision making process. Although I told him that I'd go home and think about whether I could live with the consequences, the die had been cast. Inside, I had already decided to take the part. This was one of the major themes of my life at that time in action! My constant search for approval from men was such a driving force that now propelled me down this mysterious and notorious path.

The cool of the satin sheets took me back to the reality of the Sexworld set again. My heart pounded and I realized that I was hyperventilating. I looked up to perhaps catch eye contact with someone whose glance would re-assure me - or something! But, this was not the time to be looking for re-assurance outside of myself. I was mere seconds away from recording on film, for all time most likely, my first sex scene!

How could I possibly have known the deeper significance of that moment and how could I have known the lifelong ramifications of my choice. Oh yes, I *had* chosen, because even as the many voices inside of me cried out their fears and concern, the fact was that I was resigned to go through with it! I knew deep in my soul that this was right for me, although I didn't know why. Had I been able to, as I always say, "Go upstairs and take a look down," I might have known why it felt so right, for this one action most assuredly set up a series of life experiences the likes of which I couldn't possibly have imagined. How on earth could I have known that this one situation, out of which I would carve a career and dramatic public platform, would then also provide the door, through which a few select individuals would come, persons I was destined to meet in this lifetime? I often speculate upon how I might have connected with those persons had they not seen me in a video at a certain point in time and been motivated to track me down.

How indeed would Charles have found me. Charles, with whom I had a huge chunk of karma and much to accomplish during a ten year period of time? Conjuring up alternative scenarios in answer to those questions remains a real stretch of my imagination. How also could I, or anyone for that matter, have imagined a global computer network that would broadcast these images to every corner of the World? Paradoxically, the Internet has become a venue through which I now do the major portion of my life's work.

A rustle beside me revealed the make-up artist who smiled as he dabbed away at my perspiring upper lip, in that moment far from being stiff (no pun intended!) I wondered if my emotions were showing. Was I as transparent as I felt? As my actress persona clicked in, I wondered if I should be concerned about my appearance. How did

I look through the eye of the camera? How far did my responsibility as an actress go? Did I need to ask more questions about angles and eye-levels? Then I reminded myself that the character Millicent was no spring chicken, she was more mature than the other women. So, I concluded that I should let her be authentic, let her look and be her age. Why compare myself with all the other actresses on the set, all younger than me and certainly more glamorous even without their make-up, or so I felt? Feeling painfully shy and very self-conscious, I had watched them, taking tips where I could, aware of just how alien to me these issues were. Glamorous was a label I certainly had never pinned on myself. I was much more comfortable with my earth-mother persona. Now, circumstances were insisting that I coax forward my siren persona. She was definitely there, deep within, although she didn't fully bloom until years later. Indeed, I jokingly referred to myself as "The Prude of Porn" for most of my career, aware of the dramatic splits in my personality.

In that moment, I felt profoundly intimidated, awkward and insecure beyond words. I looked into the make-up artist's face and recalled an earlier conversation with him. During his career this gentleman had applied make-up to the faces of some of the World's most famous women, including Jackie Kennedy and Elizabeth Taylor. Now little 'ole me, I mused. Unbelievable! With a final dab, he was gone, and I lay there on the white satin sheets, alone again.

I looked around for Joey, my partner in the scene. In that moment he was nowhere to be found. Where was this person with whom I was momentarily to engage in sex? In acting class exercises, it seemed that we would spend an eternity connecting eye to eye, building the emotion and intensity of the relationship between characters. At that moment, anticipating actual physical intimacy, I felt an almost desperate need for closeness with my fellow actor. Yet, to have asked for what I needed in that moment, was of course out of the question for me. I was entirely too new to the experience, unfamiliar with protocol and far too intimidated with the range of emotion I was feeling.

Joey and I had met fleetingly at John Leslie's house a couple of days prior. He seemed nice enough with a shy reserve and a dry off-the-wall humor, reminiscent of an awkward schoolboy. Of course, at the time, I hadn't known I would be *working* with him within a few short days.

The technicians labored away adjusting one thing and another. I just lay on the bed alone, feeling helpless, to say the least. Just how much time transpired as I weaved in and out of my thoughts and emotions, I had no idea.

"Well, maybe all this waiting was to give us one last opportunity to reconsider. We could still renege on our agreement to perform sex and they'd be forced to rewrite it out of the scene!" an inner voice of logic quipped. Then Spinelli's voice rang out,

"Here we go folks...!"

My emotions came to rest, and my very vocal inner cast of characters disappeared instantaneously! As if by magic, the set came alive and Joey appeared on cue. The camera operator positioned himself on his crane, the boom man lifted the mike high overhead; all hands were on deck and Sam leaned over us for last-minute directions.

"Sexworld" was a take-off on the movie "Westworld", only in the X-rated version, **sexual** fantasies were fulfilled and, as in the Hollywood version, some with robot characters and others with humans. We were on a San Francisco sound stage shooting the fantasy sequences. Previously, we had filmed the counseling scenes in which each guest spells out their fantasy to their individual counselors. Millicent, my character, hot for *a real man*, had already stated her desires to her counselor,

"I want that son of a bitch to have a huge gorgeous cock with huge balls. My guy won't care if I want to do it or not. He'll throw me down and talk dirty to me. I may fight it but he won't care. My guy's gotta have balls!"

When I first read those lines in the script I panicked. I wondered if I could meet the challenge of this character. The dialogue alone was offensive to my sensibilities and so very much out of my own realm of expression. "Balls" to me inferred grit, or a mild oath my Mother was known to utter on occasion. Used in a sexual context, such expressions were way out of my comfort zone! It slowly began to dawn on me just how much stretching I was going to have to do, sexually and otherwise. "I'm an actress, I can do it," inside a quiet voice assured me. It remained to be seen whether or not that was true.

Sam had painstakingly worked with me on the dialogue, motivating me with real personal life issues I'd shared with him earlier during rehearsals. (Yes, we had lengthy rehearsals in those days.) I had confided in him as to my inability to ask for what I wanted in relationships, and how, when it came to sex, I belonged to the majority of women who were painfully self-conscious and un-demonstrative. Slowly Sam had coaxed the words out of my mouth. Millicent gets her fantasy! She gets her guy who doesn't care "if she wants to do it or not," who is the total opposite of her husband; an impotent whiny Mama's boy. She asks for rough and she gets it!

"And, speed!" Film was rolling!

As rehearsed, Joey, my robot lover, grabbed my head and faked a couple of slaps. On the third, however we missed our timing and the back of his hand met my cheek. The slap stunned me yet, deeply in character, the thought of stopping the action didn't even enter my mind. With an even firmer grasp Joey proceeded to thrust his member vigorously in and out of my mouth. By this point, my adrenalin was racing and I *became* Millicent, the sex-starved housewife, simultaneously protesting and begging for more. Joey straddled me, pinning me down in a most uncomfortable position. Other than flapping my legs, all I could do with my limited span of movement was to grab his rear end with my right hand. I was subtly aware of blocking the camera, but there was naught to be done, there simply was no other way to keep my head up. Off camera I heard Sam's voice giving direction, but my own sounds drowned him out. Joey thrust hard until he suddenly pulled out and I felt his warm liquid squirt onto my face. Caught up in the momentum, I let my head drop back, smearing it all over my face until I heard, "Cut!"

Joey rolled over and collapsed beside me on the bed and, looking over to our director, queried with a grin,

"Did I cum Sam, did I cum?" There was that schoolboy humor and his way of creating levity! The whole crew broke up.

"That was great guys, just great!" Sam was beside us on the bed adjusting his trademark baseball cap and grinning with approval. Again, he reiterated to me,

"Great, honey, you were great!"

I was in a state of shock, hardly knowing what to think. The intensity of the scene was certainly more than I had bargained for.

You can always tell when a scene has really worked. Although it isn't always verbalized, there is an air of unanimous approval, of collective satisfaction. Everybody did their job and the result was felt--it's called teamwork! The actors are the last of that team to contribute and, when they perform their part well too, everyone feels that team spirit and a deep sense of satisfaction. This was one of those times.

I snapped out of the character and, still feeling the numbness where Joey's hand had accidentally slapped my face, I raced into the make-up room to see if I had been injured. Although there was no blood, to my shock, what I discovered instead, was that Joey's slug had chipped my front tooth. As I stood there looking at my mirror image, I saw my Father staring back at me. The one mutual physical characteristic Dad and I shared, was an overlapping front tooth. Dad's had, for as long as I could remember, a slight chip on the outer edge. Now mine was chipped in the identical place. This had been a bitter and most ironic blow!

"Karma," I deduced.

Up until that point I hadn't given but a split second of a thought to how my parents or family would ever react to this journey I was taking. Later I did ponder the issue, yet always, I knew deep down inside that this was something I had to do. (In terms of my dental mishap, fortunately the next day I was not scheduled to work. A visit to my dentist assured me that no further damage was done and he filed the tooth down.)

The shock subsided as the make-up man, shaking his head in annoyance after seeing the condition of my face, instructed me to go and,

"Wash that stuff off your face!"

In that moment, a very logical thought occurred to me. We were by no means finished with the scene and my make-up had to be completely re-applied. Such situations are, I discovered later, a make-up artist's nightmare. It meant stopping in the middle of what he was doing, to redo a makeover on a face that had originally taken thirty minutes or so to prepare. Inevitably it threw him off his schedule. But, there was naught to do about it; I was needed back on the set, stat! Despite my actor's ethics of being in the moment, I would think twice next time before smearing my face. I also learned quickly that one did **not** require seniority to stipulate "no ejaculation shots in the face."

I was soon back on the set with fresh makeup, powdered and ready to resume. Further technical adjustments were underway, and once again I lay in waiting. It hit me at that point that the camera had been repositioned for tight angles of our lower bodies. Nervous anticipation hit me again as I realized that, although I had been captured on film delivering "fellatio," Joey had not yet entered me. There had been no penetration.

I waited to see if my inner cast of characters would make another pitch to reconsider and talk us out of going all the way. This time, they were but a faint echo. Collectively, *we* were finally resigned.

"Whenever you're ready Joey..." Spinelli's voice was slightly lowered due to the sensitivity of the upcoming scene. From somewhere off the set, Joey appeared quite ready for action, brandishing a giant hard-on. I was taken aback in that moment for I intuited that he had assistance in becoming aroused. There was no shortage of young attractive female "production assistants" on the set, and it was obvious that they were totally available to assist in any way necessary! Somehow though, I felt slighted and even insulted that I was not the one who aroused him. This was so impersonal! My own indignation caught me by surprise and I quickly reminded myself that this was not real life. All the same, my ego was deflated and, as the action resumed, I found my personal response to the situation affecting my character's performance.

"Want some more Baby?" hissed my robot stud, as he forcefully entered me. And with that, it was done, recorded on film for all eternity! In that particular moment I was lost in time, split somewhere between my authentic self and my character, pinned to those cold white satin sheets by this person I hardly knew. I heard my character whimper,

"Stop, please stop!" But I, Kay, meant it.

Perfectly in character, Joey as The Robot, ignored my plea and we played the scene to the end climaxing with his obligatory "money shot."

Ironic, I thought later, that Joey indeed had remained true to his character, whereas I, the "actress" had, in the end, stepped way out of character. Or had I? Either way, the moment I had so anxiously anticipated was over. I had now entered the ranks of porno actress, sealed my fate, branded myself with an indelible "X" and joined a unique group of individuals who choose to go public in the most extreme sense of the word.

I felt strangely like I had just lost my virginity for the second time. Indeed, my feelings were significantly similar to those I had experienced in Germany, just prior to my nineteenth birthday, when my sweetheart Wolfgang had sneaked me into his dormitory room in Stuttgart and there, clandestinely, we made love. It was my first time. Wolfie was gentle, not forceful in any way. We adored each other, smitten with that youthful innocence which knows no boundaries. We had to do it, there and then, there seemed to be no question about that, yet when it was all over, I felt strangely empty. Lying there in that stark dormitory room, less in an afterglow, rather more in a quandary about the new bizarre world of sex into which I had just been introduced, the dorm mother had discovered us. Now, once again, as the adrenalin rush of my virgin film performance wound down and my rational mind stirred once again, the icy stare of the hausfrau surfaced from the deep recesses of my memory into full consciousness. She came fully alive again, towering in the door-way, dramatically flourishing the key to Wolfie's room, and threatening to throw him out of the house if I wasn't out of there immediately. This was such a harsh blow to me, a lowly teen hitchhiker with only a handful of dollars to my name, a stranger to the land in which I found myself (although later, during a past life regression, I discovered that I was merely retracing steps from my last lifetime to begin my worldly journey in this life.)

Wolfgang and I had met a few days prior at a public swimming bath and we were already inseparable. My traveling companion Loraine had been summoned home to England by her parents after her remaining funds were stolen from the youth hostel where we were staying. They had sent her a ticket and instructions to take the next train back to England. This was fine with her. She lamented that she missed her boyfriend, a statement I thought strange coming from someone with such promiscuous tendencies; a trait which both bothered and yet strangely awed me.

Loraine was an overtly sexual person, who flirted with just about every man she encountered and, in that, I felt that she flirted constantly with danger. I was so very much the opposite. So I watched her, shocked and yet fascinated with her loose mannerism. At sixteen she had already been pregnant and had had an abortion, yet she continued to go through men at what to me was an alarming rate. The fact that, of all my friends, she was the one who showed interest in going with me to the Continent was ironic to say the least. We truly were an odd couple. Shortly after she returned to England, she did in fact settle down and marry her boyfriend. I, on the other hand, simply could not return and give my Father the satisfaction of fulfilling his prediction of.

"You'll be home within six weeks, mark my words!"

Unable to express any form of blessing, Dad had simply thrust a few pounds into my hand at the train station at the onset of our trip, and offered his prediction as farewell. A mere few weeks later, I was nowhere near ready to return. So I stayed, secure with Wolfgang's promise to take me home to meet his family, and to help me find a job!

The imprint left by the eavesdropping hausfrau had added yet another layer to the already considerable burden of sexual issues I had carried through from my past lives, which would take me years to fully resolve and heal.

Now, on that San Francisco sound-stage, the memory of that moment was revived. Despite feeling elated knowing that I had performed well, I was confused by the mixture of emotions erupting inside. I suddenly felt very alone.

Once again I heard Sam's inimitable,

"Great honey, just great!"

Quickly returning my full consciousness to the soundstage, I looked up to numerous nods of approval from those on the set, and met with even more kudos as I returned to the wardrobe room. The whole experience had taken probably less than a couple of hours, yet it seemed an eternity. I was amazed that it was all over. To everyone on the set, it was just another scene, but in that moment, a profound truth occurred to me — this singular decision to perform a role which involved sex, and even beyond that, actually fulfilling the decision, changed everything for me.

Was this manifest destiny or had I just re-written the script of my life? What now?

Just a few weeks prior, I had completed a year of intense study with a small improvisational acting company. My then live-in boyfriend Joe, who knew of my passion for the theater, had encouraged me take advantage of the fact that his friend Roy was starting up a new group. I was foolish not to jump at the opportunity and so, for the next twelve months, I re-focused and adjusted my work schedule so that I could fulfill my long-time dream. Roy was a committed and passionate teacher who referred primarily to the Stanislavski method of acting. The experience felt wildly eccentric, not to mention challenging, yet served to bring me out of my shell to begin my love affair with the art form. In no uncertain terms, my life was fuller and much changed from my experiences. Roy of course, was none too pleased when I later shared with him the news of my foray into the world of porn. But there was naught to do, I had chosen, and I would conscientiously use all I had learned from him. I believe it showed.

My co-actors on "Sexworld" had taken note of my technique and, no sooner had the movie wrapped, the porno grapevine went to work. The film had a large cast, employing at least a dozen or so of the top stars of the business. Performers who could carry a line and fulfill more challenging character roles were in high demand; this was after all a brand new and growing industry—a far cry from the video industry that emerged a decade or so later. Consequently, within a very short time, days even, I began to receive more film offers. But I wondered, as I allowed myself to get caught up in the momentum, was this all too easy and too fast?

Next came "Seven into Snowy," an x-rated version of—yes, you guessed it, "Snow White and the Seven Dwarfs." In this case, the dwarfs were studs! My role of Fedora, the wicked stepmother, provided an opportunity for me to camp it up, mixing spells and demanding that the magic mirror declare me "...the fairest of all." It was fun, fun, fun and I was being paid for it! The sex aspect of my part was minor, to say the least.

Then came an offer that proved to be one of those cosmic links, where invisible lines converge to create change in our lives through people and circumstances. Many call such occurrences chance or coincidence; I call them destiny and synchronicity. A call came in for a part in a small but quality film called "Health Spa," whose producer remains a friend of mine to this day and whose director, I was immediately informed, was a young actress named Emily Smith. That fact was very appealing since I was already aware that this was a male-dominated arena and female innovation was a welcome addition. I met the major players of the cast and crew for a script reading and pizza at Emily's home, where I felt most comfortable. I subsequently agreed to do the part. There was no problem scheduling my shooting days. Although my day job took me on the road—I was a sales representative for a large line of imported jewelry, I could pretty much call the shots, as long as I produced orders. However, the truth was, by that point, weary from lugging heavy sample-cases, I was phasing out of the job.

On the first day of the shoot, I walked into the make-up room and felt immediately enveloped by an aura of warmth and familiarity. The energy emanated from the beautiful Afro-American make-up artist, with whom I felt an immediate bond. To say that I instantly knew her to be a member of my soul family is saying the least. She spoke freely of the Light and of Spirit with a power of strength she had obviously found on the path she was embarked upon. Never one to mince words, my new friend, who I will refer to as Gina, gently confronted individuals, men and women alike, by baby talking to them. This was a clever and effective device to put them at ease and get them to lower their barriers. Her technique bored a hole in the most rigid and inaccessible of egos and was one to which I surrendered immediately. Whatever she had, I wanted some! I deeply desired the kind of spiritual connection she exhibited.

Little did I know how pivotal Gina would become in helping me to realize my dream of a deeper connection to my spiritual beingness. Later that day, we exchanged phone numbers and I discovered that she was from Los Angeles. In those days, many technicians working in adult films were moonlighters from mainstream Hollywood productions. Like so many, Gina had flown to San Francisco for the five to seven days of shooting.

During the filming of "Health Spa," I decided that if, in fact, I was serious about the business of acting, there was but one place to be--Los Angeles. Pornography prevailed in San Francisco, but other opportunities for acting were limited. (During the Golden Era days, we often joked about the fact that, except for a few productions coming out of New York, almost every adult film was photographed in the City-By-The-Bay or Marin County. With the Golden Gate Bridge as the dividing landmark between the two, the bridge was inevitably featured during exterior footage in each film, to the point of being totally predictable.)

Although I had never cared for Los Angeles from my earlier visits, it made sense for me to move. Now I was motivated and made my plans to uproot. Meeting Gina was profoundly synchronistic and had cinched my decision.

Mere days before piling my belongings into my car and heading south, I was selling off a few things at the Sausalito flea market when a familiar face appeared. It was Johnine, the script supervisor from "Health Spa."

"I'm moving to Los Angeles in a few days," she told me.

"No kidding," I said, "me too!"

We also exchanged phone numbers and agreed to meet. I had no idea that she and I had such a significant past together. Strangely, I felt no indication of it at the time.

But the tribes had begun to gather!

"Sam" Spinelli and I, January 1977

*With Seka and Annette Haven,
At the Sixth World Congress of Sexuality"*

Sam, Annette, Producer Marga Aulbach, Seka and Jimmy Johnson (the preseident of Pussycat Theaters) at the Sixth World Congress of Sexuality.

Chapter Seven: Orgasm

Within days of my arrival in Los Angeles in January of 1978, my new spiritual Sister, Gina the make-up artist, set me on a path of discovery that changed my life. She was very persuasive and insisted that I have a reading with a numerologist she knew named John. I was awed by what John told me. He seemed to know so much about me and we had only just met. But John also spoke of meditation, an area I had mildly pursued, and he added that he was starting up a group to focus on specific meditation techniques. I signed up right away.

During our conversations, Gina had repeatedly mentioned two other men who were profoundly instrumental to her own spiritual growth. I was introduced initially to the first, her spiritual teacher, through a audio-taped seminar at a private home, soon after the numerology reading from which I was still reeling. We drove to a very pleasant home in West Hollywood one evening and, as I entered the living room where a dozen or so individuals sat, I felt the same sense of deep familiarity and resonance which had struck me when I first met my friend on the set of "Health Spa" back in San Francisco. I felt nervous with anticipation as the hostess and seminar leader delivered a brief invocation I would come to know as "calling in the Light."

She followed with other protocol, and for new-comers she offered a brief explanation about the taped seminars: a person was required to attend three taped seminars before being permitted to hear the teacher live. Finally we were invited to sit back and listen to the taped message.

As soon as I heard the voice on the tape, my head began to buzz. I was immediately lightheaded and I even felt slightly nauseous. The next thing I knew, my Spirit lifted out of my body and hovered over everyone else in the room. I was literally on the ceiling looking down at everyone present. Oh boy, that had not happened to me since I was a child. Why now? It was clear that I had connected to something profoundly mystical and timely. In fact, this event marked my embarkation on a seven-year study period with the teacher. There was never a question in my mind; I knew it was right for me. I had asked for a focus and guidance and it had manifested – big time! In a sense I felt I was going back to school, but one unlike any conventional institution, with no walls or boundaries. Rules? Yes, there were rules but these were more like life principles: "Don't hurt yourself and don't hurt others, love yourself and love others." That pretty much summed it up although, as in any other form of study, work is required to accomplish results. Meditation, spiritual exercises and techniques in addition to living the principles, *this* was the work.

Simultaneous to all my other new adventures, including my rise to stardom in X-rated films, I also met Rhyen, the other individual Gina had often mentioned. Could my life have been more diverse? I don't think so! Rhyen's influence immediately became an intricate part of my development and growth for which I am so infinitely grateful. We met frequently, more times in a mentor-student capacity, yet at other times, it was a dramatically different exchange; a friendship unlike any I had ever experienced. The man-woman thing *was* there–the magnetic attraction, a combination of basic-self (inner child) desire and karmic bleed-through, but our relationship would remain undefined and unconditional. Years later, I understood why, as I found myself in similar situations with individuals who were also at a dramatically different point in their spiritual development than me yet who wanted a different kind of relationship than I was willing - or even able - to offer.

One evening a couple of years after we met, Rhyen visited me in the apartment I then shared with Johnine, my long-time roomie. We were alone, and relishing a quiet and deep, although non-sexual connection. His dark eyes stared intensely into mine. I swayed slightly and adjusted my footing to balance myself. Suddenly I felt self-conscious in every way imaginable as my emotions intensified, rising up into my chest like a tsunami wave. Strangely, at the wave's peak, sensing what was happening in me, he seemed to switch an inner gear and he bore yet deeper and gentler into my being with his gaze. As he did so the wave dissipated and my breathing relaxed.

What finite attunement! Simultaneously I wondered how he did it. It was as if I was held suspended in a kind of supernatural tractor-beam of loving frequency. I was literally frozen in place by this most mystical and powerful force. Although I was anchored in place, I felt completely safe. Moments, or minutes passed – It was impossible to tell. The indescribable emotion and feeling welled up inside over and over, yet each time he countered with his inner adjustment. I felt nurtured, caressed without being touched, and blissful almost to bursting point. Had I expressed what I was feeling, the result would most certainly have been uncontrollable laughing or crying. Either way, in terms of vibration, it would have been the same.

The penetrating force increased more and more and neither one of us budged. To an observer this scenario might have looked like a futuristic sex ritual. In fact I have often described this unique experience as Future Sex — the kind of sexual exchange I fantasize will be the norm in future times, as we move away from raw animalistic sexual expression. (Remember the love scene from the movie Barbarella.) I believe that as we continue to raise our spiritual consciousness, we will choose a more *Tantric approach to love-making and to living, and in doing so, we will automatically align more and more with the transcendental energies that are available to us. Our collective shame and self-consciousness regarding our sexuality binds us to our attitudes and behavior regarding the exchange of sexual energies. Those of us pursuing a relationship to our higher soul being-ness have already discovered that the old way just doesn't cut it, and now we have little or no choice but to apply consciousness awareness throughout all of our experiences.

To expel anger, aggression or negative emotion through the sexual channels is harmful and unacceptable.

Rhyen and I stood glued in place, as if our souls had made a pact not to budge until what wanted to express itself was purely and fully transmitted. Though normally we were ones to touch and hug constantly, there was no physical contact in this moment. We were transcending space and time. What was taking place was far beyond third-dimensional reality. I felt that I had indeed entered into a time warp cocooned by the sweet, vibrating supernatural energy. In no uncertain terms, this was an altered state of a most amazing kind. I simply had never experienced intimacy like this!

I inhaled, releasing even further in total surrender, sinking deeper with every second as if stretching a most delicate muscle. The outside world evaporated as our energy capsule expanded. Throughout our exchange our faces remained expressionless and all need to overtly "do" anything was non-existent. Then I was floating, not charged up and aflame with emotional passion like being "in love." This was so different. Had this been a more classic romantic situation, the kind where you lead up to a certain climatic experience by holding each other close, where you kiss deeply and melt into each other's body, I might have closed my eyes to enhance my experience. What was so profoundly different here though, was that our souls were in deep communion through our eye connection and *we* could not interfere.

This was surrender, as I had never known it before. There was no coercion of any kind, no conditions or expectations, and no limitations. Part of me wanted to cry out of pure appreciation, to myself for what I was allowing to happen and to him — just for being him! Each time that feeling welled up in me again, I was lifted once more into an even deeper state until finally, my body didn't exist. I was weightless, matter-less, and I was sheer energy itself.

THEN IT HAPPENED! A trickle of cool liquid ran down the inside of my thighs - a release so subtle, so beautiful I hardly knew what was happening! In fact, for a few seconds I *didn't* realize what had happened.

He stepped back in surprise sensing what had transpired, and with eyes wide, he asked,

"Did you just...?"

I nodded in shocked response, scarcely believing it myself. His face lit up with the softest of smiles as he tweaked my cheek endearingly,

"Well, well, isn't that something..." he purred.

Speechless, slightly embarrassed and totally baffled I tried to grasp the fact that I had spontaneously and magically climaxed. Just how it had happened was a mystery to me. A moment later, I felt strangely proud in a child-like kind of way, a feeling boasting,

"Look Ma, no hands!"

Our experience had involved no touching, fondling, bumping or grinding, heavy breathing (deep yes, but not heavy,) and no words! In fact I did feel proud of my accomplishment, as well as being amazed that I had been able to surrender to such a degree, to step outside of my reality and into a whole other realm of experience. It was also clear that I was only able to do that because of my profound trust in Rhyen and in the fact that I felt completely safe and confident of his integrity and caring.

Although not without his human flaws, my dear friend seemed quite eccentric to me because of his weird yet wonderful idiosyncrasies. It was difficult to imagine that earlier in his life my beloved mystic had studied law. Yet perhaps, like me, the journey for which he opted was one where he could be more of service, illuminating the ways we perpetuate the lies and conditions which man has created. Rhyen therefore retreated into his world of philosophy and mysticism and created what to me was a very unique way of counseling others. His consciousness and wisdom, in no uncertain terms, knocked my proverbial socks off!

So many times he and I had literally talked the night away, although it would be more accurate to say that we "tested" the night away—using Applied Kinesiology—to identify the layers of issues, conditioning, negative consciousness and belief systems I hadn't dealt with and which blocked my power, my worthiness and ultimately my authentic self. My most unusual friend taught me the dynamics of this profoundly revealing technique, otherwise known as Muscle Testing. For those unfamiliar with this amazing science, it provides access to the storehouse of information locked away in the body, the unconscious mind and cellular memory. A vast new world had opened to me which would provide a springboard to my own inner reservoir of talents.

Rhyen was my teacher. Of course I was also his, although I couldn't see it at the time. I wasn't ready to acknowledge the gifts I brought to him. Our evenings together were usually preceded by a phone call just to check in. Typically however, unless I was in a pretty clear state of being, the conversation would continue at his house. He had an uncanny ability to hear the slightest glitch or imbalance in my voice, and would suggest that I "Come over and look at it." Naturally I always jumped at the opportunity; I *wanted* to be squeaky clean!

There, typically at his house, we would proceed to explore issues that threw me off balance. I would resist, groan and grimace at the process I knew lay ahead, but this was met with his familiar tweak of the cheek and gentle teasing. He just didn't take no for an answer; *his* intention was clear, for he knew only too well how fickle the human animal is, and that given half a chance, we will avoid our truth. He gave unconditionally and accepted no limitation and each time I was gently and lovingly coaxed into releasing my blocks and restoring my inner harmony.

My dear friend's house was situated at the foot of a hill. Along the side of the building and leading up to the street on the level above, were several flights of stairs - about 150 steps in all. Most times, those of us who came to visit or to consult with him professionally would be challenged to scale the steps up and back as fast as they could. Ryhen would time us, after which the session would begin. Hours later, after the lengthy process of clearing negative mindsets, emotions and consciousness, a person was invited, to "do the steps" again. Though most were likely to feel thoroughly exhausted from the testing experience they had just undergone, typically we scaled the steps at a significantly faster time than previously, with energy to spare! Such exercises proved indisputably the power not only of Rhyen's work, but also of the human consciousness when which unfettered and free of disempowering emotions and mind-sets, is unlimited.

It was Rhyen who sized things up for me during a period when I struggled with the direction my life seemed to be heading—further into my adult film career rather than out of it. I couldn't seem to break loose and it bothered me immensely. He looked me squarely in the eye and said,

"Someone has to go behind enemy lines and bring the Light. Who's better equipped than you?"

His statement took me totally by surprise. The unworthy me screamed out silently in objection of such a statement—I couldn't possibly be that significant. My purpose couldn't possibly be that defined—could it? How could he make such a statement? Yet deep inside I resonated with his truth, although I could not have explained or identified its origin. He continued,

"When it's time, you'll just leave—there will be no question."

This was of course, how my transition out of the business happened—several years later. As Rhyen had suggested, when it was time to take my leave, I knew. A year and a half after taking a position with Caballero Control Corp. as Director of Public Relations, I made my swansong, a film called "Careful He May Be Watching," one of the last substantially budgeted, shot-on-film movies of the era. I had seen the writing on the wall. AIDS was upon us, the video age had arrived, and it was finally time for me to make my exit.

It was also dear wizardly Rhyen, who called me one evening in late 1985 to report,
"I have discovered the muscle test for Passion!"
From the enthusiastic way he announced his discovery, I knew it was significant, not to mention how thrilled I felt that he wanted to share it with me. Through his studies with Applied Kinesiology he had discovered dozens of tests for different levels of consciousness, all of which he had named and catalogued meticulously on 3x5 index cards. Most were tests conducted in a standing position, where simply an outstretched arm was used to ask questions of the body's own "inner computer," as I like to call it. (Whether the arm holds or weakens when pushed down upon provides a negative or affirmative response to questions posed. These answers unravel the mysteries of the person's life issues and problems, for truly the body doesn't lie. Today many holistic doctors, chiropractors and other practitioners, utilize this amazing diagnostic science.) Other tests Rhyen designed seemed strange and quirky, but proved to be accurate in terms of the level of consciousness in question. (Dr. David Hawkins' profound book, "Power Versus Force, is based on a twenty year study using Kinesiology.) Back then it was still new and a little strange to me although my confidence in Ryhen's work was unfaltering.

"Passion?" my ears pricked up, "Really? You've found a test for passion? I'll be right over!"
I drove to his house in record time. We were like two kids who had just discovered new treasure. Rhyen was waiting at the door when I arrived and, without so much of a greeting, pulled me in and immediately instructed me to,
"Sit on the couch with your knees about a foot apart. Now place your hands behind your neck with your fingers interlaced."
I was just as excited and followed his order without hesitation.
"Now," he further instructed, "think of a time of passion."

That was easy. I pondered for a moment or two, and then I automatically chose a romantic evening in the early 1970's with my great love TM (the young man I had banished in Atlantis). I was to hold the memory in my mind and Rhyen would try to push my knees together while I resisted. I concentrated for a moment, returning my thoughts to that idyllic time and then followed his instruction. But I had no holding power, my knees collapsed together. I was astounded.

"Wasn't passion," he declared matter-of-factly.

I protested. How could this be? With TM I always felt completely blissful. I quickly deducted that I hadn't held the thought strongly enough.

We tested again and, to be sure, I chose another romantic and deeply memorable interlude also involving TM. I was confident the test would prove that *this* was a time of true passion. I sank into reminiscences of yellow roses, sipping sherry and sharing beautiful embraces in front of a crackling fire. My hands were behind my neck with my fingers interlaced as Ryhen crouched in front of me and once again tried to push my knees together. I resisted but, as before, my knees flopped together.

"Wasn't passion," he insisted, shaking his head.

"I don't get it," I was now quite confused.

Was my memory not true? Had what I had experienced not been love, was it not pure?

Ryhen looked closely at me with one of his trademark stares, boring deeply into my third eye, into that place where my truth resides. In an instant, a message was transmitted. The proverbial light bulb went off. Something was wrong with both memories. If it tested weak, there had to be a glitch. Maybe I had *wanted* them to be perfect and I was choosing to overlook the truth — in other words, I was in denial of the overall reality of the situation of the person being unavailable to me on a consistent basis. I felt a pang of confirmation in my diaphragm as the *higher* reality about the process underway clicked into gear. This process was profound and was forcing me to a level of honesty I had not previously been willing to go to. In a moment I felt confident I knew what was really going on.

"OK," I instructed him, "try me again, I know this will test strong."

This time I held in my mind the seduction scene from my best-known movie, "Taboo." In the scenario I make love with "my son," played in the film by a young actor named Mike Ranger (who was twenty-six at that time). I secured the memory firmly in my thoughts, and then gestured to Ryhen I was ready. Once again he pushed against my knees, only this time they held as if cemented in place. He pushed harder, they didn't budge.

"*That* was passion!" he proclaimed confidently.

I jumped to my feet, "No wonder that sucker sold so many copies!" I exclaimed!

To this day, more than thirty years after the release of "Taboo," it remains an all-time top-selling video, and my character of Barbara Scott is the role for which I am most remembered. During the eighties, at the height of my adult film career, I was frequently recognized in public. More times than not the recognition was due to the "Taboo" movies although, most specifically, it was the seduction scene from the original that people responded to and which caught the most attention. It was not unusual in those days for adult film aficionados I encountered to greet me with comments along the lines of,

"Wow, the scene with you and your son...!"

They would then just shake their heads with a funny kind of awed expression on their faces. Video store owners told me that not only was "Taboo" so popular they had a hard time keeping it in stock, the other dubious distinction was that it was stolen more than any other title!

The implication of the discovery with Ryhen literally took

my breath away.

"Yup, the soul knows what it sees," Rhyen pronounced, his voice resonant with wisdom.

I distinctly remembered the energy during the shooting of "Taboo." I felt a strong attraction for Mike and I believe the feeling was mutual. Although we had appeared in several movies together, we had not *worked* together, meaning we had not previously been cast as sex partners. Now we were playing mother and son and portraying the ultimate "oedipal" scenario. There were several other sex scenes in the film, three of which I performed in, but it is without doubt the seduction scene which captured an intense magnetism far beyond the others. In all of my films, no single other scene I performed in captured such potency.

When I was first approached to play the role of Barbara Scott I turned down the offer because of the incest subject matter. Admittedly, I was surprised that the writer of the script was a woman (the wife of the producer/director) and a mother of two children. But I had friends who had been victims of incest, and I was deeply aware of their pain and life challenges resulting from their traumas. Just a week prior to being offered the part, I had been an audience member at the taping of a TV show on child incest on which a friend of mine's sister was a guest. She had been one of several children incested by their Father, who also used them in child pornography. He had finally been brought to trial and convicted. It *was* a very sensitive subject and I caught the irony of the timing.

Yet the film was about to be made, with or without me. I spoke with several friends and deeply reckoned within myself. In the adult film industry I had come to know I already knew that there was a code of ethics about children. No one I ever met in over ten years of involvement with adult films had the slightest connection to child pornography, although it bothers me to this day that much of the public assumes otherwise. In fact, many people I had met in the business were family people with normal balanced home lives, people who loved their children very much. Ironically, children I knew of who grew up with liberal attitudes about sex, escaped the pain of sexual shame for the most part.

After I read over the script of "Taboo" several times, I concluded, albeit perhaps idealistically, that if *I* played the part, at least I could lend some sensitivity to the role. The film at least deserved that. I called the producer back and accepted the part. There were times when I felt that maybe I was taking my career too seriously—certainly I heard that statement from several actors in the business. I learned later that most viewers take the plots of X-rated films very lightly, that they expect a comedic edge to any subject tackled. In fact, many don't even notice the story line and some even fast forward to the sex scenes ignoring the story line completely. Historically, films of the genre attempting to handle more serious themes didn't fare well at the box office. (One example of this was "Body Talk," an ambitious drama by first-time producers and a female Hollywood veteran director. In the plot, the main character played by Anjelique Pettyjohn, whose main claim to fame had been a featured role on an episode of the original "Star Trek" television series dies of cancer. Although it was a quality film with some redeeming factors, and was satisfying from a performance point of view for me, it did poorly in sales.)

Regardless, I felt a deep level of responsibility about the nature of my work. I discovered along the way that a handful of my female and male peers had similar sentiments—we were allied in our cause to make a difference and to add sensuality and humanity to adult films. Up until that point, I had personally only seen a few sex films, yet it was conspicuous to me that once the sex began, the characters normally flew the coup. This element was offensive to my artistic sensibilities; after all, in acting training we spent hours developing characters and breathing life into them. Acting was serious business to me and I wasn't about to abandon the techniques and tools

I had learned. Most importantly, I was committed to maintaining my character throughout each film, most especially during the sex scenes. After all, so much is revealed through our sexual natures.

Whether or not I accomplished that level of honesty with my character in "Taboo" is hard for me to say because it was as though another energy took over; something quite mystical in essence. "Intense" is the word which many have used to describe the pivotal seduction scene with "my son." I think that's putting it mildly. Perhaps one contributing element was that I had given myself permission to be absolutely true to the character, thereby allowing passion to prevail. In retrospect, it occurred to me that I surrendered to the character of Barbara Scott more wholly than perhaps I ever had in my private sexual encounters. And, if the feedback I have received from so many (men primarily) about my performance in all the years since the film's release, is any indication of the potency of the energy captured on screen, I have to believe that Spirit indeed intervened. This was true synergy; a blending of physical and meta-physical energies recorded on film for people to witness for a long time to come. Its purpose went way beyond what I could have known and understood at the time.

I had prepared myself for the seduction scene in "Taboo" as I always did (especially for explicit scenes), I called in the Light, asked for higher guidance and protection on all levels. In the scene, my character, a frustrated divorcee, awakens from a restless sleep and fumbles for a sleeping pill. The previous evening she had been invited out on a blind date with a guy who turned out to be a real jerk who, much to her dismay took her to an orgy. Barbara had watched horrified as her date indulged with the rest of the swingers, until she was finally able to convince him to take her home. Visions of the orgy are still haunting her as she realizes she is fresh out of her sedatives, so she rises from her bed to search elsewhere. As she moves down the hall from her bedroom past her grown son Paul's room, she hears him moaning in his sleep and is drawn into his room. She lingers, watching him sleep, amazed at the urges she is feeling and tries to fight them. Finally she succumbs and the rest, as they say, is history...

Once I, totally in character, was sitting on his bed contemplating my "son's" glorious erection, the passion had clicked in. Yes, indeed, this had been passion, no glitches or blocks; a pure energy unencumbered by any linear thought or negative emotion: total surrender to the moment.

Clearly the two memories I had recalled for Rhyen's first two muscle tests were not even close to passion. But it was all I knew back then. I reveled in the romance and fantasy I created around the person I loved for so many years. A gentle and sensitive lover who made me feel so wanted, he was never the less emotionally unavailable to me. His visits were sporadic. Sometimes a year would pass between our encounters. It pained me to my core, yet I accepted the situation and held on to the idyllic memories we shared. This dynamic was my relationship with my Father manifest again in my life. No wonder the memories I selected didn't test as passion! It wasn't until much later, as I began pealing off the layers and truly healing my relationship with my Father, that I would come to realize that I *was* of course, worthy of having the type of relationship of which I had always dreamed.

There was another significant contributing element to the passion in Taboo to be considered—Gina, the mutual friend who introduced Rhyen to me, had been hired on as the make-up artist. At one of the initial meetings with the director, I recommended my new friend, who fortunately was available for work. I fully believe that her special (Light) presence on the set added much to the overall resonance of the energies of that magical scene.

It had become most obvious that Gina and I had a significant past together–in fact, we had shared several lifetimes. It was also a given that there were spiritual promises being fulfilled, since she single-handedly connected me to, and securely placed me on my path of self-discovery. The synchronicities were profound. In one particular lifetime well over two thousand years BC, she had been my Mother who, having witnessed my seduction and ultimate demise, vowed that she would protect me against it ever happening again. History always repeats itself. The same person who seduced me then entered into my current lifetime as I was exiting adult films. Gina had a profound and strong reaction to the news of my introduction to him, a person known to her as having a subtle Svengali type personality. Sadly, at that point our relationship waned. Despite the telltale signals of my patterns with men, my karmic ties with the new man pulled me into a relationship, if only for a short while (although he and I have remained friends.)

Gina's promise to protect me was an overlay of another promise from a yet earlier existence as a male scientist in Atlantis, where I became involved in deviant scientific experiments. Here she also vowed to keep me on an honest conscious path. The two promises combined were evident and manifested as the driving force behind her protective relationship to me resulting in a somewhat controlling mannerism. Much as I later fulfilled my spiritual promises to dear Johnine, so Gina had pointed the way for me. And both women had come into my life through the film "Health Spa"—a true little window of destiny.

My friendship and study with Rhyen continued until the mid '80's. Without question what I learned from my amazing friend set the precedence for my own career as a counselor. His wisdom had rubbed off on me in infinite ways, and I built a repertoire of tools and techniques from my personal experiences with him. To this day I continue to share anecdotal stories of my experiences with him in my own teaching, including a profound incident involving Johnine.

One afternoon, in the mid 1980's, Rhyen stopped by our apartment. In true form, he immediately began to work with my dear roomie to balance her energies. As I prepared a snack in the kitchen, I saw him muscle-testing her, applying his gentle teasing mannerism to help break down her defenses. Johnine had a lazy eye, an astigmatism which was corrected by a contact lens. While at home, she usually didn't wear her lenses, as was the case on that particular day and from where I stood, I could clearly see my roommate's eyes as Ryhen proceeded with his testing process, addressing whatever issues which were throwing her out of balance. Although I could not hear their verbal exchange, I suddenly saw her lazy eye straighten up totally of its own accord. It was an amazing thing to see. He turned slightly to me and asked if I had seen it.

"I most certainly did!" I gasped.

Whatever level of consciousness they were addressing had hit a truth nerve causing her eye muscles to respond, pulling her eye into its natural position.

"What—what did you see?" Elizabeth quipped suspiciously. And, of course, as her doubt set in, her eye returned to its lazy position. I told her what Ryhen and I had both witnessed, but she didn't believe us and thought we were exaggerating. It was beyond her comprehension that by shifting her consciousness, she possessed the power to create that miracle.

In contemplating a true definition of passion, it would seem clear to me that if the mind or consciousness is pre-occupied at all, true passion cannot exist. Passion requires total surrender into that state of child-like vulnerability where magic and miracles happen and one-ness with God is automatic. Whether in a sexual context or otherwise, the mind-body-spirit-soul connection must be intact. That means that the heart must be fully open and resonating with the energy of pure unconditional love for self as well, as for any others involved.

This reality is one embraced in the practice of *Tantra (the yoga of sex,) whose philosophy is many centuries old. The Tantrics teach methods of prolonging and elevating the lovemaking experience into a celebration of spiritual unity. In that pure state of passion, of complete connection to the supreme one-ness, we may catch a glimpse of God consciousness, if only for a moment.

But this state of pure unconditionality is rare. Most who experience such bliss stumble into it as if by accident; a newborn baby or animal may evoke it, or an event where the soul is deeply touched and moved in the human experience. Yet those who are aware of the higher truths about the times in which we live, and who are committed to applying the ways of the new paradigm in their experiences, will know of what I speak. This new model of living is one in which we choose to move past fear, competition, lack and martyr consciousness, into trust and willingness to look at the higher purpose *of all things*. As we literally lighten up, and begin to align with this higher reality, we may on the one hand, become more sensitive to our toxic environment, yet on the other hand, we might find ourselves entering into a sort of natural immunity against the dis-ease and disharmony in our world. It becomes an infinitely fine line to travel, and travel it we must. Collectively there is still so much karmic density to be transformed, before we fully recognize that level of personal power where we can walk through muck and mire and not be affected.

In 1993 I was approached by a manufacturer of adult marital aids to help create a video, an introduction to the art of Tantric yoga for the layman. It was eventually called "The Tantric Guide to Sexual Potency." I had always wanted to participate in a project introducing higher consciousness into sex and lovemaking, so initially I was thrilled. The deal was that I would produce a script for the video, I would co-direct and I was to be the on-camera hostess.

Although I would have preferred otherwise, the producers naturally wanted to include explicit sex footage, that way, their market was broader. Consequently the producers were super-sensitive about using the correct traditional names of certain yoga postures, which for the most part are animal names such as the cat pose, downward facing dog, fish etc. I could not persuade them that their fears, reflective of the paranoia of the adult entertainment arena where any reference to animals is strictly a no-no, were unfounded, and that these terms have been used for thousands of years.

There were other limitations and challenges to overcome, not the least of which were time and budget. Beyond that was the task of re-training porno actors who were used to performing sex the Western way, to bring their performance energy down and into a quieter, slower and more sensual exchange with their partners. My old friend Wesley Emmerson, producer of the film "Health Spa" was line-producer and director and had already hired the actors for our project. I was relieved that, of the eight actors he had cast, two of them, Sharon Kane and Mike Horner, were my contemporaries and both were very adept at yoga. To instruct the four couples in the video, I brought in my friend and avid yogini, Diana, who gave the performers a crash course in the exercises and postures. Diana and I had written the script together and had carefully worked out an appropriate program of stretches and postures designed to prepare the body for the tantric practice.

Ironically, the actor who was the most challenged with his role had the simplest of tasks. All he had to do was to make deep eye connection with his partner, while lying on his side quite passively, making the subtlest of movements. This was so alien to him he became very frustrated, even angry. During the shooting of his segment he got up, stomped around the set and exploded into a verbal tirade,

"I have never done anything so unsexual! I just wanna fuck!"

I quietly replied, "You weren't hired to fuck. You were hired to do a yoga video. You have the easiest job here and you're complaining?"

He growled and completed the task to the best of his ability. It was not only obvious that he was looking for a place to dump his chaotic misplaced energy; sadly he had hoped to do it on the video set. As it turned out, after seeing a rough cut of our project, the actor's anger and frustration were sorely evident on the tape. I insisted that the editor cut out as much of his segment as possible. The energy of that one scene had the potential to disrupt the energy of the entire

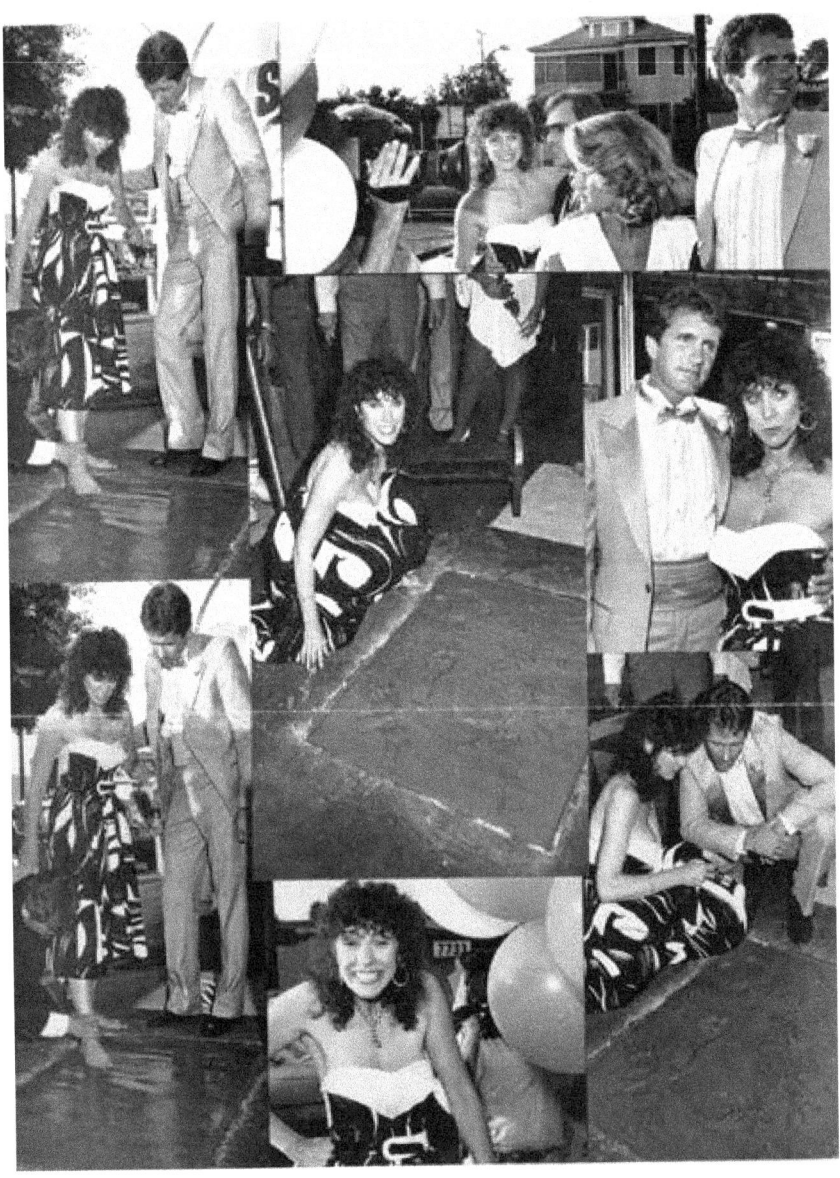

The Great Cement Event
July 12, 1984

Chapter Eight: The Princess's Tears

I have incarnated approximately 182 times since my arrival on Earth in ancient Atlantis. Less than a third of those lifetimes have been male, perhaps an indication of the required emphasis on the female experience as an integral part of my soul's overall mission. With this in mind, it is not surprising therefore that a conspicuous theme has shown up time and again throughout my female experiences, where I was forced to power down and stifle my God-given talents and abilities.

Whether I found myself as wife, mother, sister, lover or consort, each role of course was dominated by the social climate and the prevailing patriarchal attitudes of the times. For the most part, the only talents I *was* free to express were those supporting the men in my life. Consequently I remained subservient as have millions of women globally. One would think or hope that this situation would have improved but clearly the change has only been a minor one, even after sending people into space and advances in technology reaching amazing new heights.

The "submissive female syndrome," as I call it, continues on then as humanity struggles to evolve. Over the ages, it has been a significant component in the collective human experience, providing the opportunity for right choice: love and harmony or violence and competition. Now, more than ever, the choice is clear; awaken to our soul reality, embrace the Goddess, and recognize our individual responsibility of creating balance and harmony in all of our relationships — to ourselves, to each other and to our environment, or continue to wreak havoc on our planet and bury our heads in the sand.

In my experiences as a counselor, I consistently find remnants of this submissive female syndrome equally in modern men as in women and, although each gender manifests the signals differently, according to the individual life lessons and challenges, the end result is normally a subtle passive or martyr quality.

Several of the lifetimes where I had to conform to the culture of the day and hide, suppress, or otherwise stifle my true nature are pivotal to my experiences today. By revisiting those past life events, I have been able to systematically re-instate what I believe my authentic essence to be. It might be said that the purpose of those past life dynamics was to demonstrate the very best examples of oppression, submission, futility and a host of other emotions and conditions.

This is, after all, the Universal classroom.

My past life exploration is strictly for the purpose of understanding and realizing greater truths--Universal truths, as they apply to myself and essential not to apply the information in a negative manner, thus reinforcing the ways we classically hold ourselves victim to our circumstances and the collective conditioning. When applied positively, past life work can clarify and identify free-floating feelings, emotions, patterns, phobias, and attitudes. Most significantly, we may finally identify the origin of our oldest **shame** and reinstate our worthiness. In a time when depression afflicts hundreds of thousands and suicide numbers are increasing at a staggering rate, past-life regression provides an unparalleled avenue of self-exploration and understanding. In most cases it can illuminate the bigger picture of a person's life path and destiny. The classic "no reason to live" feeling prompts many, especially young people, to end their lives. In many cases, to assist a person in identifying their purpose for living: their soul's mission, can be to save a life.

Some years ago, a woman who was in total futility came to me for counseling. She was a special being indeed with whom I felt a deep heart connection. In her short life (she was around 40,) she had survived many surgeries, deep physical and emotional pain, and profound suffering.) Regardless of her travails, she had found a reason to fight and place meaning in her life. As a very spiritually oriented and deeply responsible person, she prayed, meditated and worked in the holistic health field where she assisted others. Circumstances had required her to raise two sons alone, so despite all her other struggles, she had even sustained those challenges involved in being a single mother. Why she sought my counsel and what had so profoundly thrown her for a loop was the fact that suddenly, both her sons had developed drug habits.

She implored me,

"I need to know what this is all about — I cannot survive this, I won't survive this without deeper understanding."

Through gentle and careful probing of a couple of lifetimes relevant to the situation where she and her sons were also related, we were able to determine a pattern where, as an over-bearing parent, she had denied her sons their sovereignty. The consequences both times were tragic and highly dramatic. What we derived from the session was that neither son was an addictive personality per se, and that their experiences would ultimately serve them in their soul growth patterns. It seemed clear that, once again finding herself in the role of their parent, my client needed to allow them to have their experiences. Her challenge was to resist her inclination to dominate them, while at the same time not condoning their actions. The fact that the issue was about drugs, served to dramatize the lessons for all of them.

"Love them through this, don't judge them, and know that there is a gift for them in their experience. The gift for *you* is not to personalize their actions. Meditate — see them whole. *That's* how you can help them," was the guidance provided from my own guides.

I empathized deeply with her situation, yet felt intuitively that both young men would come through relatively unscathed. So would she, I suggested, as long as she remained aligned to the bigger picture. By the end of the session, the tension in her face had eased, her breathing was less labored and she had once again embraced her life. She was most grateful, and both she and her sons survived their drug experiences.

In the handful of female lifetimes I have recognized, many of my innate gifts of shaman, seer and clairvoyant remained dormant, and I inevitably experienced great futility--not to mention feelings of desperate helplessness. Worse yet, in most of that particular grouping of lifetimes, I also felt guilt-ridden knowing there was so much more I could have done, so many ways I could have served mankind had it been acceptable for a woman to take a more dynamic role. This is true for many people – the fact of having the tools to make a difference but social mores not allowing them to do so.

Of the over seventy lifetimes I actually chronicled during my research in the 1980's and '90's, there were several exceptional female incarnations where I did stand in my power, if only for a short while. This is with the exception of two - the first as a scientist in Atlantis, the other as a German monarch. Both of these lives were totally power-based and positive. Yet in each of the others, due to the conflicting standards and laws of the day, there were highly dramatic, even tragic consequences resulting in loss or modification of my power. Never the less, the emotional residue from those lives is similar in resonance to those incarnations where I experienced total subservience. These energies of futility and despair from this particular life group carried forward in my DNA allows me the opportunity to serve a greater collective in terms of healing and empowerment, now as we approach Planetary Ascension into the fourth dimension. Many of us who work as Light workers are aware of the many levels on which we may work, not just here, in our third dimensional existence, but in other dimensions as well. Much of this work may be accomplished in the night time as we sleep.

In the 1990's, I became familiar with well-known gifted and dynamic speaker Caroline Myss, through her brilliant audio-tape series called "Energy Anatomy." Caroline has commented on the fact that she believes every thought and emotion we have ever had, at any time, in any of our lifetimes, is stored in our bodies—in our cellular memory. I agree. To gain access to that information for self-healing requires an individual search and discern the perfect modality and/or facilitator for their specific needs and personality. Of course, I believe that when the student is ready, the teacher magically appears.

In striving to be absolutely responsible for what I believe I agreed to accomplish in my life, the divine tapestry of my history has been revealed, piece by piece, to help me clear away all the scars and dross from my past. Incrementally, in perfect timing, and with impeccable wisdom guided by my Higher Selves, the ancient memories have surfaced, allowing me to understand the intricacies and essence of my Soul's journey here today. And I can say with certain adamancy,

"No wonder I've never married in this life!"

-For I simply could not walk in a man's shadow. The conditioned me brought me to that point several times in my current lifetime, but my Soul just wouldn't have it and my unworthiness blocked it. I can walk at the side, in front of, together with, but **not** behind a mate. I've been there, done that —to death! Yet, I hasten to add, I do not say this in a woman's liberation kind of way--my goal is and always has been unity not separation. But to do the work for which I contracted, to align with my most authentic self, my focus must remain on my relationship with God. Does this rule out intimate relationships? Not as far as I'm concerned. In my prayers I always ask that if there is a mate for me, it must be someone who is equal to me, or more. I suggest this affirmation for everyone seeking a relationship.

I first learned of my lifetime as the young Macedonian noblewoman Quigopa (pronounced Wee-kay-pay, I'm told by my guides) when Aaron, my deceased friend and mentor, channeled an amazing document chronicling several past lives where our own histories had intersected. It was shortly after my friend Charles and I met. Charles came into my life, made an indelible impression and is now gone. He was involved in world affairs — on a somewhat covert level — or so he told us. Constantly on the move, he met with high dignitaries from countries where there was unrest, political or otherwise. We listened to his stories and, in the way we know to be of assistance, offered moral and spiritual support, as well as speculation as to the higher purpose of the events that so deeply disturbed our new friend. Aaron and I also contemplated the possible part the three of us, as well as other close friends and spiritual allies, were to play in each other's life drama. As High Priest, mentor, or shaman, Aaron had repeatedly been at Charles' side throughout the ages, as he had been at mine. He had been prolifically involved in my most significant Egyptian life, where he taught me the sacred codes of alchemy and then was forced to retrieve them from my consciousness--but that story comes later.

Aaron's "Lifetimes Chronicle" outlined a dozen or more incarnations where our combined destinies had been purposefully interwoven. I therefore did not realize the deep significance of my Macedonian life until much later. Here was another situation where I was born into a noble family lineage. In fact, my guides tell me that I was a descendant of Alexander the Great. Once again I was deeply intuitive and clairvoyant, yet my gifts for the most part would remain suppressed.

A marriage to a powerful Egyptian prince was arranged for me, a union taking me far away from my home into foreign lands while I was still a teenager. Aaron was my husband's chief advisor — stern, protective, and quite aware of my dormant gifts. This much I knew then from Aaron's document, although it wasn't until a decade later when I met Marcus, who played a major role in that lifetime, that my memory of the tragic events that occurred, opened wide the floodgates for the emotions and unresolved feelings to surface to be healed. The tremendous pain and futility I experienced in those ancient times surged up inside me like a powerful drug, and there was naught to do but to ride it out. It took almost two years to consciously and thoroughly process every last emotion and to heal every scar.

CHAPTER EIGHT: THE PRINCESS'S TEARS

Born in the wake of the enormous impact of Alexander's conquering exploits, I, as Quigopa, found myself in what was unequivocally one of the most notorious families in the world. During the short time I was on the planet there were no significant wars, therefore trading with the territories to the North was in full swing. When I turned eighteen I began a journey abroad to the lands of the Nile Delta to join my new husband to procure new and wealthy trade agreements. It was my first trip away from home, and it both scared and excited me. But after all, I was a monarch-in-training, and it was appropriate for me to be at my husband's side. As Quigopa, I was apparently both energetic and enchanting, with an insatiable curiosity and a powerful imagination that, unbeknownst by most, was considerably fueled by my great gift of precognition.

The huge caravan carrying me and my entourage to our remote destinations was a veritable traveling palace, and my every need and comfort was catered to by a team of servants and handmaidens. During the long journey, I began to experience prophetic visions and disturbing dreams of a major earthquake and other cataclysmic events. I spoke of my visions to those close to me, passionately voicing my concerns and insisting that those in power should take steps to prepare to minimize the potential death and destruction. Once I arrived at my husband's court, I was bitterly disappointed when even he would not take my concerns seriously. In a desperate attempt for recognition, I used my flair for the dramatic, drawing groups of individuals to me while my husband and his officials were preoccupied with their affairs.

My audience of mostly women—since few men dared to be seen with me without the prince's presence—was inspired by my passion and magnetism. Quigopa's diplomatic finesse was, for the most part, lacking; I was a diamond in the rough and still very much an adolescent. I held nothing back as I described my visions exactly as I had seen them: ominous and threatening. Sadly, what most of my critics failed to see, was the wisdom and caring behind my mask of defiance.

After a while I became an embarrassment to my husband, whose advisors considered me a nuisance and felt my continued presence would adversely affect my husband's business—not to mention his goals. It was therefore Aaron who recommended the obvious solution that I should return to Macedonia. Naturally, I had no say in the matter and any resistance would have proved futile. Scorned and saddened, I complied with my husband's wishes, and embarked upon the long trip home with my proverbial tail between my legs.

Once back in my homeland, I, the young princess, again united with the young sculptor who had been my best childhood friend and playmate. During childhood we had been inseparable, close as only soul mates are. We had never lacked games to play and our fertile little imaginations concocted adventures and stories, busying ourselves for hours in the gardens of the family compound. The lad was the son of a mason, one of the court's primary craftsmen and, as such, had led a fairly privileged life. But his greatest joy was our friendship and he pledged eternal love to me. When he reached an appropriate age, he became his father's apprentice, putting to good use his creative imagination and skills throughout the vast porticos of the estate.

When I returned, the young artist was one of the first to console me. The gossipmongers had already been busy spreading elaborate rumors as to the circumstances surrounding my separation from my husband and return home. But my friend knew well of my gifts, and chose to ignore all the stories, opting to hear the truth from me. With great compassion and his heart full, he had watched me mature into womanhood and begin my tutelage into the ways of a noble wife. He knew that no amount of training could help me integrate my extraordinary gifts into the role for which I was destined. No doubt he was the only one who understood and could see me for who I was, and his fears for me were justified.

Lonely and at odds with my life, I threw myself into my friend's arms and, fueled by our soul-connection, I surrendered to his tenderness. He also was unable to resist *his* inner stirrings, thirsty as he was for *my* love. Our passion was ignited, propelled perhaps by the fact that time seemed short—the earthquake would soon happen. We gave no consideration to the consequences of our union and consummated our relationship. Naturally, after the fact, I not only felt ashamed of my actions, I also feared the consequences of my infidelity being discovered—there was no shortage of spies around the family compound. I wondered if I had submitted too fast to my carnal and emotional needs, thereby endangering myself and my lover.

Two months later, the predicted earthquake struck, causing much death and destruction. Despite their skepticism, a number of Quigopa's family and court members *had* taken certain precautions beyond the structural reinforcements that were already a standard procedure on the estate. Consequently they suffered very little damage and injury.

Then, however, a strange and spiteful pattern began to emerge. Those who had heard of my visions began to blame me and accused me of sorcery. To add insult to injury, a family court advisor (who was my friend Charles) overheard a conversation between the clandestine lovers. Our affair was exposed and overnight my notoriety escalated to fever pitch. With the family name besmirched, life in the palace became tense and challenging. Still, my family's anger was far easier to cope with than the public attitudes that I prayed, would in time, abate.

It seemed this was occurring until shortly after my 23rd birthday when, as I strolled outside the palace grounds with several female court members, a group of commoners rushed towards me, pelting me with stones. Their ringleader and the person who cast the first stone was an earlier lover of mine in present times whose own guilt, at the time, caused him to so direly accuse me. The crowd was relentless, cursing and accusing me of conspiring with the gods to bring about the earthquake. They had continued to blame me. My companions fled in terror back to the confines of the palace grounds. Paralyzed with shock and helplessness I was hit time after time, and within moments, I collapsed to my knees.

My lover, hearing the commotion and the screams of the attendants, raced to my side. He bravely forced his way through the crowd that was growing considerably in numbers, picked me up, battered and bleeding, and carried me to an abandoned hut at the side of the road. By the time he reached the tiny refuge, he too had become a bloodied victim of rock and stone missiles. Inside the hut he barricaded the door against our aggressors and laid me gently on the floor. Oblivious to the merciless onslaught continuing outside and barely conscious, I and my lover declared our eternal love to each other, securing within each of us a frequency that would remain with us for two millennia. And then, in an instant, flames engulfed the hut ignited by a torch thrown by one of our attackers. The wrath of the crowd seemed to increase the intensity of the inferno and within minutes there was little left of the tiny structure. When the flames died down, all that remained of the ill-fated lovers were the charred remains of our bodies entwined in a final embrace.

In moments when I have attuned to Quigopa in me, I have felt a curious mixture of energies: the female adolescent straining against her innate wisdom, ill at ease with the force of her power rising inside of her. I have felt her frustration of being so sadly misunderstood by those around her; so many it would seem who, despite her position in life, had power over her. The futility she felt that her predictions were not taken seriously is as deeply familiar to me as is her sadness at being ordered back to Macedonia by her unsympathetic husband, whom she genuinely loved and respected. I have also felt the great joy she experienced with her soul mate and, later, her great love. Most poignantly, of all the data from that fated lifetime I've discovered, none is more poignant than the fact that I was pregnant with my lover's child when together we met our demise in the blazing hut. This was the final piece of the puzzle I needed to fully heal the scars from that lifetime, to finally release the fear attached to her dramas and integrate her energy and gifts into my current life experiences.

The memory of this lifetime fully surfaced in 1993 when I met the person who had been my childhood friend and lover in ancient Greece. At a time when I continued to look for ways to supplement my still meager income from counseling, I answered an advertisement in a film industry newspaper for a small role in an independent movie. The role called for some nudity, yet the ad was written in such a way as to indicate that it was an art film. Some months had passed after I responded by mail and, for the most part; I had forgotten all about it, when on June 16th, I received a call from the person who had placed the ad. Despite the fact that my needs had shifted, and my interest in the part had certainly waned, I agreed to meet with Marcus.

The young filmmaker arrived at my home as I was dealing with a plumbing problem in the upstairs apartment of the house I lived in and cared for, owned by a friend of mine living overseas. I sensed his presence even before he came into my vision. As he crossed the street and moved towards my gate, I caught my first glimpse of him. There was an immediate recognition on a soul level. Outwardly his physical appearance reflected his deeply artistic nature; his mannerism was polite and sensitive.

"You're Marcus," I greeted him, not doubting for a moment who he was. "Go ahead inside and make yourself comfortable--I'll be right there after I handle the plumber."

When I came back downstairs, Marcus was standing in my garden under a large palm, as if in an altered state. He silently followed me inside my apartment and sat down. We shared some polite conversation, most of which I didn't hear because of an intense ringing in my ears. These sensations are very familiar to me, and are always indicative of soul recognition and reunion, and often portend adventures into past-life discovery. This time it was significantly more intense than usual. (On one such occasion, in a meeting with a very powerful individual to whom I had been married in an ancient lifetime, I almost fainted—the energy was so potent.) Although I mostly consider such reunions to be good and positive events, it can also be a little unnerving. In the case of Marcus, it was apparent that we had come together for a purpose far beyond what was evident in that moment—something mystical and probably transformational.

On a purely physical level, there was an immediate attraction; this was clear for both of us. Simultaneously, however, was the practical reality of the purpose of the meeting. I was aware of multi-dimensions of reality clicking into gear. It was as if all my chakras, from the base of my spine to my crown, were charged and vibrating at an alarming rate. But, as challenging as the moment was, we focused on the matter at hand: the film and the necessary details. I honestly wasn't sure that I could bring myself to do the nudity required in one of the character's scenes. It had been a number of years since I had appeared nude on film; my body had changed and my self-consciousness had returned. But there was one other element holding significant weight: the scene in question was a fantasy sequence with Marcus himself! All facts considered, this felt like dangerous territory. The bottom line, I admitted frankly, was that I would have to mull it over. Marcus deposited the script on my coffee table and left.

Much later, after our entire interaction had passed, I wrote Marcus a letter reflecting on that first meeting. I quote from that letter:

"So we sat you and me, and we talked. Truthfully, I could barely hear what you were saying to me. The sub-plot was profound, loud in an inaudible way, stunning in a non-visual sense. I know you felt it too. You made a comment as you left, something to the effect of, "This is

deep." My inner judge by that time was already at work wagging her finger and running her dialogue…"attractive younger man…taking off your clothes again…tsch, tsch."

After you left, I read your script. Mostly I loved it, yet as you know, I was split down the middle when I read the part of the "alluring woman." Again my practical mind stepped in and assured me that this was my opportunity to just say no - something which has always been hard for me. It seems simple enough; I don't have to do anything I don't feel completely comfortable with. Back on the phone with you the next day, I initially declined your offer, but you asked me what you could do to make me feel more comfortable with the part. You could so easily have let it go at that point. Maybe it wasn't so easy to find someone to do the role — I'm not sure, but I do know that you knew there was something else going on: the resonance of our past together."

"Well, let's talk some more about it," I was surprised to hear myself reply. As the words came out of my mouth, I once again felt the familiar feeling sweep over me, rendering me dizzy and a bit overwhelmed. Simultaneously I was afraid that I'd scare you away because of who I am. I've often been accused of being too deep, but I am a sensitive and I view life multi-dimensionally. I guess that automatically makes me deep. The way I see it, we are here to clean up our stuff' so I am always alert as to the anyway I may do that. For me, there is nothing more important. I spend time every day looking for ways to grow and release the past. We seers have the ability to see so much more than is obvious to most people. That's the good and the bad news, but a God-given talent, regardless.

I also feared that you'd think I was a horny middle-aged woman (yuck!) who just wanted your body. Truth is, I would like to experience a beautiful kind of intimacy with you, whether sexual or not — sex is not the criteria for me but intimacy requires willingness to be vulnerable. I think we're both a little afraid of that — no?

In one of our earlier conversations you expressed a fear of losing me, echoing my own sentiments. I didn't ask you any more about your statement, rather I felt moved to assure you I wouldn't go away.

My own fear comes from a deep-feeling place where past life memory exists, where vows or promises made are recorded along with the pain of non-fulfillment and loss.

I also feared that you were afraid I'd try to manipulate you in some way. It was in your eyes that had it had happened to you in the past..."

I did not finish the letter or send it. My critical self talked me out of it and wrote it off as another exercise in personal processing.

My part in the movie was shot over two days in a quaint old gold-mining town outside of Los Angeles. The basis for my decision to take the role in Marcus's film was more about a sense of destiny playing out rather than for any other reason. Certainly the diminutive fee I received could not be factored into my choice since, if I broke it down into an hourly rate, it was completely ludicrous. If there was any higher purpose, I was always willing. I knew there was in this case. Marcus was a prince on the shoot, and went out of his way to make me feel comfortable, despite the infinite pressure on him from all angles. Not only had he written the script, he was also directing and starring—a feat requiring the utmost concentration and impeccable decision-making. When it came down to the scene I had dreaded, it was handled with the utmost sensitivity and executed in a matter of moments.

When it was all over, I experienced a mixture of relief and sadness. I was sad because, although initially we had expressed a mutual desire to stay in touch, I knew it would most likely not happen. Regardless, in the weeks and months following, lifetime after lifetime surfaced in which Marcus and I had been together, providing countless opportunities for me to heal ancient scars and balance energies. It was like having a relationship with all of our past lives, again—alone. Still I felt grateful.

One day, a close friend observing my process and witnessing the depth of emotion involved in the lifetimes with Marcus, commented, "You fell in love with him!"

Wow! Her statement threw me for a loop. Really? Was that how falling in love looks and feels? True to my Virgoan nature, I immediately drew an analytical definition. So what was it- falling in love? What is the invisible force, the dynamic by which two individuals are drawn together? Against all odds, and many times illogical, reckless, and often resulting in deep drama, falling in love may be anything but blissful and easy. I deducted that in fact, that mystical, magnetic force is, for most people, a combination of unresolved past-life resonance and basic-self (inner child or adolescent-self) attraction. Are we not mirrors for each other and do we not witness the best and the worst of ourselves in those with whom we are relating the closest? This is why so many relationships are so challenging; there's a lot going on. It may, and usually does, require constant vigilance to maintain a sense of harmony while functioning in a union, whether intimate or otherwise. What is crucial is that both parties are willing to be responsible for their own growth, while not placing blame on the other and allowing each the space to be authentic.

Almost exactly a year after Marcus' film was shot, I received a phone call from the film's producer inviting me to a screening for the movie. So much had transpired in the interim. I felt reluctance to attend the event but my high-self compelled me to go. When I saw Marcus, the same familiar energies; at once poignant and uncomfortable, rose up inside again. My soul was happy to see him but my heart was still sad. After the screening, there was a quick hug, no time for any conversation, and I went home. I couldn't let it go like that, and I thought he might want to know about my discoveries––after all, there could well be residue from those lives in his own present-life experience. Once again I decided to write him a letter.

Dear Marcus,

How good it was to see you last night. As you greeted your audience and stated that it had been exactly a year since you began production on your film, I had just whispered to my friend who was with me, that it was about a year ago we met and I began my adventure with you this time around. We didn't have a chance to speak last night and so I decided to pen this letter to you.

My adventure with Marcus...I have often mused over these last months...he'll never know the half of it. But after seeing you again, all these months later, I thought you might be interested in knowing about my discoveries in regards to you and me. After all, we promised to stay in touch with each other --so here I am. Then I remembered the letter I began to write to you last year, primarily for my own process. It seemed appropriate now to send you a copy of that as the first chapter of the adventure, so-to-speak. Read that first, it's on the green paper...

Then the story continues:

In my reality our journey began many eons ago. The person who attended your screening last night is not the same person you met a year ago--my growth has been amazing, and for your part in that, I am grateful. Freedom holds top priority for me so I use every opportunity to release whatever I can from the past in order to move closer to my fullest potential. I've never seen the paradox of life more clearly than now—on one hand I've always been a late bloomer, yet I have also felt way ahead of my time....

So, what magical discoveries I have made about our past! As issues have come up day after day, the lifetimes began to filter up to the surface to clarify my feelings and assist me to release countless layers of shame, guilt, rage, etc. In late August of last year I had a dream in which I was an American Indian. I actually heard the name of the tribe in my dream: Chippewa. In the dream an elder handed me a ceremonial robe and said,

"Put this on, it's time—you've earned it!"

I explored this dream in the way I do and discovered a lifetime in the 1700's as a Chippewa. I was a female shaman and you were my father. A friend of mine, Charles, who until recently was a most significant player in my life for over seven years, was the chief. Both you and he wanted me to marry. You had someone in mind within the tribe, and he desired me to marry outside the tribe for reasons of accruing power. You won, and I married a brave who is a friend of mine today. But my passion was stifled and I made a promise in that life never to marry again—ever! Interesting that I haven't in this life so far (there have been other layers related to this issue I've found along the way). Furthermore, in that lifetime, I fell into a deep depression caused by deep grief, anger, and shame for not having practiced my gifts.

In October a past life surfaced as a result of examining why, when I was 27, I shut down a piece of belief in myself. Someone with whom I was briefly involved had turned me against myself. The root issue traced back to a lifetime where the same person was a slave owner who purchased my husband (a long-time love of mine in this lifetime) and me. You were our love child born in the South after our journey from Africa. The "Master," whose personality in current times fits the profile from the past, fell in love with me and claimed me for himself. He sent my husband away, but you were allowed to stay with me. Forced into a relationship with him, I bore him four children. You watched closely over me and his wrath for you grew, not only because I continued to grieve for your father, but because I adored you over the other children. Then something happened for which he falsely accused you and, in a fit of rage, he whipped you severely. You died in my arms. It was too much to bear, and shortly after, I also passed this plane. I harbored deep remorse at not being able to save you, and for leaving my other children—all of whom are in my life today.

(Synchronistically, the same day I was processing all of that, you sent me the Polaroid of yourself holding the shaman wand I made for you.)

Also, in October I was examining an issue about being accepted by boys relating back to when I was thirteen. This referred to a lifetime in the Orient where the fact I had large breasts was not only unusual but was challenging. You worked for my parents as an artist in some fashion and we became endeared to each other. Because I was so young our relationship left an indelible mark on my entire life. You said something to the effect that I would always be your dream woman. In *your film my role was that of a woman in a dream sequence. Later in that lifetime I became a Geisha.*

There was another American Indian lifetime in which you were once again my child. The significance here is that many of us made a pact to return to this place called California, to help heal the land we so loved. A handful of us, who had the sight, foresaw the devastation in the future and we vowed that, God willing, we would reincarnate to play our part in balancing Earth energies.

Let me not forget the Greek lifetime where I was married to a powerful man. You were a sculptor, son of a master craftsman who worked for my family. We were childhood soul mates who later became lovers. As in so many lives, I had the sight, and experienced frequent premonitions of a major earthquake. Although I was constantly admonished for speaking of such things, my conscience propelled me to do so since I felt the calamity was imminent. Of course most would not believe me, and yet the earthquake came to pass, causing great death and destruction. It was then that the non-believers turned on me, accusing me of sorcery. Long after I thought things were rebuilding and returning to normal, I was attacked by a group of civilians who relentlessly assaulted me with rocks. You came to my rescue following which we died tragically in a hut ignited by one of my assailants. (I remember something you shared with me—a dream about a house on fire that I feel is eerily synchronous with, and relative to, that event.)

My discovery of that lifetime has helped me to clarify deep-rooted feelings I've long wanted to understand as to why, when I ask for anything, I don't feel anyone is listening. More accurately I now realize that it's more to do with being heard. Again, it was my shame about those individuals killed or harmed by the earthquake I predicted, compounded by your death, which had held the resonance in place for so many centuries.

Last night after the sweet experience of seeing your beautiful film, I sat at home in deep reflection, and in an instant found myself in a pool of intense perspiration. I remembered that the same thing happened after

CHAPTER EIGHT: THE PRINCESS'S TEARS

I met you and throughout the time we were making the film. Many would call this the vapors or proclaim it to be menopause-related, but I know better. My truth says that it has more to do with karma burning off. Suddenly I saw an Atlantinian lifetime in which I was a man and you were a woman. Our love for each other was deep and profound, but I was duty-bound to leave in search of new horizons. We sensed we might never see each other again and made a promise that, should it come to pass, we would find each other again in another lifetime. Perhaps this explains the mutual fear we expressed shortly after we met; a fear that we would lose each other.

Well, I guess we fulfilled the promise, again and again. We've been many things to each other over many journeys. How sweet it is.

I just wanted to share a little from my year's experiences since I know how much you appreciate stories. The beautiful book of stories you brought me shortly after we met, continues to inspire. Yet what greater story is there than our own, from which we may inspire others. And speaking of books, "Mists of Avalon" has been coming up for me again. Did you ever read it? I made a call to see what's happening with the film adaptation. I'm told that Warner Brothers has the rights.

So the journey to Tintagel begins again!

Much love, Kay

I finally decided to mail both letters. Marcus responded in writing, thanking me for sharing. Sadly, since that time, our paths have not crossed again. I am struck, however, by how much a brief encounter can affect a person's life – how he affected mine, although it was not our destiny to remain connected. In the end, it would seem that the gifts involved in reuniting, for however brief a time, for me were related to more deeply connecting to my power and my gifts.

What has constantly struck me about relationships throughout the years, whether brief or otherwise, is their function in bringing me in closer union with God. This is the gift of all human interaction. If only we could know this across the board, we might celebrate all of our unions, whatever their nature. It boils down to the issue of greater responsibility for all we create, and *who* we create, as our divine mirrors. Therefore, in the most challenging of relationships we have the greatest opportunity to unfold and embrace the gift *we* are. The traps we fall into are when we take things personally and *falsely* identify with what or who is standing in front of us. In the new paradigm of human relationships and partnering, particularly those of a romantic and emotional nature, we know that the old ways of co-dependency do not and cannot work. Why? Because we are here to be all that we are—total beings! I used to cringe when I would hear someone refer to their partner as their "better half." Although I believe the term was intended as acknowledgment of the spouse or mate, it seemed self-deprecating on the part of the speaker. And back in the 60's and 70's we referred to our partners as "old lady" or "old man." Not too reverent either, although old was perhaps a tad better than "half." In either case, it seemed to me that attitudes in relationships deserved a face-lift.

I am reminded of a deeply poignant scene from the movie, "Enemy Mine," a story of a reptilian alien and a human trapped on a deserted planet together. The androgynous alien, played so sensitively by Lou Gossett Jr., begins a metamorphosis of reproduction as the outraged human (Dennis Quaid), replete with his biases and homophobic small thinking, struggles to conceive of such a phenomenon without the involvement of male and female counterparts. In the simultaneous blissful and painful throes of birthing from which it knows it will not survive, the alien scoffs at the human condition requiring two genders that struggle to be whole. The alien dies as the human is forced to assist in extracting the tiny reptile from its parent's body and bringing it into life. And, as fate has it, he becomes the newborn's guardian and a much bigger person for the experience.

We would do well to take note of such a scenario in these times, as we boldly go to the other ends of the Universe in our imagination by way of film, radio and television programs, publishing, the Internet, and the undisputable fact of world-wide UFO sightings. In no uncertain terms, we seem to be readying ourselves for contact with other species. Will *we* be intelligent enough to interface with extra-terrestrials, all a part of God's vast creation, if we still cannot grasp how to love and embrace each other here on planet Earth?

I believe that one primary way we may prepare is to look more deeply than ever before within ourselves and at our relationship to our very existence. Clues to the gifts and purpose we are here to fulfill may be found in the threads to our major life lessons, running through many of our lifetimes. For me personally, it has been crucial to consciously connect to my distant past for the bigger picture of why I'm here. Specifically, by reuniting with young Quigopa's energy and her pains that carried through into my current lifetime, I have recognized not only deeper significance to the innate power in me, but also the fear and resistance which might have held it back.

But the Macedonian princess was just one layer for me to heal and integrate into the present; there were many others. The scars from both male and female lifetimes have provided a most unique journey--as a sort of spiritual anthropologist--to find the pieces to guide me back to my divine nature. However, there was one lifetime above all others that left its mark and provided the greatest challenge of exploration.

Ancient Egypt was its location.

Chapter Nine: Merlin

But before I introduce my most pivotal past lifetime I must more fully introduce Merlin, because if history truly does repeat itself, then second only to the creator Him/Herself, this man may have had the greatest influence on my existence.

The way I see it, each person we meet is a potential teacher if we choose to only look for highest purpose in all of our experiences, whether challenging or not. Those we are the closest to in any moment offer great gifts in what they reflect back to us through their humanity. And perhaps those persons who push our buttons, relatives, friends and so-called foes alike, are *most* especially our greatest teachers. Through each of them we see our own foibles, the chinks in our armor and the unworthiness from our past needing to be healed. These individuals cause us to rear up defensively with knee-jerk responses and defenses illuminating the "hot spots" within our consciousness; the hidden scars of our past. It's true, however, that had these persons nothing to teach us, we would unlikely have any reaction to their idiosyncratic behavior at all. Through our relationships we learn and evolve – we self-actualize. That's the beauty of them.

Then there are souls along the way who inspire us to seek the greatness in ourselves. They exemplify all that is good in humanity, and they remind us of the sacredness of the human spirit and of its beauty and resilience. Through them we witness the virtues and traits of the human potential made manifest. Through them we see our own greatness-- perhaps yet in its infancy—awaiting maturity, and its perfect voice and expression. To say that I have been blessed with magical and profound teachers is an understatement. My gratitude to them is eternal, my love deep beyond words.

In all of these ways Merlin was my most precious teacher, second only to my Father in current times. Naturally I've also had my share of relationships, both romantic and otherwise, each providing me with a mirror par excellence to view my own shortcomings, as well as the gifts I am here to bring. Yet my dear friend and mentor's influence in my life peaked at what was undoubtedly the most potent time of my life—when I was to throw caution to the wind, and finally allow the whole me to emerge. The nature of Merlin's and my Earth past lives together and the destiny which reunited us in our current lifetime would require us, at the very least, to recognize that we were continuing a mission that began almost six thousand years ago in ancient Egypt. Apparently we have known each other for an eternity dating back to another far distant world, but in more recent times, here in twenty-first century America, we reconnected shortly after my arrival in Los Angeles in 1977.

My first impression of this very unusual man (he referred to himself as weird) was rather baffling to me. I had signed up for a course called "Ministering Consciousness" which was offered at the seminary of the spiritual movement to which I was connected for a few years. (In fact, he had been responsible in large part for establishing the school and writing its' syllabus.) During that time I was passionately ensconced in my spiritual studies, and I spent up to two hours daily in meditation. I had made my choice—my relationship to God Source held central focus in my life. My journey home had begun! So the idea of pursuing ministerial credentials seemed like the natural thing to do.

Friends and acquaintances, impressed by my natural nurturing tendencies, told me that they saw me as a minister. Even during the years I spent in Northern California they acknowledged that quality in me, far more than I recognized it myself. It earned me the nickname of "Mama Kay." Giving advice and providing a shoulder to cry on, plus administering herbal tinctures to soothe their souls, came infinitely naturally to me. The door to my little Victorian cottage was open to all. Apparently, at that time, I didn't recognize the fledgling shaman and minister stirring within me.

It was the seventies after all—the Flower Child era—and the mood was very conducive. In keeping with the mode of the day I wore skirts made from Indian bedspreads, leather moccasins, scarves around my head and rings on every finger—I looked and dressed the part. For a while, my day job was as manager of a local head-shop called Afro-Asian Gifts, a tiny emporium of jewelry and trinkets from around the world. It was a little gold mine, a tourist trap on the main road through the picturesque, bayside hamlet of Sausalito. The owner of the store was an East Indian who owned a thriving chain of shops called India Imports. I had briefly worked at his San Francisco location where and he and several of his relatives, who were also involved in the business, became impressed with my retailing abilities. I sensed that I had had past lives in India since I had always been attracted to its culture.

Then, quite synchronistically, the opportunity to relocate to Marin County occurred. I moved into the cottage and took up my position with the little store within days. It was heavenly. Each day I walked to work along the beautiful San Francisco Bay to work, hardly believing my good fortune.

An amazing assortment of individuals found their way people to the tiny shop, some were locals who frequently came for rolling papers, roach clips, pipes, incense and other smoking paraphernalia, while yet others enjoyed the vast array of jewelry, clothing, Indian bedspreads, sandals and other minor art treasures and knick-knacks.

During those days, due to the recording opportunities and the environmental allure, Marin County teemed with musicians and rock bands, many of whom made their homes there among the redwood trees, and others who were foreign performers and bands passing through. Somehow many found their way into my little Afro-Asian gifts. Joey, a one-time drummer with The Jefferson Airplane, became a regular and good customer, asked me out on a date. Before too long we were living together, with most of the merchandise he had purchased from me, a rather ironic twist I thought!

Some time later, as our relationship was winding down, Joey encouraged me with his "sh...t or get off the pot" attitude, to sign up for an improvisational acting workshop a good friend of his was teaching. He knew of my love for the theater and was acquainted with the handful of friends of mine who studied with the American Conservatory Theater of San Francisco. He knew, as did I, that it was time for me to relinquish my wallflower persona.

And so, my life changed dramatically. Roy's group became my new family and focus for a whole year. Now, there simply wasn't enough time to give of myself to others, as had been the norm for me. Before too long I also signed up for classes in voice and dance. My outer image changed too — jeans and shirts replaced my long skirts and baubles, a uniform more conducive to my new lifestyle. This dramatic turn of events was an unwitting step towards a period of a different kind of "service," the dimensions of which I could not possibly have imagined. (I am referring here to my adult film career during which time I felt every inch a minister.)

From that point on, events happened in fast progression – in the bigger picture and Cosmic sense, all designed to relocate me to Los Angeles to reunite with the members of my Soul family already living there. (Years later I ran into countless individuals who had spent time in Marin County when I was there - but for reasons unknown our paths were not meant to cross at that time.)

Several years hence and already consciously on my spiritual path for some time, I imagined a framed credential upon my wall proclaiming me a minister, and so it was a logical move for me to sign up for the Ministering Consciousness class.

On the first night of the course, I walked into the designated classroom and came face to face with the two facilitators, a man and a woman seated before the students at the front of the room. My friend and teacher Ryhen had mentioned that he knew the female, a devotee of renowned Indian avatar Sai Baba. She was easy to recognize, draped in a sari with a red kumkum gracing the center of her forehead. I was curious about her and had looked forward to making her acquaintance.

Merlin, however, looked totally out of place. He sat languidly sideways, dangling a leg over the arm of the chair and chewing gum. His shining countenance was one of playful yet staunch defiance of conformity; his laugh was nothing less than a bellow. This was not my picture of a minister, let alone one who was to be my instructor. An odd couple, I thought. The course promised to be very interesting.

And it was! It was also one full of rich experiences. Right off the bat, to set the tone of my experience, I learned not to judge by appearances.

The first evening began with a general sharing from each person as to the reason why they had chosen the course, followed by a series of exercises for breaking the ice, so to speak. One exercise in particular, designed to release inhibitions and mindsets, had us crawling around on all fours as our favorite animals, interacting with the other critters and breaking up with gut-wrenching laughter. Such exercises had been a staple in acting classes and not so much of a stretch for me as for others, although it did seem a little out of place. I obviously had a few preconceptions. But I soon realized that this exercise was designed to free us from rigid ideas about how ministers should behave. Merlin was big on basic-self techniques designed to induce the inner child to play and express joy. The animal exercise was, I decided later, brilliant.

A couple of women who had shown up that first night didn't return and it was obvious that they had been intimidated by the process. Many years later, Merlin and I were reminiscing about that evening, and he shared with me that he had previously known the women and had intuited they weren't ready for the material covered in the course. He sensed that their resistance would be detrimental to the group as a whole, so he had chosen the exercise to challenge their willingness to be open. As anticipated, it shook them loose so that the others in the group could flow forward. Years later in groups which Merlin and I led together at my own home, I learned that maintaining harmony within a group is a fine art.

By enlarge, that first evening's activities impressed upon its students that being a minister was not about being serious, and it encouraged us to let go of any stereotypical ideals we may have assumed about ministerial behavior. Instead what was stressed was the importance of joy and laughter, two elements I had certainly never experienced in the church I attended as a child.

As kids, our parents insisted that my Sister and I attend Sunday church services, although I always wondered why Mum and Dad never came themselves. We would make a beeline for the musty pews in the back of the local church in Rainham, Kent, as far removed from the sinister beings we knew as vicars. Chilled to our bones from the dampness and cold of the thousand year old building (beautifully restored recently I discovered during a trip to the UK to visit my family,) we huddled together for warmth, exchanging sweets and pondering the reason we were there.

What child could understand the antiquated language the preacher used or, for that matter, the Bible language? Who were "ye" and what did "shalt" mean? Nothing I heard made any sense to me. If it was the great God whose word was being preached, why did He feel as unavailable to me as my own Father, and if He was love, why did I not feel it—there in that dusty, eerie old church. Why was "His House" not friendly and warm with laughter and joy and attractive people? I just didn't get it. As if that wasn't enough, I was just as unimpressed with the compulsory Sunday religious study classes held in a local high school. I do, however, remember one lady teacher who felt kindly and gentle. She was the exception to the rule, her mannerism alone made the material much more palatable.

So perhaps it was ironic that a quarter of a century later, I would be looking towards ordination. Clearly on that first night of the "Ministering Consciousness" course, the first lesson was that one's ministry must come from the heart and not the head. Merlin was a master of demonstrating that.

CHAPTER NINE: MERLIN

The next nine weeks were rich in self-examination and study, both conventional and unconventional, beyond what I could have imagined. In my final paper I offered,

"My ministry as I see it today is sharing my awakenings and awareness, helping others to find their own inner keys, and using my insights about inner balancing, self-discovery and self-love. My truth is simple, that by humanly be-ing, I am serving in God's perfect love!"

Proudly I received an A-plus for my effort.

Isn't it curious how friendships are formed? We come together through an event or series of events or meetings, molding and shaping a relationship and then, one day, we find that we have evolved from acquaintance to friend. But do we ever forget the initial spark? In the case of Merlin, it was impossible to forget.

A while after the Ministering Consciousness class, my dear friend and I were drawn to spending long interludes together. And, over the next several years, I spent more time with him than with any other friend. A deep spiritual bond already existed between us, evidence of lifetimes of adventures together. Yet in current times, our relationship was of purely platonic design to allow fulfillment of our destiny and commitment to our mission.

So many times I was moved to tears with gratitude for the support Merlin gave me over the years. Whatever the spiritual contract between us, it's clear that it was agreed he would act as a major guide and spiritual buddy to me during a major part of my own development. Indeed, it was he who coached me out of my Monday blues-

For as long as I could remember, I was depressed on Mondays. Weekends would pass and unless I had a specific plan or job to engage my attention, I would retreat under a blanket of futility and sink into depression. A computer printout someone gave me during that time period revealed that I was born on a Monday. That was a revelation for me, although it certainly made no dent in the futility I felt at the onset of each week. So I continued to research the trigger mechanism for the oppressive onslaughts. It was clear that the cause stemmed from a very early period of my life; I just hadn't discovered the exact dynamics of how it manifested. I knew that it was related to a time in early childhood during my temper tantrums period. As an adult, when the identical feelings of despondency and frustration would sweep over me, I would continue to perpetuate the pattern on myself, as if pulling an imaginary gray blanket of gloom down over me. There I would remain in hiding, isolated and inaccessible.

Merlin was my houseguest for a few days in 1982 since he was in transition from one living situation to another. Monday had arrived and I had no job or prospects of employment and no leads to follow. I felt that familiar, all too encompassing feeling sweep over me. Slowly my energy level dropped and the numbness took over. No positive thinking or motivational exercises I knew could pull me out of my state. Once again, I had lowered the impenetrable blanket down over me, locking out the outside world.

My dear friend was fixing himself some breakfast in the kitchenette and I sensed him observing me from across the room. Outwardly I tried to pretend that nothing was wrong but Merlin, every inch the sensitive, saw my pain. He simply could not stand by and watch my struggle without offering his assistance.

"Would you like a hug?" he offered gently.

I immediately tensed, realizing that the dynamics of our friendship would require a confrontation of some kind. If he persisted, I would have to come clean and move through my pain. I wasn't sure that I was ready to do that in that moment.

"I'm fine thanks," I insisted through clenched teeth.

He came and stood beside me, still tempering his rather large persona. Again he offered,

"I'd still like to give you a hug."

I shrugged, "OK," as a myriad of emotions began to stir uncomfortably in my chest. In our circle, one just didn't refuse hugs and even though I was sure that my veneer was quite transparent, to refuse a hug would have aroused even more suspicion as to my state of mind. My entire behavior was illogical, given the overall circumstance, but I was too deeply into my pattern to pull out. Some part of my personality was hell-bent on continuing with my cover-up behavior, futile as it was. As Merlin stooped to deliver his hug, I felt uncontrollable anger and rage welling up in my chest. My initial impulse was to push my dear friend away, I was in such self-abandonment. But you just didn't do that with him! He wrapped his arms around me and held firmly. I resisted for a few seconds, but his love was too big, too potent. My gray blanket disintegrated, releasing waves of indescribable pain into my chest. I began to sob and the sobs turned into wailing. I couldn't believe the sounds coming out of me. Merlin gently coached me through the experience, encouraging me to talk about the myriad of emotions gushing forth. Memories of my childhood experiences surfaced; the root of my debilitating pattern—the oppression I felt in my environment, the bleak energies around me and the dire feeling of not belonging. My little inner child, "Babsie," I called her, came through loud and clear expressing her anger and frustration and holding open wide her arms to dear Merlin's love.

This incident was a turning point for me, a major step in receiving love and just one of many I would take with my dear friend. On countless occasions, we took long walks together in the park or on the beach. We shared the most incredible conversations, exploring every corner of the Universe and marveling at God's infinite creation. Little did I know back then that our exploratory work would later take us into dimensions I didn't even know existed, and would open up the way for a major life's project to become manifest.

Always, my time spent with Merlin required complete surrender. Again and again he helped me to see how I tried to control my life and how pushing against the grain; trying to make things happen, only stifled my flow. In lightening up and entering into what he called the vacuum or emptiness, a person could experience Grace and allow the Universe to shower them with its fruits and abundance. In that void magic happened - always! The day of my gray-blanket break-through was no exception.

As my tears subsided a feeling of blissful renewal filled me. My self-confidence restored, I was now perfectly assured that I would get work. I knew God always provided for me.

"What you need is a comedy! " Pronounced Merlin, "so you can see what a big joke this all is."

My friend had never questioned my adult film career rather he seemed to have a deep understanding of the lines of destiny which had pulled me in that seemingly incongruous direction.

As I resonated in deep gratitude once again for his support, the phone rang. It was a producer I knew and he had a job offer for me. This kind of instant response from my Universe inevitably happened when I was willing to move through my blocks and self-heal. It was in moments like these when I truly believed, not only in the existence of realms where thoughts were instantly manifested, but that at some point in time in my Soul's evolution, I *had* lived in such a manner. In the years since that experience I have come to *know* it. As a child I knew it.

The role the producer was offering me was for three days work on a film shooting in Las Vegas, for less than my usual fee. He briefly described the part in question. For the most part it sounded uninspiring, hardly the comedy Merlin had suggested. Nevertheless, I accepted the offer, applying the conditional classic "I should, since I need the money" response. I assumed this was the amazing synchronicity I had come to expect from exchanges with Merlin. An audition was unnecessary—my work was known, as were my parameters in terms of what kind of sex I would perform. Usually, when I received a call, it was a given that I had specifically been chosen for the part, since the roles offered to me were typically older women, housewives or rich-bitch types. There simply weren't that many women in the business to fit those stereo-types. I felt relieved knowing that my rent would be paid, and gave thanks.

Shortly after the phone call, Merlin and I left for the beach and spent our usual mirthful time soaking up negative ions, chasing seagulls and engaging in our usual deep contemplation of spiritual matters. We returned to the apartment several hours later, windswept and refreshed. Barely had I shaken the sand from my sandals when the phone rang and I was offered yet another film role. This one was for five days at my usual fee in a co-staring role opposite Paul Thomas, an actor I had known since my early days in the business and with whom I had a good rapport. As the director on the phone described the role and a basic outline of the script, it was clear that *here* was the silly comedy my friend had prescribed for me. This was Merlin wizardry at its best and once again, a demonstration of the fine art of surrender reaping untold rewards.

For the first time in my career, I reneged on one offer for another. I called the original producer and told him I had decided against accepting his offer. A while later I learned from a friend in the business that the Las Vegas film had been raided. Apparently, residents at the shooting location in a residential neighborhood noticed the unusually heavy stream of people coming and going, and what they deemed to be suspicious goings-on. They notified the local police who quickly determined the nature of the gathering and shut down the production. Consequently, all the existing film footage was confiscated; several actors were arrested and were severely harassed before being released. These were the kinds of indignities I was consistently spared throughout my career, proof to me that I was protected and guided.

Although originally entitled "*The History of Sex*," the film I was about to make was later renamed "*Intimate Lessons*." The story took place in a quasi "sex college" where the kinky deans, played by myself and Paul Thomas, instructed and acted out sexual scenarios from points in history to an assortment of young over-sexed individuals. I had worked with the director once before on the X-rated Dracula film later renamed "Lust at First Bite." He was a highly creative man, yet once again I felt that he was overly ambitious about the project given the realities of budget and genre. Known as one to bite off more than he could chew, his productions typically began with high energy and good intention but several days into the shooting schedule, things would begin to fall apart. It was sadly evident that cocaine played a part in this energy breakdown.

Still, it promised to be a fun time. Paul, or PT as he is affectionately known in the industry, is one of the male legends of porn who is still active as a director and producer. He and I met in San Francisco just prior to shooting my fourth film, entitled "*Untamed*," in which we were paired. PT's aristocratic good looks and suave though restrained demeanor were very attractive to me yet, after our first meeting, I just didn't get it—I didn't understand what a nice boy like him was doing in X-rated movies any more than I could figure out my own involvement. A multi-talented actor and performer who appeared as the apostle Peter in "Jesus Christ Superstar" both on the Broadway stage and in the movie adaptation, Paul also appeared in the long-running musical show called "Beach Blanket Babylon" in San Francisco, which I was fortunate to see. Why someone with such talents and an existing quorum of success in the world of mainstream entertainment would opt for a career in porno was baffling to me. But I knew that the answers to my query were probably as complex as my own psycho-dynamics.

Paul and I decided to drive to the location in Encinitas together. We embarked upon our trip with a mutual commitment to having a fun time. En route to the film's location, as we drove south on the San Diego freeway, Paul chose an audio tape from the collection in my car as traveling music. He opted for Kenny Loggins' "*Celebrate Me Home,*" the title song on the album of the same name. That song remains a huge favorite of mine, not only because it reminds me of that experience, but because of the chorus for me has deep spiritual implications.

"Please celebrate me home, gimme a number
Please celebrate me home, play me one more song
That I'll always remember, I can recall whenever
I find myself too all alone, so I can make believe I've never gone
Won't you let me know where I belong—Sing me home!"

This became our theme song for the ensuing adventure. Neither one of us could get the music out of our minds and, throughout the shoot, in moments of tedium and endless waiting for "action," we would burst into another rousing chorus. One such moment occurred when we were shooting our bathtub sex-scene sequence. We sat immersed in lukewarm water for what seemed like a small eternity as the technicians shuffled around us solving lighting and sound problems, as our bodies slowly turned into prune-skin. It was easy to lament at such times and to lose any sensuality which might have previously existed. But, such is the art of filmmaking. Suddenly Paul rose to the spirit once more and bellowed out in his rich tenor voice,

"*Please celebrate me home..,*" immediately diffusing the impatience on the entire set. In an instant, harmony and levity was restored as well as a reminder of the ridiculousness of the moment.

The location for the film was a "Swinger Ranch" in pristine surroundings just north of San Diego. Our accommodations were a charming rustic little motel just ten minutes away in Encinitas. The adult industry was at its peak and on-location expenditures were commonplace. Later, as budgets plummeted, location shooting practically became obsolete. On this occasion, I was assigned a suite with a kitchenette and total privacy to create my own little haven. But the icing on the cake was my discovery that my temporary digs were situated a mere mile or so from the Encinitas branch of the Self-Realization Foundation retreat.

Of all the places I have visited in my life, one of my favorites remains the Lake Shrine, located in Pacific Palisades, on Sunset Boulevard just before it meets the Pacific Ocean. It is one of the California centers of the "Self-Realization Foundation," founded by the beloved Indian guru Yogananda Paramahansa. It's a perfect sanctuary and for years I have personally found incredible peace of mind there when I've needed a respite from life. The exquisite gardens are awash with a wide variety of plant life, the beautiful lake teams with ducks, swans, turtles and huge koi fish, and the houseboat where the guru stayed during his visits nestles on the lake. A little windmill serves as a chapel, and there is a tiny yet fascinating museum with relics of Yogananda's life. Under the huge golden lotus archway is a sarcophagus bearing some of Mahatma Gandhi's ashes. What I most particularly love about the foundation is its ecumenical attitude. It is a monument to and embraces all religions. Any visitor to the Los Angeles area should not miss it.

I had known there was a branch of Self-Realization in Encinitas, but this was my first opportunity to visit and I was thrilled.

No sooner had I unpacked a few clothes and checked in with the production crew, I jumped back in my car and headed to the retreat. Unfortunately by the time I arrived at the location it was closed. I peeked through the wrought iron gates into a beautiful garden with a path leading to what surely had to be an incredible ocean view. For sure, scheduling permitting, I would return the following day.

My call time for the next day turned out to be early afternoon. Perfect. My Universe had heard me! The next morning, after a light breakfast, I headed back to the retreat. Once inside the gates, I felt transported to another world, serene and sacred. The grounds were every bit as gorgeous as those in the Lake Shrine and likewise immaculately manicured. I found my way to the cliff top and to a bench around which a fragrant hedge was sculpted, overlooking the ocean. This was all too reminiscent of Atlantis—so blue was the ocean, so infinite an expanse. A subtle haze over a surreal view transported me back in time. Far below the cliff the waves broke against the rocks and I could subtly taste and feel the salty spray on my face. I remained in the gardens for about an hour, drifting in and out of consciousness. Finally I realized it was time to return to the other reality and to the film I was there to make.

The producers of the film, a group of young Canadians, were new to the business. Like many others at that time, they saw the potential of the expanding industry, so they had come to town to make their bid for a piece of the pie. Right off the bat I liked them. For purely selfish reasons I was always eager to work with new people in the business. They were the ones most likely to dare to be innovative and to break away from the existing formula of seven sex scenes per film. Unfortunately for them however, their venture into the business often turned out to be a one-time-only experience. Innovation rarely paid off for X-rated film producers, perhaps largely in part because their distributors lacked creative marketing skills. But for us actors, these were our chances to do something a little different.

At our initial meeting the producers appeared a little unsure to me, most especially in the area of preparation and shooting sex scenes. No first-timer, whether performer or technician, can truly be prepared for the unique circumstances involving capturing sexual situations on film. I felt inclined to forewarn the newcomers of some of the elements to be expected, as well as making sure that their makeup and wardrobe personnel were familiar with the pre-requisites of sex scenes. It was my opportunity to educate them and to put in a request for the optimally equipped hygiene department: towels, douches, contraceptive gels, lubricants and, most especially, clean and private washrooms. Of course, in this case, since the location was a swinger ranch, the latter was already quite adequate since there were numerous bathrooms throughout the facility. In fact, this proved to be one of the most comfortable locations of my entire career.

The dichotomy of my life was never as apparent as when I left the magnificent sanctuary overlooking the ocean, and contemplated what the next few days of filming would bring. Before commencing shooting I spent time to meditate, to ask for protection and guidance, not to mention reminding myself to stay balanced and conscious at all times of the subtle energies at play. Irresponsible and misguided sexual energies can produce chaos and potentially effect the entire production. I saw it happen more than once. Even the most conscientious of crews and talent could find themselves swept up in indefinable energy fields, reeking havoc on a well-flowing production. In an instant shooting could slow, even to a standstill, equipment could break down and tempers quicken for no apparent reason. All this can happen because of irresponsible and misdirected adolescent behavior. (I learned years later that this is the stuff of poltergeists—defiant teen-ager energy running rampant.) I carefully steered clear of such energies by keeping my imaginary shield up, placing myself inside a bubble of white light, and by projecting various positive images on those around me who felt off balance. My spiritual protocol always paid off. At the same time, I allowed myself to have fun and enjoy the mirth—something not always easy for me in a work situation.

The next few days were in fact some of the silliest I ever spent on a film shoot, with moments of sheer sidesplitting humor. It started off well and then, as anticipated, we fell a bit behind schedule. This was the point at which the director would begin to panic and apparently resort to cocaine, a profound hindrance to *his* performance. It seemed to me this might sabotage the entire production, so I took it upon myself to address the issue. I went to him and spoke honestly yet diplomatically with him about his drug usage. He sensed my genuine concern for the greater good of everyone involved and seemed to rally for a few moments. Yet as he lapsed once again into his angst, the sensual banquet scene in progress became a free-for-all.

As anticipated, things became rather riotous, with several of the actors themselves pitching in to help direct the scene. But we know only too well that too many cooks can certainly spoil the broth. The story became quickly distorted, transforming the action into an all-out food orgy with very surrealistic overtones. My memory as to how we actually completed the scene has faded, more likely because I either lost interest at that point, or I became disgusted as a roasted chicken carcass took center stage.

Despite the insanity of the final hours on the set, Merlin had been right—it was just what I had needed. This had been the perfect antidote for my heavy heart. I marveled at the fact that I was actually getting paid for being there. At the film's conclusion, I returned to Los Angeles where Merlin and I began a series of workshops at my home dealing with The Archetypical Inner Personae and healing the Inner Child. Within the next month I, along with many others, was baptized in a beautiful ceremony around the pool at my spiritual teacher's rustic home. My personal spiritual studies continued, culminating in another weeklong workshop.

Following that, I once again flew to San Francisco to make another film. My diverse and strange life continued!

Some time later I wrote my letter to apply for ordination within my spiritual organization. A friend with whom I had taken numerous workshops happened to be on the ministerial board at the time. He knew of my film career and at the review of my application, he felt compelled to bring it to the attention of the board members. My friend had approached me with his dilemma. He was torn because, although he knew of my affiliation with the world of porno, he also knew of my deep spiritual commitment and of the time I devoted in service. I believe he felt as if he was preparing to betray me. It was a challenging moment, yet I assured him that whatever his decision, I would not hold it against him.

I was aware that some people within my spiritual community knew of my rather unusual career and several of them seemed challenged by it. Although we rarely discussed the fact, I could feel their conflict. From time to time their struggle certainly mirrored my own. Under the umbrella of our spiritual movement we were all equal and there was no overt judgment or rejection; we all worked side by side in consummate unity. But the issues of my ordination involved legalities—this I knew.

My application was therefore declined. However, the letter I received from the Ministerial Board was less of a rejection, rather a glowing acknowledgment. But they collectively agreed that there was a gray area and, because of that, it could reflect badly upon our Teacher since the organization held the status of a church.

So, ultimately I was declined ordination on account of my association with the world of X-rated films. I couldn't and didn't blame them for their decision and imagined I might have voted likewise had I been in their shoes.

For a short while afterwards my ego did feel little bruised, but in a meditation, a greater reality hit me. I realized that I had placed far too much emphasis and energy upon the document. Did I really need a piece of paper to proclaim my spiritual status? Suddenly I saw the challenge as a perfect lesson in self-acknowledgment. Again the phrase, *"God's Laws versus Man's Laws"* echoed through my consciousness, a phrase an astrologer had once applied to my natal chart. I was challenged to look inside, not outside. Only *I* needed to know who *I* was and of my worth—therein lay my true foundation.

Years later, I received a phone call from a woman named Barbara who knew of both my film and my spiritual work and who had heard me lecture on several occasions (including once when I read this chapter, before many rewrites.)

"Do you still want to be ordained? "She asked me.

I was surprised. I hadn't spoken with her in a couple of years."Why, sure," I replied somewhat nonchalantly, "Although, I don't have the energy on the issue I once did."

"Well," she said, "I would like to make it happen for you."

My acquaintance went on to explain that she was a minister of the Universal Life Church, a somewhat revolutionary, non-denominational entity promoting an ideology of "acceptance of human beings, just as they are, in their process of cosmic becoming." The church champions above all else Liberty of Thought, equality of man and woman, peace, prosperity and good will to all. They also promote the Golden Rule that a person does right, harms no one, lives honestly and gives everyone their due.

I began to hear about the Church back in the 1970s when it was common place to hear of individuals becoming ministers of the Universal Life church. Their desire to be of service was the only requirement, yet I believe that for many it was more of a novelty. Most of those individuals were drawn in by the extremely liberal attitudes of the church, whose postures included a belief that adults may well have become the ignorant in our culture while the young were the oppressed, judged and harassed by their elders. And, they further intimated, if what was going on in our world was any measurement of this fact, there needed to be serious re-thinking of the values by which many children were being raised.

Based on my own experiences and my cognizance of the lies and misguidance which had been perpetrated for so long by those who came before us, by conventional religion and other gubernatorial bodies, I had to agree with most of their thinking.

Barbara explained that the church was promoting ordinations over the Internet at that time, to get people more involved in ministerial work. She would handle whatever paperwork was necessary for me, she said, and even pay the small fee. It was her way of giving back, of being of service. So with no fuss or red tape, no forms to fill out or ministerial boards to apply to, I was ordained—sight unseen. Barbara also made sure that I received my ministerial diploma in the mail a few days later.

Things we desire often come to us when we let go…

Did I frame my credential and put it on my wall? Although I was grateful and moved by my friend's gesture, by that time the tone of my life was quite different from when I had first applied for ordination. The years of counseling, lecturing and other kinds of ministering in between had altered my ideals somewhat. I *knew* who I was, I didn't need a piece of paper to confirm it.

However, it was my great joy in 1995, to perform the wedding ceremony for two of my oldest friends who had met and fallen in love at my birthday party, two years prior.

As for Merlin and me, our journey in this lifetime was really just beginning. I was to discover that my dear friend—whose real name is Aaron—and I were to eventually play pivotal parts in each other's lives beyond what I could ever have imagined. First, however, we had other things to do, lives to touch and much growth to endure. Most importantly, I had to come face to face with ancient wounds for which I initially blamed him—and that was part of the plan!

Chapter Ten: The Gay Italian Lifetime

One of the deep scars I initially pinned to Aaron (Merlin) dated back to the early days of opera in Italy. I can trace threads of this lifetime throughout most of my current life adulthood.

The earliest clue is found in the form of my first boyfriend, a tall distinguished looking German lad I met in 1961 in Margate, a popular British seaside resort. Hundreds of foreign exchange students poured into the British beach towns in summertime to improve their command of the English language and to party. My girlfriends and I were hungry for variety and the chance to interact with the very suntanned and often physically beautiful German and Nordic boys. On the short train ride South to Margate we often fancied ourselves to be foreigners also opting to speak to each other in gibberish for extra effect.

I met Christoph in one of the many dance cafes typical of the era, where we danced to popular tunes blasting over the ever-present jukeboxes. I was at once infatuated with him. He exuded power and self-confidence, humor and a zest for life, traits I hadn't witnessed in English lads I knew. His English was excellent, a result of time spent with American friends, he informed me, and so there was no language barrier. We seemed to find lots to talk about despite my shyness. Later, with zero regard to how we would explain our absence to our families, my girlfriend and I decided to break curfew and stay overnight with him and his fellow students. Their accommodation was a modest private home, which provided just the basic needs of the visitors. The boys sneaked us into their room, a small and very crowded space with four single cots, and there we stayed and talked the night away, and there was no hanky-panky!

The following day we exchanged addresses and agreed to stay in touch and, for the next two years my life force hung on our trans-continental exchange of letters.

Chris came from a prestigious family in Munich, where his Father was the head of a camera-manufacturing corporation. His upbringing therefore was privileged. But he was the perfect gentleman, a very fun-loving and ethical being with a huge heart. We had connected on a soul level in the first few seconds of meeting, indicative I now realize, of a sibling resonance from the Italian lifetime where the world of opera was so significant. Chris therefore provided the impetus for me to leave England: He was my carrot, my excuse to leave home and travel. In fact, some time later, my traveling companion Loraine and I did visit him in Munich, where he assisted us in acquiring work permits enabling us to seek out temporary jobs in a restaurant located in the "Englischer Garten," the city's most beautiful park, which runs along the river Isar. After several weeks of work, we had replenished our finances adequately to proceed on our way. Chris had by that time returned to his boarding school in the South of Germany and his life style, realms from my own reality.

Some weeks later, at the tail end of our hitchhiking adventure through Germany, Loraine's money was stolen from our room in the youth hostel in Stuttgart. She quickly notified her parents who insisted that she return to England which she did willingly, claiming she missed her boyfriend, which I thought a little strange given her tendency to pop into bed with the next male who showed up in our travels.

However, there was no way I was willing or ready to return to the U.K. especially in light of my Father's insistence that I would "…be back in six weeks, mark my words."

What was I to do…?

Prior to Loraine's departure, we had spent a few afternoons at the local schwimmbad. It seemed the Germans loved to soak up the sun and as soon as the weather permitted, the swimming pools were crowded to overflowing with students and locals alike looking to bronze their physics.

CHAPTER TEN: THE GAY ITALIAN LIFETIME 177

It was a given then that this would be where we would spend a few hours daily among the hunks and fellow travelers. On the very first day I met Wolfgang, a tall bronzed hunk who took to me as I to him. We connected on all levels including physically and it was with Wolfie that I surrendered my virginity, in his dorm room at the Daimler Benz factory in Stuttgart where he was studying engineering.

With my traveling companion's imminent return to England, the question became, where was I to go?

Wolfgang insisted that I accompany him to his home in Wurtzburg, where he was convinced his Mother would find me a job of some sort. It seemed to be my only feasible option. He told me that his Mother was a member of the German-American women's club in her city, which hosted a U.S. military presence. I was nineteen, practically out of money, naïve and without any other direction. The one thing clear to me was that I wanted to spend more time with Wolfie since we were already quite infatuated with each other.

By the time we arrived in Wurtzburg, Frau Raith had already arranged an interview for me at her home with a Major Eubank and his wife. We settled an agreement on the spot and I began working as a domestic help for the couple and their three boys the following day.

A few months after being hired by my new American friends, the reality set in that my relationship with Wolfie was overshadowed by the pressure of his familial duties, to say the least. Even though, by that time, I had secured some independence by renting a one-room apartment on the other side of town, it remained a challenge for Wolfie and me to find quality private time together. And although we actually discussed engagement and had even begun to look for a ring, I was unable to imagine what married life together might be like. I was nineteen years old, lacking in skills, and I still didn't speak German. He was in college and was very much the head of the family whose patriarch had died some years earlier. I was frustrated and confused as to what my next step should be, and I began to doubt if, in fact, there was a future for us.

The obvious answer for me was to change jobs and enter into a new environment, hopefully one where I could at least fulfill my goal of speaking another language.

Wolfgang's Mother suggested Munich as a good place to start searching for a position as an 'au pair,' and assisted me in composing a personal advertisement for the Munchner Zeitung, Bavaria's best known daily newspaper. I could sense that she was very wisely guiding me out of her son's life and onward in my life.

Frau Raith was a remarkable woman, mother of four grown children, traditional, tall, and dignified in an Ingrid Bergman kind of way. And she was profoundly kind. Sight unseen, at her son's bidding; she had welcomed me into her home and had treated me as one of the family. For this I was deeply grateful. But as any good mother, she had plans for her son and, realistically speaking, I didn't fit the picture. Her wisdom prevailed and in fact, she played a most important role in my destiny, not only by introducing me to Major and Mrs. Eubank, my eventual link to the US, but also by pointing me towards Bavaria and a brand new experience.

It amazes me that we accomplished most communication by 'snail' mail in those days. How far we've come! Mere days after placing my ad, I received two responses from families looking for live-in domestic help. Consequently, I arranged to take a day's excursion South for interviews, figuring that it was possible to accomplish the task in one day. Both parties were located in close proximity to Munich, yet in significantly different parts of beautiful, verdant Bavaria. The journey there was easy as the train from Wurtzburg was convenient, fast and comfortable.

My first meeting was in Lake Sternberg, just to the southwest of the city, requiring me to transfer to a local train that stopped very close to my destination. My interview with the particular doctor's family was brief, and despite the appeal of the location, it was evident that it was not the job for me; the energy was wrong.

I turned around and headed back to Munich, where I transferred to yet another local train line to the suburb of Pullach, where I easily found my way to the home of Dr. and Frau Rennert. From the moment I walked into their lovely home, it felt right. The atmosphere was immediately inviting and warm, elegant yet unpretentious. This was a place of love and creativity and I felt enveloped in its spirit. I was equally moved by Frau Rennert's own unique personality. She was buoyant and open, and she touched my heart right away.

I was ushered into the living room and served tea and kuchen while my hostess explained in excellent English what would be expected of me—should I choose to accept the position. The chores would be light ones, since they already employed a cleaning lady. Some cooking, ironing and errand running would be the extent of my domestic tasks. Mostly, I would be there to cater to her three children—two daughters, eleven and fourteen, from a former marriage, and a son aged six, by her husband Doktor Rennert, who apparently was rarely home.

Frau Rennert herself was a retired opera performer, and her husband an established figurehead in the world of international opera and theater, who some years later assumed the esteemed position of Director of the Bavarian State Opera. Frau Doktor, as I would address her, was a petite woman with tiny feet and bad eyesight, a typical Cancerian (if memory serves me,) who was overtly friendly and amiable and who went out of her way to entertain and make others feel good. She had retired from performing to raise her family and was a dedicated and wonderful Mother.

My decision to take the job was made within moments of my arrival—I knew it was right for me. Far beyond the fact of how comfortable I felt, was a knowing that I needed to be there. The family, who also took well to me, later teased me about how, in my very broken German, I had accepted their offer, endearing me to them also. Since by the time of our interview it was late afternoon and unwise for me to travel back to Wurtzburg alone, I was invited to spend the night in the room I would occupy in my position as 'au pair'. Like the rest of the house, the room was cozy and comfortable, decorated with antique furniture, oriental rugs and a lovely garden view.

From the first day I arrived in Pullach to assume my duties, I was treated as one of the family and, as such, indulged in most of their activities. Any challenging aspects of my duties were completely over-ruled by the many gifts I received from my year with the Rennert family. I learned to cook, shop wisely, to tend the children without giving in to their wiles and whims, and I became expert in carrying groceries on the handlebars of my bicycle on my daily shopping expeditions.

My bedtime story reading sessions became a family favorite—everyone gathered around as I read in German to young Oliver, a precocious yet brilliant child (who I met again years later in San Francisco, where the pimply teen visited his Father who was directing an opera and, more recently we fondly reconnected via the Internet). It was a great opportunity to practice my pronunciation of the often-difficult German vocabulary. In fact, it was the children who taught me their language—who better? I essentially parroted them, and paid close attention to their corrections.

Within three months I had mastered spoken German to the point where at times, were it not for grammatical errors I made, I could fool certain individuals into believing that I was a native. I thought it was curious that it came so easily to me. (Little did I realize that I was actually experiencing a past-life bleed-through, in particular, my very last incarnation prior to this.)

It was the beautiful and sensitive Claudia, the eldest daughter with whom I had a special and close relationship, who broke it to me delicately that, while on the one hand it was admirable that I was doing so well with my pronunciation of the language, my grammar was often terrible. Practically every day phone calls came in from dignitaries and celebrities from the opera and theater world from all over Europe. Claudia suggested with her gentle humor that when I answered the phone, my ability to converse fluidly was quickly muddied by my errors and I tended to sound like a country bumpkin.

We laughed together about the fact, and I adjusted my speech patterns so that it was obvious that I was an 'auslanderin' and not from those parts.

And speaking of laughter, the greatest gift I received during my year with the family was the gift of joy and mirth that flowed relentlessly in their home. "Mami" Rennert was a gifted entertainer whose stories held us spellbound. Tales of her days as a young member of the Hamburg Opera company during the war, and of survival escapades she and her fellow performers pulled off while risking their skins left me with mouth agape. Yet, as a mirth-maker whose clowning frequently reduced us all to howling heaps, rolling on the floor and begging for mercy, she was truly a genius. Many an 'accident' occurred as the children, frantically grabbing their crotches, attempted to reach the bathroom in time to avoid the inevitable. I had never laughed so hard with such abandon. It was a brand new and healthy experience.

There was also the gift of culture. I was introduced to the theater and, more specifically, the world of opera. Frau Rennert's generosity laid open a rich new medium that filled me with wonder and a joy so deep and resonant I could hardly believe it. But how could it have been otherwise when, for my virginal live opera experience, I was invited to sit in the royal box at Munich's National Theater. That evening, seated on plush velvet in the best seat of the house, I felt more a part of the performance, a Puccini opera, than an audience member. The music moved to my core, triggering the cellular memory of a significant past life where opera played a pivotal role. This experience was as far removed from life in England as it could be. The girl-child from Kent was blossoming!

Almost exactly a year after I joined the Rennert household Claudia announced she was going to attend a party in Grunwald, an elite suburb of Munich. Although I was barely four years older than she, I had occasionally chaperoned at her social events, but since this particular party was in a private home, she was going solo. It occurred to me that I had lost touch with Christoph whose home was in the same area and so I casually mentioned him to Claudia,

"If you run into my old friend, give him my best wishes. You never know, he might be there, this is his home turf."

The following day was Sunday and my day off. I ventured into the kitchen for breakfast where Frau Doktor was serving. She greeted me,

"Kay, did Claudia tell you she ran into your friend?"

My mouth fell open as her daughter entered the room brimming with excitement of the uncanny story of the previous evening. She told me that upon her arrival at the designated location, she rang the doorbell and was greeted by a tall stately young man, who, in true German tradition clicked his heels, extended his hand and introduced himself,

"Guten abend, ich bin Christoph..."

My sweet Claudia admitted to bursting into laughter and then composing herself to explain to him that she brought greetings from someone he had not seen in a while. As she related the story of what had been my last thoughts to her the previous evening, he was speechless. She added,

"He'll be calling you momentarily!"

I gasped again, not quite sure I was ready for the imminent reunion. Sure enough though, not fifteen minutes later, with the rest of the family eagerly listening in, my pen pal from years past called me. We hadn't spoken to each other in close to two years and were conversing in his native tongue.

The feeling of that moment, of pure accomplishment, is one I'll never forget. Christoph was in awe of the fact that, not only had I remained in Germany, but that I had indeed learned the language as well as I had. We met that same afternoon and for a while after re-ignited the flame of our two kindred souls. He subsequently introduced me to his family and to more of the beauty of Munich I had not experienced up until that point. We spoke of a more definitive relationship, but it was not to be. My father was taken seriously ill and I had to return to England immediately.

Once again my Father became the catharsis for change in my life. With great sadness I gave notice to my beloved family Rennert intuiting that I would not be back. I knew it was time to move on with my life.

Three months later, after Dad's recovery, I returned briefly to Germany to follow my course of destiny — to America. I met Christoph and shared with him my decision to cross the pond. He was angry and insisted that, if it didn't work out for me in the U.S., I would return to Germany and he would marry me. He meant it! That was a notion I couldn't even digest given my idea that we were from such different worlds. Could I have ever really been worthy of him – I wondered?

We saw each other only twice after that when he visited San Francisco. He told me that he had leukemia and that his future was very unsure. I felt numbed by this information and didn't know how to respond. Subsequently, life continued on and we dropped out of touch.

From time to time, I checked in with my friend in the soul dimensions and I sensed him doing likewise. A channeler I consulted with during the 1980's told me during one session that he had survived his leukemia, much to the chagrin of his doctors!! Yay! This made me very happy.

Then in 1987, whilst in Bavaria at the wedding of a friend to a German chef and Gasthof proprietor, I decided to throw caution to the wind and phone Christoph's home since I still had the phone number. His Mother answered, and in rusty German I explained who I was and that I wanted to inquire as to her Son's well-being. She remembered me and quite willingly shared with me that indeed he was married and living in Hamburg. She even gave me his phone number.

When I returned to California I called the number and left a message with his house-keeper – he was on vacation, she told me. Immediately following my Father died and I was off to the U.K. again for his funeral and family affairs. When I returned to California Chris' familiar voice had recorded a message on my answering device. It felt good to hear him. He mentioned that he visited California once in a while on business and said he would notify me when he due for another trip.

And that was that. We haven't connected again since.

I had taken to opera as naturally as I took to the German language, and for years after, it was the music I listened to the most. As I continued along my path, both in Santa Fe and San Francisco, the opportunity to usher at each city's opera house magically availed itself. But how deeply woven into the fabric of my life was Germany and opera?

The answer to this question was revealed years later in Los Angeles in 1978 during a session with one of my health practitioners -

-As his fingers probed my face coming to rest below my left cheekbone, he coaxed me to relax deeper and to let my mind totally come to rest. He was applying only the subtlest of pressure as he focused on the one point he had intuitively targeted. A few moments later there was a blinding flash of light behind my eyelids and a sensation of tearing of flesh and complete horror. I gasped in absolute shock and then fell into a void of coldness, confusion and total non-comprehension.

"Oh my God," I uttered, "I was shot in the face!"

My Doctor continued to guide me through the process in which he had quite unwittingly triggered a past life regression. His technique was unlike anything I had experienced until that point and yet it was one of the most beneficial. Although primarily a practitioner of Chinese medicine, acupuncture and herbology, he also occasionally employed other processes to achieve the required results. The particular body release technique he used that day was Hawaiian in origin, called Lomi Lomi he told me. It involved the very slightest of body manipulation and, at times, it was difficult to tell if he was even touching you. Because of the nature of the exchange, a patient clearly had to be in a place of total trust, as I was that day. I say 'exchange' because, as in the case of naturopathic healing, it requires a joint effort to reach a particular goal of healing. An individual's level of commitment as an equal participant in the healing process is crucial. (Herein, from my point of view, lies a significant part of the difference between the worlds of homeopathic and allopathic medicine, where individuals tend to give their power up to doctors and relinquish dominion over their bodies.)

The appropriate course of treatment for me that day was a deeply intuited decision by my practitioner in alignment with my spiritual guide. We were working in tandem to release the old memory from my cellular body. I believe that every negative thought we have ever had, in all of our lifetimes, is stored in our cellular memory and will at some point in time, in some way, manifest to be healed and released. This is the human experience at its core, to discard the veils of inauthenticity and return to God—our divine nature. Our process therefore, as third dimensional beings, becomes one of restoring our whole-ness, balance and integrity of all our cells, in all of our dimensional awareness. This was never more evident than now, here in the twenty-first century, as we witness the external manifestation of this dynamic; our beloved planet Earth struggling to survive the overwhelming toxicity and disease we have collectively allowed and perpetrated.

Billy, my Doctor (I was on familiar terms with him because I had known his Sister from my Marin County days) guided me to stay with the energy. He suggested there might be more information to be gleaned from my experience, to assist in healing the centuries old memory that had been lodged in my cheek. For a few minutes I allowed myself to sink into the spectrum of emotions encoded in the cellular memory of that wound. I felt the disorientation of the fatal blast deep in the pit of my stomach, sudden, unexpected, brutal, and the strangest of the feelings surfacing, that the perpetration of the act had been profoundly unfounded!

The sensations washed over and through me, and finally, when I was able to move beyond them, I wondered if they were the emotions of a dying man. Somehow the fact of me having been a male person was clear. But had this been a battle, a vendetta, or just a random event, an accident even? It felt otherwise. Had I been murdered? That didn't resonate as truth either.

In fact, the truth about what had happened was not and could not be revealed until certain individuals had come into my life. And, like players waiting in the wings of the stage to make their entrance and act out their parts, the primary five people from that lifetime had either just entered my reality or were just around the proverbial corner. The design for our collective karmic experience in the current time period was still unfolding, as we embarked upon our various relationships and journey together.

Over the next few years the story took shape piece by piece, like a magnificent tapestry. One of my closest friends at the time played the central character to the drama that had happened in Italy. She had been a famous opera singer who, despite her remarkable talent, was unhappy with her life. I was a patron of the arts enamored with her unusual gift, a heavenly voice that touched me to my core. My interest was far from romantic, for despite a marriage to a wonderful woman with whom I had sired three children, my actual sexual proclivity was far from heterosexual. The true focus of my emotions was my partner in a successful art dealing business. Although unconsummated, our relationship had all the markings of a tragic romance, impossible and unacceptable by society and personal circumstance. We worked side by side in great harmony and mutual respect, and our secret remained sacred. The music of the relatively new world of opera became not only a great passion for me, but also an escape from the matters of my heart.

Enter a nobleman who, upon witnessing the Diva's beauty and talent, fell head over heels in love with her. Over a period of time, he became aware of the deep soul connection between the two of us, falsely identifying the nature of my attention. He courted her at great length, eventually becoming baffled and confused that his overtures were to no avail. The truth was that she had earlier been enamored of a young tenor with the opera corps whom her parents felt was unworthy of her. They were very much the stage parents who navigated her career with impeccability and who felt that a relationship with the young man would be disruptive to their future plans for her. She was devastated and found solace in our friendship. Her innocence was as refreshing as it was tragic, and although she was aware of my marriage, she had no notion of my sexual leanings. The foundation for our deep bond was the common thread of a yearning for the kind of freedom we were not destined to find in that particular century. In addition were our deeper karmic ties from ancient Egypt where we were siblings.

The Diva turned her affections to another fellow artist of the opera, a man with a fine baritone voice who unfortunately was completely uninterested in her advances. His dedication to his craft and affinity to the music was every ounce a spiritual union with God. One day, out of sheer exasperation of her repeated attempts to engage him romantically, he responded in a way that sealed the fate of all concerned. Although he knew of my marital status, he was also quite aware of my affiliation and the innocent affection

I harbored for the young woman. Acting quite irrationally, he sent her running to me, insisting I was the one to love her in the way she desperately desired. Neither had considered the fact of my family status and neither knew of my secret sexual yearning. This set of circumstances sent the Diva into emotional turmoil and spiraling out of control as I finally confessed to her details of my own situation, truths she was emotionally unable to integrate. It was a situation of damned if I said anything and damned if I didn't. Either way, she took it as a rejection that proved to be the last straw for both of us.

The dejected nobleman suitor received news of the Diva's deep sorrow and despairing and, caught up in his own ability to determine and accept the truth of the situation, in yet another reflex reaction, blamed me for her state of mind. He threw down his glove and challenged me to a duel, an action both irrational and manic, not to mention profoundly self-invested, as if he thought that by engaging me in a fight to the death he could win her affections.

It was a chilly spring day when the buckshot exploded in my face, thus martyring me for a cause that would not be resolved in that lifetime. Maimed and weak from the blast that disintegrated a good portion of my face, the attendants took me home to be nursed by my grieving wife. Within a few weeks the infection from my wound spread throughout my body. It was a slow and painful death. Naturally, the worst part was my emotional pain of the injustice of my demise, as well as the guilt I felt towards all those I left behind; my family, my pregnant wife, my children and my true love, the man I adored.

After my death the total truth was revealed. The nobleman and my partner agreed to divide the responsibility of making sure my wife and children were taken care off and supported. In a rather ironic turn of events the grief stricken young woman agreed to marry the nobleman, thus finally freeing herself from the clutches of her stage parents. Somehow, through their commitment to one another, they were able to find some degree of atonement for what had happened to me. But a huge talent was laid waste, the diva never sang again.

The karma from this lifetime would play a major role for all those of us involved…

Of my German 'family' in current time and space, beautiful Claudia had been one of my children. Dear Christoph was my Sister, a fact that partly explains why, despite our deep soul connection, ours was not a physical romantic relationship this time around. Aaron's part naturally was pivotal; he was the baritone whose attitude, perhaps more than his actions, set in motion the events resulting in my death. The fact of his involvement came to light long after I first began exploring the residual energy from this ifetime. I had long forgiven Charles for his role as the nobleman suitor, for his outlandish jealousy and irrational behavior, as well as making peace with the memory of him pointing the pistol and delivering the fatal shot. (There were similar traits in his personality in current times.)

The Diva was my friend Dianna with whom I had researched this past life as well as significant other lives. As usual, we discovered the familiar theme as to our karma together, as well as with the other key players. We had systematically researched many of our past lives, working out the issues pertinent to each time and circumstance. We each experienced a slightly different relationship with Charles who came into my life in 1985 at a time when Dianna and I were close friends. This time around he focused his romantic overtures on me and, whereas I deeply cared and cherished him, I immediately recognized what my role was to be with and for him. His emotional scars were deeply related to his abusive childhood and he clung for dear life to old paradigm values. Naturally, he felt his love for me was unrequited. Conscious of his wounds, I provided a solid, supportive and unconditional friendship and spiritual mentorship. That was the best way I felt I could serve him.

(There is much more to Charles' story, but that is in and of itself another book.)

The other major player in the Italian experience, the man I had loved, turned out to be none other than a dear friend and co-conspirator (I use that word quite intentionally) during a period spanning much of the late eighties and nineties when she and I became the closest of pals. We often mused over this particular past life together and its implications. And even though we are both strictly heterosexually oriented, we felt a loyalty and co-creatorship every bit as potent as we did in Italy.

In the 1990's, I introduced her to Aaron and the three of us embarked upon an adventure of enormous proportions, but I'll get into more about that later too.

So if, in the bigger picture, I co-designed this experience for higher purposes and understanding, what were my lessons? I concluded that, primarily it was about Power and Truth, or perhaps more appropriately the Power of Truth. Of those of us involved in the drama of this past lifetime, the one person who was living in truth was the baritone Aaron. Each of the other characters was, to some degree, involved in lies, deceit, envy, denial and false concepts of power. And look where it got us!

CHAPTER TEN: THE GAY ITALIAN LIFETIME **191**

Manifesting My Authentic Self

Chapter Eleven: New Beginnings

The year was nineteen eighty-five. AIDS was upon us, as was the new kid on the block—video! The new medium heralded a revolution in communications beyond what many of us could possibly have imagined and sent all the production houses scuffling for new equipment and digital know-how.

Despite the fact that I had entered my forties, the offers for acting parts in adult films were still forthcoming. I could have continued to work indefinitely but I knew that it was time to make a change. I had reluctantly accepted roles in a few videos, but the experience was like a bitter culture shock, a totally different experience from shooting on film. Video was so much more immediate, so in-your-face, unflattering and lacking the depth and breadth of film. The technicians were learning as they went along, thus practically every step was experimental. I found this most disconcerting. Gone were the secure feelings of being in the hands of professionals who knew what they were doing. Trial and error was the name of this game. Lighting, make-up, colors, just about everything had to be re-configured for video. On video, colors as well as textures translated quite differently than on film. In the beginning some of the rules were no white or blacks, no stripes, small patterns or tweeds. These were just a few of the initial no-nos. Satins and shiny fabrics, however, worked well. As to whether or not video added ten pounds, as was the case with film –well, in the beginning, we weren't quite sure.

There was so much new information that had to be added to the overall equation, it was nerve-racking. Worst of all were the shrinking budgets that this new medium dictated. The days of multiple takes of a shot disappeared; we were lucky to get one re-take. I felt disoriented and vulnerable. For almost a decade my reputation had been synonymous with quality and class. I had carefully chosen my projects and I had placed stringent perimeters around what I would or wouldn't do – what or how I was willing to perform sexually. Many roles I was offered left me cold. If I could find no redeeming factors about the part in terms of the character or the story line, I inevitably declined the offer. In fact, over the years I turned down more work than I accepted. With video as a glaring reality then, the margins of possibility for decent roles and satisfying performances were shrinking even further.

I succumbed briefly to the new medium, yet the few video roles I accepted were, for the most part, uncomfortable experiences. In addition to my own resistance, I felt extremely badly for the directors and technicians who essentially were taking significant pay cuts. The days of Panavision, large crews and multiple day or even weeks shooting schedules were over. Suddenly, two and three day shoots were considered big budget productions. The whole scenario felt ludicrous to me, but change was upon us and resistance was futile.

It broke my heart to see my dear Anthony Spinelli, certainly by then a legendary director in the business, also forced to conform to these new conditions. Around the time of this major transition, I accepted a part in a project written by his son for this new medium. It coupled me with Richard Pacheco, one of my favorite actors in the business and one of the only people from those days with who I remain in touch.

"Spectators," had no story line per se; in a simple scenario that took place in a single location, the characters play psychological/sexual games with each other. Although my role contained some pretty meaty dialogue, a rare and well-appreciated factor, I nevertheless felt that I had compromised my integrity. In one scene I am bound with rope while I observe my partner having sex with another woman. I am not one to easily regret my actions or decisions but I deeply rued my choice in participating in this one. One of my rules had been that I would not participate in anything that remotely suggested bondage or sado-masochistic behavior. I had broken my rule and in doing so, I had moved into self- contempt.

As the first day of shooting wore on, I felt deeply self-conscious and embarrassed and I began to spiral down emotionally. I immersed myself in self-judgment for my involvement and, in doing so I activated my old asthmatic pattern. The more I resisted my situation, the more constricted my breathing became. But I knew I had to fulfill my obligation and so I struggled on. Despite everything I knew of my own psychology, I could not bring myself back to a place of harmony that day.

Worst of all, when I finally viewed the edited video some time later, I was horrified as I heard my distinctive wheezing over my dialogue.

My dear Mum always used to say to me,
"You bring it on yourself!"
She meant that my asthma attacks (or "turns," as she called them) were self-induced, brought on by my state of mind. Mum never knew just how right she was. In fact, once in my teens, witnessing my pattern of working myself up, she grabbed me by my shoulders, shook me sharply and told me to, "Buck up." I was caught totally off guard and the shock of her action literally shook it out of me! I gasped, and when I exhaled my normal breathing pattern resumed. Bless her heart, she knew my patterns well. It probably frustrated her as much as it did me when I obsessed over something or when I was as upset as I was that day.

The following day I reluctantly finished and vowed "No more videos!" It was time for me to move on. This experience had been the clincher.

I do not believe in random events. I do however belief in what I call divine synchronicities, occurrences which happen in seemingly perfect timing, too perfect to ignore or write off as coincidence or luck. In fact, I believe that to pay attention to the synchronicities in our lives, whether welcomed or not, is a sure way out of victim consciousness. It offers an individual the opportunity to align with destiny unfolding as opposed to being a victim to one's so-called fate.

Within a few days of shooting "Spectators" I received a call from a company called Caballero Control Corporation offering me a job as their public-relations director. At that time the company was a large and powerful voice in the adult film industry. Along the way I had made a couple of films for them and so I was aware of the fact that they were self-contained with a full in-house film production staff, as well as a large distribution network. Their name was synonymous with quality and their reputation seemed solid. I interviewed and decided to take the job. The opportunity provided a comfortable and welcomed bridge into retirement from my nine years or so in the business as an actress.

My position promised me not only a steady paycheck but other fringe benefits as well. What a welcome change from my otherwise financially unstable lifestyle. In no uncertain terms my presence was also a big plus for Caballero since my media work was widely known. During the preceding years I had become a major spokesperson for the industry at large. Now, finally, I would be getting paid for it!

My responsibilities as PR director entailed promoting the company's film and video releases and acting as a liaison to the outside world at large. I knew the business and I had a good rapport with many of its key personnel. All in all, the opportunity provided a comfortable and very natural segue from my career in front of the camera.

For the most part the transition from film actress to production executive was relatively effortless. My challenge fell in the "nine to five" area, as well as the necessity of commuting from my beloved Santa Monica by-the-bay to hot and dusty San Fernando Valley. But I adapted quickly.

Preceding my assignment it wasn't unusual for me to receive several phone calls a week from the media wanting either statements or interviews pertaining to sex or the industry at large for one or another news report or program. At certain times of the year the phone would seem to ring off the hook with requests.

"Must be sweeps time!" I'd comment to myself.

Indeed, during sweeps week, when TV stations all vie for the highest ratings, programming with sexual content is always in high demand, for it remains that sex sells! It always has and probably always will, as long as our consciousness remains preoccupied with the subject. Finally perhaps, when collectively we have healed our shame and our self-conscious attitudes towards sex, when our consciousness at large has risen to a new plateau in terms of self-love and self-worthiness, maybe this will change. Until then, at least here in the West, sex programming and controversy will continue to feed the lowest common denominator and reap billions upon billions of dollars.

Several years earlier I had embarked upon my virgin media experience with painful naiveté. It came in the form of an invitation to appear on a San Francisco talk show called "Front Line Video." The topic of the show escapes me but, as the only guest, I welcomed what I thought would be an opportunity to speak about sexuality and to share highlights of my own quest for personal freedom through my experiences in films.

My heart was wide open as I prepared for the live taping. I was directed to take a position on a stool, center stage. The moderator began his questions and within a few moments I felt as if an all-out attack on me was underway. It seemed as if the audience had been stacked with anti-porn fundamentalists and other irate individuals. Their collective wrath, which in retrospect seemed strangely inauthentic (I have since wondered if they were paid antagonists,) came at me like a huge slap in the face. I was knocked off guard and deeply shocked at such a demonstration of pre-judgment.

For a moment I felt angry and betrayed at having been misled by the producers who had painted such an inviting picture to me.

I considered walking off the show. My mind changed in an instant as a striking woman with long blonde hair stood up and acknowledged my contribution to the Adult Film industry and my "body of work." She spoke in a compelling manner with a gentle intelligence. Several people sitting close to her nodded in agreement. I felt their support and sighed with relief. At least I had a few friends there!

I later learned that this woman was Kat Sunlove, a well-known dominatrix from Oakland. This seemed ironic to me since I had never personally embraced the acts or practice of Sado Masochism or Bondage and Domination. Despite my personal feelings, it is a large and powerful genre within the realm of sexual expression and entertainment. And, if it provides a safe space in which people can release certain energies without any lasting pain for themselves or others, far be it from me to judge.

A one-time casual friend of mine, who is in fact a mainstream film director, once admitted to me that a particular scene in one of my films was the "single most erotic scene I have ever seen in any film in any genre." In the scene I am being spanked with a birch branch in a tongue-in-cheek mock-up of a historic sex ritual in the film "Intimate Lessons.'" In the letter which he shyly delivered to me, my acquaintance revealed his own particular penchant for spanking and very sweetly asked me if I was interested in participating in some mild B and D with him.

This was a first for me! I was completely thrown off guard.

"Wow," I later told him on the phone, "You're speaking to someone who received spankings as a child. I'm the wrong person to be asking. That's the last thing I'd want to indulge in with you."

I then questioned him about his attraction to the practice and whether he knew for what he was still punishing himself, after all, that is the obvious psychology behind the attraction to this activity. There was no doubt in my mind that what he was interested in went way beyond administering a couple of fun slaps on the bottom during love-making.

He admitted to frequenting S and M clubs. The fact that he spent money to be spanked awed me. I was curious to know if he ever even thought about why he was so into it, but my queries were met with blank looks. From my perspective I couldn't conceive that a person wouldn't want to look at why they were preoccupied with flagellation and heal what clearly translates as a psychological emotional scar. I expounded upon how I could assist him but he was completely disinterested and the fact that he had the choice to heal and change his behavior pattern seemed to go right over his head. This was obviously a comfort zone and not one he was ready to forgo.

There were several women in the audience of my first television talk show in San Francisco who stood up and angrily vented their feelings about X-rated films. One young woman insisted that she was forced to leave New York because she couldn't bear to see and hear the barkers outside adult theaters and clubs around Times Square when she walked past them. She said they made her feel dirty. I calmly suggested that a logical solution might have been to take another route to her destination and thereby not subject herself to the torment she obviously felt. My comment aroused her anger even more. I admitted that I didn't particularly like that element of the adult entertainment business either and that I was pioneering for erotica with substance and heart. But any reasoning and logic fell on deaf ears and in the few minutes I was on the air, I felt most of the female audience holding me personally responsible for their pain and suffering.

How loudly shame spoke that day! As I struggled to keep my heart open I realized that, in the true style of many of the tabloid talk shows, this was a forum for people to voice their issues and anger. In that regard I supposed it was a good thing. I did not, however, enjoy being their target. It felt profoundly unfair. I was blatantly outnumbered and any attempt to offer any conscious or logical thoughts seemed to be an exercise in futility.

I uttered a statement pleading with them not to make me their enemy when I felt I was more of an ally since my personal mission statement at the time was, "Let's put the heart back into sex." But few heard my comments over the general outburst of emotion.

After the show I went back to my hotel, took a hot bath and sobbed my heart out. I grieved not so much for my own pain but for theirs, after all, one of my patterns was to feel other's pain over my own. I understood their issues and complaints and, in many ways, I echoed them. Yet I also knew that blame is the voice of shame, and it is futility in action. It solves nothing and only rubs salt in the collective wounds.

Then I gave myself a good talking-to,

"Listen Sister, if you plan to do more of this type of thing, you'd better do your homework and learn how to prepare yourself for these kinds of situations."

In retrospect, the bruises of my virgin television experience were a gift. It taught me that it was essential to prepare emotionally and spiritually to deal with public work of this nature and to survive with heart and spirit intact.

Some years later, I ran into Kat Sunlove at an awards show and I was finally able to thank her in person for her support on that show. To this day, Kat remains a faithful and busy lobbyist for the free speech movement, someone for whom we should all feel a sense of gratitude.

After that first dramatic introduction to the media, my experiences with members of the press were quite varied, some gentler than others. I often found myself in a position where I was damned if I said anything and damned if I didn't. Only too quickly one could be thrown off guard and become victimized by an unrelenting journalist interested only in a sensationalistic approach to their story. This was tricky business. The key was to learn the art of discerning between those situations where there truly was an opportunity to share freely about my personal journey and my experiences with the industry at large, and those that already had me pigeon-holed. In cases involving the latter, my statements could easily be taken out of context and patched into a story that basically was already written before the interview had even occurred.

My defense was honesty and it is always the best policy. If interviews were for tabloid-type shows, I would ask the interviewer up-front what their slant was, since I believed that was predetermined.

"I'll work with you if you are honest with me," I would tell them. "That way I don't become a victim and maybe I'll be nicely surprised with the end result." Although I admit this approach was a bit idealistic, it worked for me. I could provide statements which could be edited into stories concisely, but which couldn't be taken out of context. My guides were always with me, and as long as I remained on purpose holding a loving consciousness, I felt that I was doing my job.

Later on I reached a point where I felt that these kinds of interviews did not serve much purpose and that I had only taken on the responsibility of being a spokesperson out of a misplaced feeling of duty; a feeling that I owed it to someone—but to whom, or to what? I had been carrying a banner upon which was inscribed my own personal issues, yet the true answer, the deeper dynamics of the issue of to whom I felt this debt, did not reveal itself until several years later. It took many hours of past life exploration to find the clues, and to eventually piece the story together as to what the heck I was doing in porno anyway.

Media work took on a different meaning after I joined Caballero. Naturally my employers welcomed all of my extra-curricular activity, it was publicity for them and so basically, whatever I chose to do was fine. Competition was fierce within the genre, with each company trying to outdo the other by releasing more video releases each month. Of course, at that time, in addition to new productions, there was still a bounty of existing films yet to be transferred to video.

The numbers of home viewers were growing at an amazing rate and a large percentage of them were women. This new female audience, it seemed, now rushed out of their proverbial sexual closets and into their local video stores to rent explicit sex movies. According to some studies, at one point in time, women renters outnumbered the men.

Because of this increasing shift in the viewing audience, I was not only encouraged to maintain a public image, but Caballero and I negotiated a deal for me to create and direct a line of "softer" videos—in other words, less hard-core—to be called "Kay Parker's Love Stories." Many of their productions were being labeled "couples tapes. These were videos with more sensuality and less of the hard-core content that had traditionally appealed to a predominantly male audience. I was encouraged therefore to spend time on the road doing promotion whenever and wherever I deemed it appropriate. There was never a shortage of offers to appear on TV talk shows. I flew from city to city appearing on one program after the next, including "A.M. Chicago," hosted by a striking, dynamic African American woman.

Prior to airtime, the two other actresses appearing on the show, Seka and Veronica Hart, and I, met Oprah for a moment in the make-up room before the show. Without doubt, one could feel a certain buzz that she was on the verge of striking gold. But how could any of us have realized how profoundly famous and influential she would become? She's definitely one of my sheroes.

Back at my home office, in my role as public relations director, I supplied magazines with promotional materials and press-kits, wrote distributor newsletters and organized screenings of Caballero's latest releases for the press. It was fun and diverse, and yet I could sense the impending changes.

Who really knew how much of an impact the video industry would have on the world, except perhaps those who were creatively involved in its conception and birth? While the mainstream film industry continued to shoot motion pictures on film, the adult film industry shifted to shooting exclusively on video. And since this was a brand new medium, and we were all learning from scratch, some of the earlier titles shot in the new format were shockingly amateurish, I felt embarrassed to promote them. But video was a reality and, by mid 1986, the impact of the shift had created a very different market place. On one hand suddenly there were dozens more titles being released monthly—a good thing, one might think for business, yet on the other hand, it created such competitiveness that price wars also quickly became reality, thus the dichotomy: the market expanded but profit margins shrank dramatically.

My original agreement with Caballero for my "Love Stories" series had included a slightly higher than average budget, but I was suddenly informed that it would be cut dramatically. Under the circumstances it wasn't a surprise to receive the news. In truth I was already prepared to let the project go, since my only other choice was to compromise my integrity. Even though I had been talking about my project publicly for months promising a departure from the accepted "formula" videos, a lesser budget would have forced me to conform to the standards of the day, which included numerous gratuitous sex scenes, inconsistent with the type of storylines I had planned. It was unthinkable to me.

The fact that I didn't even put up a fight for a project that once had meant a great deal to me was evidence that I was, in fact, resigned to the changes I knew were imminent. I was ready to move on.

Eighteen months had passed since signing on in my PR job and, for the most part I had enjoyed my experience. I was grateful for the gentle segue from acting to what was undeniably the direction of my true vocation. But was it time for me to quit? I wasn't sure, since it meant throwing myself into the unknown once more.

For two years prior to that time I had already been studying techniques that were to become a mainstay in my new work and, unofficially I had already begun to counsel privately, but it would take a while to build my new life. I also knew that my days at Caballero were numbered. Due to corporate changes, a major downsizing in the company was underway. It was inevitable that my department would be the next to be hit with personnel lay-off. The writing on the wall was clear, yet I needed distance from the situation to clear my head and to decide exactly when to hand in my resignation.

It happened that my friend Judith was planning a trip to the British Isles. She was working on a photographic project featuring megalithic standing stones around the World. She had already photographed the Pyramids and Sphinx, traveled to South America and Easter Island to shoot sites there. Now, in addition, she needed shots of various sites in England and Scotland.

Our friendship had drawn me further into my interest of metaphysics and mythology, and I deeply resonated with her work. My friend and I had spent many hours together in mystical exploration and study as we assisted each other in our individual healing and awakening. It didn't take much to convince me therefore that I should accompany her on her trip to England. I was due for a vacation, and it had been several years since I'd been back to the UK to visit my family.

In addition to seeing the standing stones, the prospect of visiting parts of the British Isles I had never seen before, such as the Lake District and Scotland, was very enticing. It also seemed timely and appropriate to re-connect with my own ancient roots in the British Isles. I knew that in addition to having been born in England this time around, I had lived there before in several lifetimes including one particular and deeply significant Druid life. The chance to visit some of the sacred sites, perhaps to tread upon familiar soil from those lifetimes hundreds of years earlier excited me to no end.

Judith and I mapped out our trip carefully, beginning with a three-day visit with my family in Kent. We decided that we would then rent a car and spend a week on the road touring as many of the stone circles as possible in the North of England and Scotland. A site called Callanish beckoned to us above the rest, and we agreed to that the trip there should be a priority above all other sites. Callanish, also known as the "Scottish Stonehenge," is located on the Island of Lewis off the Northwest coast of Scotland in the Outer Hebrides. According to Judith's research, it had been singled out by geomancy experts as a most striking and energetically potent site — a megalithic must-see. To get there we boarded a car ferry for a trip lasting several hours. We arrived after nightfall and put up in a hotel and the following day set out for the opposite end of what seemed to be a relatively barren and uninteresting island. En route, the precipitous weather had produced a most perfect rainbow arching high over the road we were driving on – what better omen?

Callanish was the highlight of our travels for me. The stones are unlike any others I saw, tall, majestic, and reminiscent of ancient robed Druids themselves, except for one, that to me looked like a giant phallus. One can only imagine what they looked like hundreds of years earlier before the exposure to the harsh elements eroded these giants, carving new and mystical forms upon their facades. It takes no stretch of the imagination to realize that, in their most potent days, this formation was truly a grand mystical energy generator — an inter-dimensional transmitter, and it is rumored, a welcoming station for Intergalactic visitors.

While we were at Callenish, a storm moved in, adding another dimension to the already profound otherworldly feeling we were experiencing. While Judith was photographing, I imagined myself clad in robes, moving between the stones in the mists of evening at the high holidays, performing ancient rituals and communicating with our off-planetary, time-traveling friends in their inter-dimensional, inter-stellar time machines. (By the way, Judith's photographs from our trip are outstanding and can be seen on her website: www.meditativemagic.com) The large format photos of Calanish are breathtaking.

And, by the way, I always point out that I was actually standing behind the most prominent stone on the foreground.

We had visited other very impressive stone circles, notable either for their specific unique characteristics or for their energies. My duty in each location was to assist in moving the animals, indisputably the guardians of the stones, out of the camera frame, and to guide my friend around their deposits on the ground, as she concentrated on her photographic mission. But as striking and unique as the other sites were, none struck me quite the way Callenish did.

After the excursion to Lewis we headed south again, where Judith continued on to the Southwest of England and Glastonbury, and I returned to my family's home for the remainder of my vacation, before returning to California.

At the time of the remarkable trip, I had been engrossed in reading "The Mists of Avalon," Marion Zimmer Bradley's saga of the Arthurian legends and the mystical time of Camelot, as seen through the eyes of the women of the time. I decided it was the perfect piece of literature to take with me.

As Judith and I trekked through the Lake District and the Scottish Highlands soaking up the rich countryside, I became increasingly awed by the parallels I found myself drawing to my life and that of the character Morgana, known as Morgaine in the book. It seemed that throughout history she was always depicted as a wicked, scheming sorceress, yet in the book, she is seen in a very different light. Morgaine is born into nobility and the bloodline of the mystics, later trained on the Island of Avalon as a priestess, and eventually becoming high priestess and Lady of the Lake. She is a shaman and alchemist and she is passionately driven to protect and uphold her heritage — that of Merlin and the mystical lineage threatened by the onslaught of Christianity and its wrathful, vengeful God, its rulings of shame and sin, and its denouncement of pagan worship: in other words, Goddess consciousness.

CHAPTER ELEVEN: NEW BEGINNINGS

From the time I arrived in Los Angeles in 1977, I had been studying with a spiritual teacher and meditating daily. My relationship to my spirituality held priority in my life. I jokingly called my film career "my madness," although I knew that it was deeply karmic. I often struggled to integrate all aspects of my life into the whole, my shame was still rooted in me, and it would take me a few years longer to disconnect and heal. Yet simultaneously I also taught, lectured, and counseled others on the integration of the total self, of intra-personal relationships, self-healing and empowerment, through a deeper responsibility to all of one's creations.

I therefore identified deeply with Morgaine's struggles when she was called out into the world to fulfill her karmic obligations with the men of power, and to influence the politics of the day. In rather obscure ways, I feel that I have also been called upon to do that.

Many times I have found myself drawn to powerfully creative and very influential men, some of who have found me through my "unusual career in the visual arts," so-named by a channeler I consulted earlier on. There is no doubt in my mind, that some degree of healing or balancing transpired through my interaction with each of them, whether sexual or not. The fact that I broke the stereotype of a woman involved in the erotic arts; that I was not what most anticipated, forced them to shift—if only slightly—their relationship to their own sexuality, and perhaps to women in general. When they related to me, they could not apply their usual seductive ruses—it just didn't fit. For some, I was too intelligent, too deep, and they simply didn't know how to handle me. Others jumped at the opportunity to relate differently, admitting that they fell into a certain rut when it came to relating to the members of the opposite sex.

An agent I signed with for a brief time after arriving in Los Angeles in 1978, called me into a meeting late one afternoon. A well-known Hollywood actor/producer was making a low-budget film and was considering casting me in a role, I was told. Later

I realized that this was not true, this man had simply wanted to meet me. I arrived at the agent's office and was introduced to the producer, who immediately ushered me into the restaurant next door. There he proceeded to drink an entire bottle of wine alone—since I don't drink—as he confided in me that he watched my films, and often "got off" to me in the privacy of his home. It was easier, he admitted, than going out and finding sex partners, especially in light of the reality of the rapidly growing AIDS epidemic. As the evening progressed I felt increasingly saddened by this person's confessions, although angry because I had been called there under false pretenses.

I resigned myself to the fact that although there had been no film part or audition, this had been one of many opportunities, my spiritual teachers had suggested would occur, where I could "hold the light" (loving consciousness) for a person or situation for a higher good.

At the conclusion of our few hours together I walked the gentleman to his car, where he took me by surprise by paying me a sober compliment,

"Lady, I don't want to go to bed with you," he proclaimed, "I'd like to wake up to you!" I thanked him knowing full well that he would not forget our experience.

So in fact, there were those men who unwittingly zipped up their pants for a far deeper experience, through heart to heart contact. I am not, nor have I ever been promiscuous by nature, and so that was a label that couldn't be pinned to me. Any stereotypical ideas a person might have had about me because of my film career were quickly dispelled. I just didn't fit the mold.

"But what about all the sex you have in your films?" people would argue. To this I would offer the following, that over a ten-year span of time, I only made fifty films and in some of those films I only had one sex scene. My private life was relatively quiet in those years.

"So, you do the math," I told the same individuals, "Since you are obviously measuring in some way, if you are having sex twice a month, you're way ahead of me!"

In "The Mists of Avalon", after years of seclusion and divinity in the convent, Morgaine is called upon by the Goddess to meet her destiny and go back out into the world to marry, to keep the bloodline alive. She must allow her body to be used for carnal pleasure once again in a way that is a far cry from the sacred fertility rituals of the Goddess. She knows that this is her destiny and, besides, she is committed to doing whatever it takes to protect her mystical lineage.

In a strange way, I have felt a parallel dedication to my life and to the purpose for which I believe I am here on Earth at this most auspicious time in history. This deep sense of destiny has always been with me. Even in my most challenging times, when I have struggled with unresolved feelings and emotions, and when things looked like they were falling apart, my faith was and remains unshakable.

I conclude that, regardless of whether Morgaine is myth or fact, to me she represents an archetype of the evolving woman in her relationship to God/Goddess, and to the reclamation of her sovereignty and essential power in a world rapidly changing. This has been my own greatest challenge, and a large part of what I call my karmic density — the stuff that keeps me anchored in third-dimensional reality, and which allows me to learn and to manifest what I came to accomplish in this lifetime. My past life study has revealed to me lifetime after lifetime, where, as a woman, I could not apply my power because of my gender. In my present life, however, I simply have no choice. This is the lifetime to complete a mission in which I believe I am intricately involved, one that began six thousand years ago. It is a task that, at its root, is about the reinstating of the bloodline of the mystics through deep, profound healing and elevation of consciousness.

For anyone who is dedicated to inspiring and anchoring a new paradigm of awareness and of living, their life challenges will guide them to awaken deeply, to connect to their authentic selves and to break away from the limitations and attachments to the physical material levels. This is our collective challenge, to prepare for the changes that I believe are inevitable in the not-too-distant future. This is the essence of the Age of Aquarius.

Within days of returning from my trip to Scotland and England, I handed in my notice to Caballero, and subsequently officially hung out my counselor "shingle," and began to see paying clients.

In that same period of time, a gentleman friend informed me, that at a social gathering in Hollywood, he heard that the film rights to "The Mists of Avalon" had just been acquired by a well-known actor. It seemed incongruous that the actor in question would be involved in such a pursuit, but I later learned that he had made the deal for his girlfriend.

Months passed and I found myself in a small meditation group one evening—in the house that would become my home and sanctuary from 1990 to 2002—when a latecomer announced that he had just acquired the film rights to "The Mists of Avalon." My mouth fell open.

Again the person standing before me seemed an unlikely guardian for this project that to me held sacred status, and towards which I felt strangely protective. My passion for the story and the character Morgaine rose up into my chest again, although I said nothing. However, once again, the project seemed destined not to move forward, and all of my subsequent efforts reaped no news or information of its progress.

"The Mists of Avalon" was ultimately made into a made-for-television mini-series. Perhaps you, the listener or reader, have seen it. My feelings were that the series could have been twice as long and still not have told the entire story as it is written in the book. The character and struggles of the Lady Morgaine, this character I feel that I know so infinitely well, although beautifully played by Juliana Marguelles, was so much larger than she seemed in the mini-series. I feel this–because of my own past life as a high priestess.

And perhaps my passionate feelings for the story and the character were fueled by my profound desire for me, and for all women, to truly emerge out of their shadows at this time, and embody Goddess consciousness. This time in which we live—perhaps the most important period in all of recorded history, calls to all to emerge from their deep sleep, to recognize that we are souls having a human experience—not the reverse, and that we are God/Goddess incarnate. For women everywhere, circumstances permitting, the pressure mounts for us to pick up the proverbial slack as many men remain attached to the old ways of greed, competition and fear-based reactiveness.

The clock is ticking–time is short.

Chapter Twelve: Channeling

Chapter Twelve Part Two: The Knodessi Trilogy

It had been my desire to channel higher messages for some time. I had asked repeatedly in my meditations for guidance in this area, although if I'd had any rational thoughts about my "eligibility," chances are that I would have deemed myself yet unready for such lofty activities. For years meditation had been a daily staple for me; I couldn't imagine a day going by without time to still my mind and simply "be." More often than not, a brief period of total surrender and relaxation refreshed and renewed me more than a full night's sleep. Yet, even after all the discipline, contemplation and spiritual exercises, the art of totally surrendering my linear mind remained a challenge, while I knew that was the essential key to higher dimensional adventures. Regardless, I was willing to expand and be of service, continuously asking to be used me in greater ways. God/Goddess was obviously listening!

On November 16th, 1989, at a small group gathering at Aaron's (my dear friend and mentor) home, we entered into meditation with the intention of opening ourselves to any messages our guides, high selves or higher dimensional allies might want to communicate to us. I had not anticipated what followed. To begin, Aaron guided us through a series of processes to silence our minds, to move past our lower selves and align with higher consciousness. We used breathing, chanting and other techniques to center ourselves and finally a verbal invocation (prayer) to give thanks, state our intention, and go deeper within. My friend is a stickler for spiritual protocol, and even though I admit to having resisted some of his steps from time to time, I have come to recognize the value of thorough preparation for any spiritual activity.

On that particular fall evening, I had obviously once again underestimated myself, not to mention taking into consideration the years, and even lifetimes, I had already spent in devout spiritual discipline.

As usual, we had set up a tape-recorder just in case any one of us tapped into frequencies beyond our third-dimensional reality. I prepared myself, silently asking and consciously moving my earth personality aside. Finally, as my mind settled and I surrendered into the void, the familiar inner lifting feeling came over me. However this time was different than all other previous exploration. Inside I began to see and experience groups of words in my consciousness. Without judging or editing, I allowed the message to speak, through my voice box. At first, the message came through fragmented, and in short phrases, as I tried to adjust to the higher frequencies. But as I allowed myself to surrender deeply to the energy, it became more fluid and impersonal...

"I see thoughts as like celestial doves because I am always excited when I can lift above the physical levels to take a closer look at an issue...

...And as we move into a state of empathy with a specific feeling or emotion, healing is immediately instigated, that is to say, without going into any judgment about the feeling, we may observe it, completely sense all of its aspects, and allow it to be a perfect expression of God. In doing that, we allow it to rise to a higher vantage point, to observe, to understand and finally to move into an even deeper empathy with it. And that action becomes like an energy wave being broadcast out from this expression of God to affect higher levels of understanding collectively. Surely to judge these feelings and expressions is to deny them. That is one of the greatest plights we've perpetuated upon the planet. Can we not live in an instant by allowing it to perfectly be simply an energy, an experience, a sense, a vibration, something that is specifically there from which to learn and grow? With that higher understanding, a great "Aha" occurs, and that energy can be dissolved into pure Light.

As you release this judgment, you can grow to understand your own perfection. The planet is yours, you created it, and as you allow yourselves to grow, you allow the planet to grow.

Be like those celestial doves, shimmering and transparent. Allow yourselves to be that Light. The need and desire to be right need be no longer. This is good."

The frequency shifted abruptly. Someone else in the room then began to speak in a stream of consciousness for a few minutes, and the session concluded. This event marked the beginning of my channeling days, although it took quite a while for me to fully understand what it was in fact that I was doing, or what was happening.

Following this experience, the transmissions, as I called them, came through regularly when I happened to be with two specific friends, in what were primarily question and answer sessions. In one of these encounters, one of my friends inquired as to who was speaking through me. The answer given was:

"We reside in a frequency where there is no time and no limitation. We are a group of, as you would say, team-workers, and you would not know us in physical form. We have colors, we have hues — we are fast like the blink of an eyelid, the speed of Light."

When asked if they were specifically my guides they replied,

"Let us say that we have aligned with this consciousness known as Kay. We align with others. We resonate, shall we say, with this vehicle. We align, and with that alignment, there is a dropping through of information, a vibration designed to resonate with your physical plane."

By Thanksgiving of that year the energy had shifted considerably. My own confidence had stabilized and a different kind of message was relayed. On Thanksgiving Day the following message came through:

"There is a thundering of hooves upon the plains of imagination, as if a thousand or more ideas are coming together for the illumination of Mankind. We are excited in the participation of our spiritual Brothers and Sisters on the planet Earth, for as you are realizing, there is little or no separation at these times, only that which would come forward as the concepts of the limited mind and consciousness. Bear

in mind that the great offerings present at this time are of Universal Mind and Consciousness working together on the spirit planes, in that harmony of which you have dreamed for so long. The offerings are for the individual consciousness to come into alignment with the greater consciousness, to release the limitation of the ego, the human bindings that trap the consciousness in its darkness.

The offering is for that which is known as Holy Communion, a communion of the whole, that whole which is God Consciousness personified, Spirit being to Spirit being. We align our frequencies once more dear friends, for the purpose of enlightenment, that is, we the Harbingers of the Ages, holding a light unto your own inner consciousness, to illumine within that consciousness those things which you now choose to remember. Like a hall of dreams — "dreams" because these memories do not seem quite real until you have that direct interaction with them which we here offer you through the quickness, shall we say, of our mind. These are the great hieroglyphics written upon the temple wall, those epic pictures representing a bygone era. Nevertheless, they are all infinitely present through this gift of channeling, this opportunity that you have created from your commitment to Spirit, to join your heart with ours. We watch with great expectation of this progress that is taking place. We listen with great anticipation for your questions, and we stand in readiness with inspiration and guidance, aligning always with your frequencies.

Do you fully understand the significance of these things coming to pass? There is such an awakening underway. Levels beyond the concepts of your human mind and emotions are being activated for this grand entry into that which is known as The Age of Aquarius, into your 21st Century, the Garden of Eden, Paradise on Earth. Step forward dear children into that grand ray of Light that is beckoning and awaiting your participation. We do so look forward to dancing and playing with you. You can sail on this ray into that new land and new time. Do not burden yourself with concepts that are from the past. They will bear down on you and send you into a spiral that, although it will not lead you astray, will momentarily take you from your path. Stay on that pure beam of Light that you recognize so divinely inside of yourselves and all will be well."

After that opening comment, a question and answer session was encouraged by those who delivered the message. One of the others in the group asked to identify the messengers, to which the response came,

"A moment please, we search the Hall Of Records."

I had heard of the "Great Hall of Records" and I understood it to be one and the same as "The Akashic Records," the records of all time residing on the higher planes. I sometimes refer to this resource as the "great computers in the sky." That I was being allowed to tap into them at that time was a bit scary and disconcerting. Was I really worthy of this? Yet I knew that I had to continue. These sessions had become the most significant part of my life.

By December of that year, I had come to know that my messengers were from "The Seventh Ray." Beyond that, I knew this energy to be the Purple Ray; a healing frequency. That was all I knew about these energies, until I suddenly began to hear other individuals speaking about them, and I also came across references to the Purple and Seventh Rays in various books. What I didn't realize was that simultaneously, many others, perhaps thousands, were also receiving similar messages from Spirit. A Cosmic door had opened and the Spiritual Hierarchies were responding to those on Earth who were choosing back.

From that point on, the transmissions came through frequently. My friends and I welcomed every opportunity to meet, specifically to initiate channeled sessions. We were excited, and our enthusiasm and hunger for more information increased as the days went on. Eventually, we began to realize that, in fact, we were fulfilling a grand mission to which we had committed eons ago.

The guidance was clear and consistent, instructional and inspiring. We were guided in our lives, our relationships and, even more significantly, in projects we were told to nurture and develop while trusting in their purpose beyond what made logical sense. Whether these endeavors were to actually physically manifest remained unclear much of the time, but we came to understand that, regardless of whether they took form or not, they held our focus in a very specific way pertinent to our growth process. I've come to realize this is true for many people: Not all projects are destined to become reality, but the journey one takes holds countless opportunities for growth and revelation, as well as providing links to significant other people and experiences with profound higher purpose. When we recognize the flow of our lives, and release our ego attachment to the outcome, grace and ease become the dominant energies, stress is diminished, and we are happier, healthier people.

Through the process of receiving the transmissions, my friends and I consistently worked on our blocks and our scars from the past and, with each session, we aligned more with what we were coming to understand as our true mission. Beyond that, the guides provided increasing clarity about the global and universal transformational process underway.

In the counseling sessions I conducted at that time, I typically began with a brief channeled message from each client's guide or guides. In many cases, this type of sharing proved to be more potent than much of the other practical work we did together. When the sessions concluded, I could hardly wait to get to my typewriter, that antiquated device I used to transcribe the recorded messages, an extra service I provided for some of my clients. The length of time I spent wasn't an issue for me, although it remains that over a decade or more, I spent literally hundreds of hours transcribing the information and guidance received in these consultations.

In early 1990, as I continued the channeling sessions, another frequency began to come through me and it was very different! For some reason, as I aligned with the energy, my head would automatically turn to the right. The first time it happened, scenes from the movie "The Exorcist" simultaneously sprang to mind. It was disconcerting and weird to say the least. What I understood to be the reason for this strange phenomenon was, much like adjusting the dial on a radio, I had to adjust my spiritual antenna by turning my head—there was a stronger frequency alignment when I was in that position. (I massaged my neck a lot in those days!)

This new energy was powerful, different in tone and resonance from the Seventh Ray and the messages tended to be more direct, more dynamic and frequently seemed to be for and about the male principle, both in men and in women. When my cohorts and I asked what collective this was, the answer came,

"*We are from the Great White Brotherhood.*"

Wow—that sounded really impressive. Deep inside of my memory banks I resonated with the name, it even sounded a bit familiar, however, on the conscious level, I was at a loss. "Brotherhood" implied a Spiritual fraternity and in fact, soon after, I was told that this was an ethereal brotherhood; "guardians of ancient wisdom," whose members incarnated from time to time. Some time later I began to pick up information about this collective whose energy was so powerful and, at the same time, deeply moving.

In May of 1991 a friend gave me a book called "The Treasure of El rado," another wonderful story of a personal, mystical journey into discovery by author Joseph Whitfield, who at one time had been a CEO of a Fortune 500 company. The timing was perfect, because woven into the story was Whitfield's account of his own encounter with, not only "The Great White Brotherhood," but also The Seventh Ray. Within a short time after that, I saw several mentions of both energies I was channeling in various books and publications. I learned from one source that there are seventy-two orders of the Great White Brotherhood, of which the most recent was called the Seventh Ray, whose last physical contingency was located in ancient Peru. So, not only did I feel it to be an enormous privilege to be channeling such a lofty consciousness, I felt profoundly blissful when the Brotherhood began to resonate in me. It was a feeling I wanted to bathe in forever.

If I had doubted myself before, it now seemed clear that indeed I was part of a collective of souls dedicated to a very specific mission of assisting in planetary upliftment. For a number of years previously I had heard myself proclaim that I was on a mission of sorts. Strangely, even in my darkest moments of inner struggle, the knowing was unshakable. I knew that I had come to be a Light-bearer, a guide of some sort. And it was the denseness of the Earth plane I found that challenged me to my core. Still, for a time, my logical mind wondered why I, a woman, would channel a brotherhood.

In 1994 a British couple visiting Los Angeles was referred to me by another person familiar with my work. Their trip to the United States was a vision quest of sorts as they pursued answers to a very troublesome issue in their lives. They had visited a number of readers and practitioners, yet had not received sufficient guidance or understanding of their problem. I was able to produce some data related to the specific past lives relevant to the issue in question. The answers proved to be revelatory and enlightening for them and seemed to ease the tension with their life's challenge.

My new friends immediately insisted that I should be their guest in Norway, where they resided. They assured me they knew of several friends who would be enthusiastic to partake of a session with me. As it turned out, I was scheduled to visit my family in England a few weeks hence and a side trip to Norway's west coast therefore was totally feasible. I had always wanted to visit Scandinavia, although the proposed trip would be primarily a working visit. Still, I looked forward to exploring new ground, as the plans fell effortlessly into place.

CHAPTER TWELVE: CHANNELING

Sure enough, it was an easy detour from London to Stavanger and my hosts' charming home. My friends were warm and generous, and provided a steady flow of clients during the few days of my stay there. Since we spent most of the time indoors, my hosts and I shared deeply and soulfully. It was clear that we had known each other before and that, as always, there were many levels of reality occurring simultaneously.

Strangely, within the first three days of my visit, I came down with a bad chest cold, my lungs labored and a hacking cough developed. Although it did not prevent me from working, I felt embarrassed and immobilized. But there was naught to do but surrender, and to receive the nurturing from those around me. My inner guides told me I was processing energy—not just for myself, but also for my friends, and that it was relevant to a past life the three of us had spent together. We had come into each other's lives in current time, to touch for a moment and release cellular memory.

While in Norway, I discovered a male lifetime in which I was told that I had been an incarnated member of the Great White Brotherhood, or the GWB, as I affectionately called them. This piece of information was profoundly humbling. My host Steve had also been a member of the fraternity, a fact that explained why we felt such an affinity for each other when we met.

I wondered if the fact of my relationship to the GWB was an indication that my work would be primarily with men. My decade in adult films placed me in a unique position to consciously influence large numbers of the opposite sex. Without doubt, working with men had always held a particular focus for me, and would continue to do so.

During my stay in Norway I was reminded of a special message from the Brotherhood, which came through in 1990, which offered,

"...for those men in general...who would be having a harder time moving into the Light consciousness than those of the female resonance. There is a shaking down within the male consciousness of ancient issues and belief systems...they experience more resistance to the changes and wrestle with the projected consequences of shifting their consciousness to the degree to which their conscience is guiding them... "

The Brotherhood continued with a very beautiful message, which was as tender as it was direct:

"My sons, all is well. You are the great male Lights of consciousness on the Planet at this time. Rise up within yourselves, let go of the history of consciousness, those past concepts, limitations, false belief systems and misunderstood loyalties. Turn your gaze inward, my sons, to the divine power that throbs within your chest cavity now, and acknowledge yourselves as one with God. In this moment you are being guided, commanded if you will, by that Universal Conscience, that true spiritual consciousness that you represent, to rise up and to fulfill your destinies. Put aside those limitations, cast off the vibrations of those who would lead you off your path. Bless them as you already do with your presence, release them and know that all the things on the tangible physical levels about which you have your consternation, will be handled accordingly. We call upon you now, we say now!

Dear Brothers, we call upon the sweetness that is innately part of the truth of who you are. We call upon that sweetness — personified through your various personalities — to speak forth the truth to all around you. That essence would know and would discern appropriately, for it represents the purity of your spiritual conscience. We say apply it now for the sake of all of us. Indeed your spiritual sisters will hold with you and love you, whoever you are.

We say, move forward in your conscience, in your higher spiritual consciousness, come forward, join, co-mingle with these sisters so that together we can go forward to represent the Aquarian relationship, the Aquarian family united by the Holy Spirit within each and dedicated to the total personification of God consciousness, to the new spiritual concepts and laws dedicated to the true loving heart."

I sensed that the reason for this particular message was because, around that time, I had conducted several consecutive counseling sessions with men. Up until that point, my female clients outnumbered my male clients four to one. My one-on-one holistic counseling could be quite confrontational, and required a person to accept full responsibility for his or her creations, beyond what was considered the norm. If an individual wasn't ready to move into that reality, they would not reap the full benefit of my work.

Beyond the pain and discomfort of any life challenge lies the "bigger picture," the person's reason for having chosen their life lessons and their purpose for being here now. For many this reality was still a tall order.

In general, the male populous seemed to be holding back, reluctant to break with stereotypical behavior and move into their authentic power. There was a broad willingness to speak and to intellectualize about it, but few seemed committed to fully living in this new reality. However, by the late 1990's, this had begun to change and I was able to track a considerable shift in male attitudes. Many more men were embracing the need to make a radical break from the accepted conventional role of the male in society. Men and women alike were all slowly grasping the true meaning of finally walking and living in truth, not just talking about it.

The main technique I used during the early years of my counseling was Applied Kinesiology, otherwise known as Muscle Testing, the remarkable science I had learned from my beloved mentor Ryhen. Through his guidance and example, remarkable truths had been revealed to me, for it is startlingly evident that the body does not lie. A single negative thought, simply the words "I can't," for instance, can weaken and dis-empower a person, no matter who they are (size, gender and body mass are irrelevant.) By the same token, a positive thought and affirmative declaration can empower. A simple muscle test demonstrates these points.

And perhaps, as the well-known author and lecturer Carolyn Myss has suggested, every thought and emotion we have ever had is stored somewhere in our bodies, in our chakras or meridians, the body's energy centers, not to mention collective thought forms, family tree miasma etc. The implications therefore are profound as to the opportunity for self-healing through accessing this stored information, by processing it, clearing it, and ultimately transforming those energies with higher wisdom.

I feel inclined to mention the Thymus Gland, which we know now to be the Seat of the Immune System, as a significant energy center of the body system. With the onslaught of immunodeficiency diseases, such as AIDS, Alzheimer's, Candida and Epstein Barr, our thymus gland becomes pivotal to our overall well-being. I see the thymus as, in no uncertain terms, a truth center, for it takes an instant hit when we experience trauma, loud disturbing noises, acts of violence, negative images, tastes and smells—anything that offends the senses. My recommendation is to thump one's thymus, located in the center of your chest, after seeing, hearing or feeling something dramatic or disturbing. It helps to reset the immune system's mechanisms.

We are all so susceptible to external energies, whether these are others' emotions projected on or around us, thought patterns, collective consciousness, or more accurately, collective unconsciousness. Any of these dynamics can dramatically influence us in numerous ways, manifesting physical symptoms such as headaches, tummy aches, nausea, angst, depression or simple confusion. It is commonplace for any of us to walk into situations where those present are not only completely unaware of what they are projecting, but are oblivious to the fact of how these kinds of toxic, free-floating emotional energies can disrupt and poison an environment. For this reason, it is essential to keep our wits about us and to pay close attention to all the signals, the red flags which our bodies communicate to us and which we all too frequently ignore.

CHAPTER TWELVE: CHANNELING

I once heard one of my teachers retort,
"…Thoughts are just thoughts…don't even worry about them… you haven't had an original one in days! "

It was kind of an offbeat statement but it gave me real food for thought! Indeed, with all the thought forms flying around, it's a wonder we can know what our own personal truth really is. (In that regard, I believe meditation to be fundamental to maintaining a clear state of mind.)

For most of us who attune to these greater realities, a further challenge then becomes maintaining balance and sovereignty in our lives, without shutting our hearts down to others who have yet to embrace such realities and how to meet them on their level without judgment or prejudice.

I believe that the answer is greater compassion and unconditional love.

Once I had decided to live my life in the new paradigm and not subscribe to any of the existing tired old belief systems, it became absolutely essential that I learn how to sustain my own energy field, and maintain sovereignty. In instances when I was unaware that I had picked up an energy emanating from someone else, I normally became disoriented and sometimes irritated. That was and remains my red flag, my cue to apply my favorite technique to balance myself and clear my field. The technique I use is to quickly and discreetly place one hand on my third eye (forehead) and the other on my second chakra (the area between navel and pubis.) At the same time, while taking a deep breath, I imagine a golden thread running up my spine and out the top of my head. The results from this simple little action are instantaneous and can create a fast return to harmony, peace and centeredness.

This tool efficiently acts as a personal reminder to be aware of what is going on around us, and to creatively discern (as apposed to judging,) whether or not to further engage in a situation or the activities of specific individuals. Secondly, it also provides a reminder to be responsible for our own personal space, to demonstrate harmony and peace and with that, to watch our lives change.

This issue of inner peace and harmony was never as present and potent as when my dear friend Charles came into my life. Charles, in his essential nature, was a peacemaker. He would probably have argued that, torn as he was by his traumatic past and deep unhealed wounds. Sadly, his humility was more indicative of deep unworthiness and patterns of shame he had inherited from a family whose values were stuck somewhere in the dark ages. My friend traveled in circles where there was an abundance of darkness and what I call Old Paradigm energy, yet he was a gift to all who met him. If I'd had one wish for him, it would have been that he could have known how special he was. But that would have gone against the grain of his conditioning: that old school of thought subscribing to the belief one has to give until it hurts, and that to acknowledge oneself is narcissistic.

Charles came into my life in early 1987 through a fan letter he wrote to me. He told me that he had been at his secretary's house one evening. This was a woman he had known for years and someone with whom he was finally entertaining a physical relationship. He claimed she also had romantic overtures towards him. She had rented some adult videos to set the tone for their evening together, but as destiny would have it, I was the video hostess on the first tape they watched. I spoke directly into the camera introducing various erotic scenarios and it was, as he later told me, "As if you were speaking directly to me. I knew that I had known you before."

Charles tracked me down through my post office box and immediately penned his first communication to me. This first letter, dated October 1986, remained in a stack of fan mail awaiting my response for an uncharacteristically long time, before I got around to answering it. This was unusual for me since I considered that area to be a special part of my life. I saw it as a sort of ministry, an opportunity to focus a little Light into the life of each person communicating with me.

Many men I received letters from at that time were incarcerated. Regardless of what actions had placed them behind bars, I felt that they were just as deserving of my attention. I was not their judge yet, aware as I am as to subtle forms of energy, I applied myself to the task of corresponding with this particular group of individuals with sensitivity and caution. My protocol in these instances was to light a candle, to offer up a prayer for guidance in choosing my words carefully and consciously, and to ask for protection. Many of these correspondents shared honestly about their errors, others mentioned nothing of them, but each was greatly appreciative of interaction from the outside world that I was glad to provide.

It had been a busy time. I had quit my job as public relations director but I was still involved in extensive public work, lecturing and appearing on TV talk shows, as well as pursuing ways to open new doors professionally. I was also in the final stages of an intimate relationship, one that had been extremely challenging and confrontational.

Dealing with the dynamics of being in a relationship which consistently tempted me to fall back into old martyr patterns of over-giving was not only exhausting, it was deeply painful. The final straw was an emotionally charged, hurtful and dramatic evening where my partner had promised he would set all business transactions aside so we might finally enjoy a night out together, a rare thing. Apparently this was not to be as, once again his business overshadowed our relationship and I found myself sitting in the back of a female associate's car en route to a concert where it became increasingly obvious he had invited numerous family members in addition to business contacts.

I was stunned and felt caught between the proverbial rock and a hard place – should I get up and leave and find my own way home, or put on a happy face and stick it out? I knew that any attempt to confront him on his actions would be met with stony silence and I didn't want to cause a scene. I felt deeply hurt and betrayed and so I silently suffered and kept my emotions hidden.

Later that night at his home, still devastated by my experiences of the evening, I became desperately ill. My boyfriend, asleep in his bed, was oblivious to my condition. My body heaved with despair and knocked the life out of me. I found myself on all fours on the floor not knowing if I was going to live or die. Then Spirit intervened and in a moment of total helplessness and weakness lifted me out of my body to witness myself in my pathetic state. That moment of being "outside of myself looking down" was shocking to say the least.

It was a harsh lesson. The adage of "healer, heal thyself" never rang more true. I knew that from that point on I had to focus on my own healing, I had to get to the bottom of my deepest pain and what stood between me and fully standing in my most authentic power. No more putting myself on hold, that became my challenge. The following morning I got up and ended the relationship.

My inner growth took a steep upturn about this time as if I was being readied for the work ahead. I could feel different synapses of my brain being sparked, attuning me to realities and awareness within the depths of my own consciousness, in preparation for my future mission.

Charles therefore did not receive a response from me until February 1987, at which point I sent him a standard brief letter of thanks, my most recent newsletter and a list of available photographs for purchase. He promptly ordered a picture, a photo-still from my last film,

"Careful, He May be Watching," where I played a character called "Amazon Annie," and he requested another, a glamour head and shoulders shot from the newsletter I had enclosed.

CHAPTER TWELVE: CHANNELING

On the day of that particular communication, I had been in deep contemplation about what I was going to do with the rest of my life. Would I be able to make a living as a counselor? Even if I could, it would take me a while to build up clientele. As I sat down to answer my fan mail, the question as to whether the logical thing for me would be to seek a manager or agent and pursue public speaking on the lecture circuit, was still very much on my mind.

I turned over the first letter on the pile of fan mail, revealing another correspondence from Charles. This time I clearly noticed his business logo that included the word "management." The word practically jumped from the page and hit me in my third eye. It stunned me for a moment as I realized the synchronicity of what had just happened. This was without doubt a message from my Higher Self.

As it turned out, Charles' expertise was in money management, but he claimed he had contacts in Hollywood, and kindly offered to make some calls on my behalf. From that point on, our communications were frequent and, before too long, we were speaking on the phone. In November of the same year, we finally met in person during a layover in Los Angeles. Charles was en route to the South Korea where, he told me, he supported orphans. I immediately sensed the deep karma that had brought us back together in this lifetime as I recognized him as the Pharaoh from what, by that time, I knew to be my most significant Egyptian lifetime! Over the years, the parallels I have discovered of that lifetime to current time and space are startling. And even though, in the end, my friend would remain somewhat of an enigma to those of us who became his California family, I deeply trusted there was a grand plan manifesting.

It was clear from the day we met that even though our two worlds were dramatically different, Charles and I would share much. The bigger picture spanned dimensions I couldn't even imagine. It was not to be a romantic liaison, I knew that right away, but I was to be a friend and an ally in the very deepest, most spiritual sense. It was extremely important for me to maintain objectivity and to constantly confer with my guides, looking only to the higher purpose, in terms of what I would share with him. In that way I could support him in the most loving and intelligent way I knew. Humor would play a large part in our communications—God knows he needed that.

Charles was an avid letter writer and, even though there were always hints of feeling his love for me was unrequited, he shared about his travels and exploits, and in between, he visited California to restore his faith in humanity. We often visited the Lake Shrine to pray for world leaders and for those individuals who had fallen in bloody conflict in the "hot spots" around the World. Mostly we prayed to calm his inner demons.

Around this time, I began to truly trust my telepathic abilities, in addition to fully grasping the concept of living and working multi-dimensionally. Inspired by what my friends and I understood Charles' work to be, we organized meditation groups to pray, and to focus our love and hope towards the areas on the Planet requiring balance. Additionally, I channeled messages specifically for him.

On Easter Sunday 1990, the following transmission came through -

"Blessed Are the Peacemakers

For they appear in many cloaks:

Each person with whom you meet, with whom you share energies, each person with mutual directive standing in agreement of the greater way at hand, because of the awareness that the things of the past have not worked, are unto themselves and therefore their countries, a peacemaker.

Each person who comes to attention and rises up inside him or herself and acknowledges that their greater conscience must be ignited becomes a peacemaker.

Each person refusing to speak out against his or her fellow man becomes a peacemaker.

All those choosing to lay down arms verbally, mentally, physically and otherwise become peacemakers.

All those choosing to take one step closer towards the true heart level acknowledging the graciousness of God become Peacemakers and...

Each man willing to make peace within himself becomes the greatest of Peacemakers."

This was clearly for and inspired by Charles. I was profoundly moved and deeply pondered peace. What exactly is it, and when and how is it achieved?

I realized that, simply stated, peace is a state of harmony. Peace occurs when an individual has reached a resolve within him or herself, or when two different sides or factions reach a mutual resolve. But what comes first, the chicken or the egg? Must the individuals involved find peace within themselves before they can initiate it? It seemed to me that if that was the case, we were in deep doo-doo. At any given point in time there are but a handful of world leaders who could even integrate such a reality.

As I pondered the state of our World and the task of creating harmony globally, it seemed too monumental to imagine. The depth of healing needed to bring about not only peace, but beyond that, the levels of responsibility the Planet was crying out for, seemed to me too enormous for words. "Blessed are the Peacemakers" ignited my personal passion and I wanted to jump to the task immediately. I handed out copies of the document to all my friends and allies. In an instant my own commitment to be all that I could be, and to more and more honestly speak about personal responsibility, had reached new depths.

The transmissions continued delivering messages about all kinds of human conditions and collective consciousness; it was like a home study course in spirituality all over again. I was no stranger to many of the ideals and concepts, since many had been covered in the lessons I had received from my Spiritual Teacher several years earlier. Now, we were being told, we had arrived and, it was time, not just to talk about compassion, acceptance, forgiveness and unconditional love, but to live it!

Be the peacemakers!

WE had to set the precedence, WE were the Spiritual Storm-troopers, and WE were the ones who had chosen to be fore-runners and trendsetters. Those of us who were willing to step into the new paradigm would now know what true responsibility was all about. Indeed it had now been two decades or so that we had been anticipating profound changes in our lives and in the way we do things. But it had always been projected,

"...down the road...future times...times to come."

Now it applied to the present and, for many of us, that was an amazing realization. We had heard so many times about how different life would be and how we would be asked to apply our true spiritual conscience in a way that would be a stretch even for us.

"Be bold!"

The transmissions of late had urged us to speak our truth more boldly than ever, not in a way that was controlling or abrasive, but full of conviction and responsibility to the task at hand. The Harmonic Convergence had already begun to see a fulfillment of the ancient Mayan prophesy of a new age. Thousands had responded spontaneously around the world in recognition of the fact that they were here on Earth to play a significant part in a huge movement of planetary transformation. We had collectively recognized that we were Star Children, that our origins were from elsewhere, and that the task was truly now at hand. From here on we had to move expediently, and the challenges that lay ahead would be beyond anything any of us could imagine.

CHANNELING PART TWO:

In 1991 Johnine, my long-time roommate, decided to buy a house. Finally, the day I had waited for, for so long, had arrived.

CHAPTER TWELVE: CHANNELING

Evidently we had sufficiently completed our karma, and were free to move on. I began to visualize and program for my new residence with great specification. It had to be special; a temple for my work. In a meditation I saw an image of a place with skylights and interesting angles and I felt that it was relatively close to where I had been living.

A few months earlier, on one of her California business trips, a friend from the East Coast had introduced me to her business partner, a young South African. Shortly after, David invited me to supper at his house, a charming tri-plex he had remodeled. We ate supper on the deck in the lovely little garden adjoining the rear of the house. Over dinner he mentioned how special the upper floor apartment was, although it wasn't possible to see it since it was occupied. Within the next few weeks, I attended several meditation groups David held in his lovely home, but the gatherings stopped when he went out of town on extended business.

About three days after I actively began looking for my new home, I picked up the local paper and scanned the listings of apartments to rent. One of the ads caught my eye. It mentioned the upper floor of a charming tri-plex, and listed several features including skylights. The phone number looked very familiar causing the hair on my arms to stand up. I felt tingly and excited as I realized the phone number was David's. I raced to the phone and called him. Sure enough, the *special* upstairs apartment in the ad was the upper floor of his house. This was synchronicity for sure. I pleaded with David not to show it until I had looked it over, and promised to drive right over. Within the hour I was standing in the very space I had seen in my meditation. I was moved to tears and, despite the fact it was a little more costly than was in my budget, I knew I was supposed to be there.

Days later I moved into my new residence which, I would later discover, was situated on a very special piece of land. I had landed in a vortex of energy waiting to be activated only I didn't know it consciously. In his own way David had recognized it. We spoke about creating a center for conscious awareness but neither of us knew just how or what that would be. But from that point on, I moved into a dramatically different phase of my channeling career, through which I discovered Knodessi, the most significant past life aspect of myself. More accurately, I should say, I re-discovered her.

Researching my past lives had been a primary part of my personal healing for a few years prior to moving into the beautiful house. Although I believe it is true that in our present lives, we create a microcosm of all of our past life issues needing to be resolved, for many however, a past-life memory will trigger a deeper level of resolve and release. I take my direction from my guides as to which will work, either for myself or any individual I happen to be counseling. I have never employed past-life recall for novelty's sake, but always as an intricate part of the awakening process.

In my daily life, as my own buttons would be pushed and issues would surface, I would trace them back to childhood or adolescence, to their earliest point of entry in this lifetime. If directed, however, either by my guides or my high self, I would retrace the issue or pattern beyond this life into my past live experience relevant to the issue. More times than not, by reaching back in my history, to the root of the issue, the bigger picture becomes illuminated and proves far more revelatory.

I am only too aware that there are those who would be of the mind set which says,

"It's over, just move on with your life. Stop dwelling on the past."

This somewhat linear concept may work for some, yet for many others it is easier said than done. It is my contention, that if you don't go to the root of an issue to heal it, the patterns associated with the particular scar will surface again and again. When the deepest root of an issue is recognized, the healing can be permanent. Personally,

I have always chosen to examine and resolve painful emotions which surface, rather than brush over them. And even when these waves of energy seem to come out of nowhere, there is always a trigger mechanism. Since I am not one to use artificial numbing devices — I don't drink, smoke or otherwise seek escape — I plunge the depths of my inner consciousness to identify the origins of my scars. I want to discover what the real lesson was, and is, and process it through. I work with my inner cast of characters on their specific areas of discomfort, past or present, put the pieces together, and at the point of absolute clarity, we embrace the higher purpose of our collective experiences, to finally arrive at a point of peace and harmony.

Over the years since I began channeling, I became increasingly aware of several lifetimes I had lived in the Middle East. Time and again a particular sensation swept over me, drawing me into deep grief. My own feelings of helplessness and impotency would be further exacerbated by current world conditions and events. It seemed to me that our leaders were still ignoring the major issues really needing to be addressed. My innate wisdom told me that the potency of my love and my personal efforts was enough, yet within me I still felt an overwhelmingly deep despair.

I searched relentlessly for the origin of this overpowering energy and was repeatedly led back to a particular Egyptian life in which my name was Knodessi. Slowly, as the pieces came together, the facts about my current lifetime made more and more sense. I came to recognize that most of the significant people in my life were also there, almost six thousand years ago. They remembered too. Judith Diana, my friend from our pilgrimage to the sacred stone sites remembered. In fact, she was the first person with whom I initially had explored the lifetime. At the time she was personally writing a book, an esoteric adventure story of the pyramids and Egypt. Researching her own history was relevant to her project and so we took many forays into our ancient past together. We discovered that we were tragic brother and sister lovers, and our history had bled-through most potently into our current lifetime.

Not the least significant of my family of friends who had a profound recall of this lifetime was Aaron. It was his first human incarnation and one in which he made an indelible impression on all those he encountered. In fact, he was the powerful and feared high priest Fahe, under whose guidance I learned the powerful tools for my destiny as High Priestess. In piecing together the story of events occurring back then, the dynamic of our present relationship became clear. As my beloved friend, teacher and co-adventurer in things metaphysical and spiritual, I would nevertheless need to retreat from our friendship every once in a while. Observers might have said there was a subtle personality conflict but that would not accurately describe the particular dynamic from which I recoiled. It was a proverbial gray area, thus I felt he was at the core of whatever had transpired in Egypt.

In August of 1994, we began to dig deeper into the story of what exactly had happened in ancient Egypt and its relevance to the present. Two female friends and I had already discovered that we were sisters in that life. Between the three of us, we began to piece the story together and, at the same time to heal our individual scars related to our experiences those many centuries ago. We tested in the way we discover most facts, by accessing higher guidance through the use of a pendulum or by muscle testing. It seemed that a curse of sorts had been placed over me, yet the details remained fuzzy and would not be clarified until later, but at least the story was beginning to take form.

Then on August 17th (Pleiadians have a strong association with the number 17 and I have identified The Pleiades as being my planet of origin), wanting so desperately to get to the bottom of the issue and to clear the oppressive feelings haunting me, I decided to take a different tactic. I turned to a technique I often recommend for the purpose of releasing negativity and began letter writing to Aaron, expressing everything I felt. It was not intended as a document I would give or mail to him, it was simply for the purpose of my personal release. I didn't know then, but it became the first of a series of letters which would assist me to clear the past, and finally reveal the truth of my circumstances, then and now. The guidance however, was not to write the letter to Aaron, rather to his past alter ego, the High Priest Fahe. That was most interesting.

I took great pains to prepare thoroughly for the process, and waited until I felt connected to my higher self to set my intention strong and purely into creating a time bridge, a link-up to my past life. As this energy came through, I wrote not just as myself but also with an alliance to my past life self.

"To you Fahe, who are Aaron in this life,

You, who were the high and most feared priest. I am Knodessi and I address you from the distant past through my lady Kay in the twentieth century, for I must finally end what I have always felt was a curse which you placed upon me, lo those many centuries past. This curse you placed over us you did so with the greatest of remorse-of the truth that you would quell and submerge. You did so with great power and control over those of us bearing the ancient knowledge, those sworn to uphold the wisdom and power of the great Mother Goddess, bringer and bearer of life. We of that ancient priestess-hood presided over and held in place the love and compassion of the Great Mother spirit throughout those most sacred and mystical dynasties.

Yet we knew that it was time to surrender our power and to relinquish our dominance in the temples and sacred sanctuaries to the new order. We grieved for what we knew we must sacrifice. I, as High Priestess, felt pain beyond words as well you know for you were privy to certain documents I scribed in which I suggested a compromise of priest and priestess serving their God, side by side in the temples.

But it was not to be, and your wrathful God proclaimed those of us women in the higher ranks of the spiritual order to be inferior--and all of womankind for that matter, such was the threat you felt from our ways of love and compassion. You pledged dominion over the feminine principle by establishing laws and doctrine designed to enslave the Human Spirit and suppress all passion. You knew of the truth of all these things and still you strived to take control. And when my dear sister, Priestess Achehehiti, out of her divine passion, attempted to halt the process already underway to empty and sack the temples, you became enraged and applied such force of will as to place upon me this curse, which has been with me over so many of my lifetimes.

But I say now — this curse now stops, ceases to have any and all effect. I remove it from my being, from my life blood, for it is my devine destiny and desire to resurrect that power which I held then in that lifetime to assist all mankind in reclaiming their power at this most crucial time in human evolution.

You have, in this our current lifetime, been our special friend and have assisted us in great ways--you have acknowledged us as sister and friend, yet a resonance which I now understand came between us, a most willful energy which would have once again dominated and had me believe that I was the stubborn one. But I have seen so often your unwillingness to end your own denial and heal - I saw your proud attachment to old principles.

With this letter we will clear the past- the curse which has been like a vice on our back, and which has not allowed us to consistently hold our power intact. I now step firmly into my power and welcome forward my new life's exciting abundant dreams and adventures! I forgive myself for having allowed this energy to have such power over me, and I forgive you for having placed the curse upon me in that lifetime."

In retrospect, I admit to being very surprised at the passion I expressed in the letter. After I reread the document, I felt self-conscious that it seemed so accusatory but I reminded myself that this was simply a technique for clearing old emotions and hurts. My sentiments had risen out of a very deep place, where all of my past memories are stored. To judge or edit what I had written would have been to disrupt or even void the process.

Within a short time after I wrote the letter to Fahe, yet more of the total picture of what happened in that lifetime began to be revealed. In clearing one layer of pain, another surfaced with a startling discovery that I had taken my own life. Surprisingly I discovered that my suicide had not been at the time of the sacking of the temples, but much later after raising two children, both of whom were in my current life's circle of friends.

I then indulged in another session. This time, unlike the first, it was not a combined effort of Knodessi and me; rather she came fully present in me. I provided a channel through which she could finally and fully express the emotions and sentiments she had taken with her into the afterlife, almost six thousand years earlier. As her energy coursed through me, my ego self became shocked as it became evident that in fact Knodessi was writing a suicide letter to the Goddess:

"To the one Divine, omnipotent lover of all and serene highness, Mother God,

This is Knodessi and this is my last discourse with you in this lifetime. Beloved Mother, I beg your forgiveness for what I am about to do. It remains difficult to believe that I would arrive at this place in this life I have known as glorious. I am tired and weak, my spirit broken by what has come to pass and for the things which I have witnessed--my power has been stripped away, and I cannot live with the shame I have come to feel. My humanity has overcome me.

Although after the take-over in the temples, I found myself with a husband who has, for the most part, provided for me, and I have borne two beautiful children, my chest heaves and my heart has become even heavier wondering what the future holds for them. What lies will they be told, and what chains will ultimately bind them to lives of mediocrity and futility, I suffer to think?

As a mother I have entered the tombs of despair countless times, disallowed as I have been to share with my children the joys of your grace and wisdom. I have been forced to teach them the ways of the new powers, of the new religion whose male God energy and truth seems devoid of compassion and harmony, and it has broken my heart repeatedly to contribute to such falsehood. What may my children believe of me when they are grown and old enough to think for themselves? I pray that they will see the willful, contriving ways of those in power, and know that, were it not for the dangers of disobedience, I would have taught them how different it was before the men came into our beloved temples.

I pray that legend survives to report to them and others of the times when you, great Mother, reigned supreme and we priestesses, your loyal representatives, taught the ways of freedom and non-reprimand, of praise for the sensual essence in all things, and of your Spirit of infinite passion and compassion for all.

My thoughts turn for a moment to those sisters of my beloved temple. How gracefully they accepted the changes and bravely left our sanctuary, the only home and most brilliant life they had known. How my heart ached for them as I witnessed their pain and fear, and for many, the terror, of being subjected to lives of emotional slavery with the men they would ultimately be forced to serve. For every one in whose eyes I saw pain and fear, a knife pierced my heart and my shame deepened.

Only a few of my beloved sisters have found some sustenance in their new duties and motherhood. I have been grateful for that. My fellow priestesses bore me no malice, for they were privy to my efforts to halt or delay the changes that we all knew were forthcoming. They knew that I tried to negotiate a co-operative alliance in the temples with the incoming priests. But it was in vain. They bore witness as I wrestled with a proposal to mix blood in marriage with our Pharaoh. Were it not for the fact that this proposal was designed by the priests themselves to usurp and abuse my power, you know that I might have considered this. But my sisters realized, as did I, that it might have been a worse fate from what eventually came to pass. At least in the outside world there might be a faint hope for us to continue our rituals and offerings to you, if only in secret. Within the confines of the Pharaoh's palace we would have lived under such scrutiny.

The love of these priestesses for me has been a mainstay, a continuous source of strength for me in these times. I pray for them and ask you to protect each and every one of them. I suffer continuously for their shame and despondency.

In moments of supreme reverence to you, when I have taken the sacrament and my spirit has soared high to find one-oneness with you oh Mother, and my Sight has been cleared to see what is to come, I have seen what I can only understand and decipher to be the future. You have shown me sights which depict another time, a new millennia and beyond, and the unimaginable events which are to succeed us here in our beloved Egypt. It has moved me to understand even more deeply the power that we have held, and the work that was your bidding, to establish precedence for future civilizations that would inspire and empower by its very existence, if only depicted in the ancient carvings, the hieroglyphics upon the walls of our temples. I, nay we, have understood that what we represented and taught, the unlimited power of the super consciousness which we brought into human-kind, would be as a lantern to light the way back to your power and wisdom a millennia or so in the future.

Now, beloved Mother, I prepare to end this existence, aided by my beloved Sister Accihehiti, who stood and defended me in the temple, whose love at one time for you must certainly have equaled mine. Please forgive her for her cursing--she is such a passionate one, and is deeply angered at her helplessness. In times like these we fall victim to our own humanity--and we strike out in resistance and fear. Forgive us that--for we find it close to impossible to forgive ourselves. Such is my own plight.

I come to you once more to pour forth my love, to ask your forgiveness for what I am about to do, for that work which I fear will be left undone because I choose to leave. I have lost faith and cannot seem to resolve this; I am fighting what I cannot fully understand. I am not trusting in your wisdom and power. I, of course, cannot see how these changes will affect the course of history from this point on. My pain is so deep and my shame overwhelms me that I could not prevent the pain of so many others.

There is one other thing I must mention; I have glimpsed in my dreams these last few nights a picture of a future time where the earth struggles to survive because of the inhumanity of man to man and to his world. There are images that are too strange for me to identify, but the circumstances prevailing are so very similar to those that have predominated in this life, here in Egypt. In this vision, I sensed an impending doom, yet I also saw a large family of souls who were willing to sacrifice their selfish wants and egos to hold the power frequency and work to stabilize the earth, thereby offering an alternative vision, that of reform and abundance for all.

In these dreams I have seen the face of a beautiful woman who sits in pain. Not only is she overwhelmed by what she sees before her and of the tasks she has undertaken, but also a deep pain that she cannot identify plagues her. Her lot seems not unlike my own, for she lives in a time when the tides are once again turning, and she must assist humanity to turn back to you Goddess, to re-attune their consciousness and embrace their power. She struggles also with her memories of her past lives which haunt her, and which weigh heavily in her heart. She is I, is she not Oh Blessed Mother, for her pain echoes my own. I hear her calling out to you for assistance, to release the bindings and suffering.

Indeed, in one of my dreams, she spoke to me by name saying, "Oh Knodessi, we are one, are we not? I know of my lifetime as you and, still to this day, I feel your pain for all that you endured, for which in a subtle way I continue to punish myself. This is a most amazing time on earth, as we prepare for a new millennia past which none have prophesied, and as those of us who promised long ago to be here, now, work most diligently to convert the hopelessness and futility into hope and passion for a new world without shame and fear, I must also heal my own past and step fully into my power. It is my destiny. Yet I cannot assimilate, as you could not so long ago in Egypt, parts of my own "fate".

My future self continued, "Oh, I have been told many times by teachers and mentors along the way that I have long since atoned for any previous wrong doings, and that one of my great challenges is to now unconditionally receive God's blessings, to receive what I have given to so many for so long. I have learned and I have healed; yet what remains for me yet to heal in this time is my shame. To do this I have remembered my lifetime as you, so that I may understand the lines of destiny more clearly and restore my worthiness.

My future Self went on to recount many of her life's adventures, of the powerful men she has encountered and served, and of another service she has rendered for many hundreds of thousands of men primarily to witness- an art form which projected images far larger than life size onto a plain wall face for those choosing to witness might see, either publicly or in their own houses. In this art form she enacted scenes of love and sex to help those watching to reinstate and accept their own sensuality, to release their sexual shame. She shared speeches about her experiences in front of many audiences in the schools of the day. She told me also that she would self-scribe her life story that others might read her words and perhaps be lifted and inspired by them. Oh Goddess Mother, she is I in the far future--we are one-- and she came to me in my dreams so that I could ask you one more thing before I leave this plane now. She needs your help. Please help her and provide what she needs so that she can move into her fullest expression. She deserves so much happiness, a life of grace and comfort. Please grant her that.

How different that future time seems. I know that it is my future Self's task to re-introduce the concept and truth of the Your divine energy, unlike now when it seems that there is no hope for the survival of Goddess worship as the black cloud descends and the wrathful male God of the priests casts its judgment on all who do not fall before him. What kind of God would do that, and yet the people fall to their knees in terror as they relinquish their truth and power. Oh, my heart aches and wants to cry out even now. It is too late but, as I prepare to leave this life, I am now strangely re-assured in a small part of my being, that these things will once again reverse and I will be there again to play my part. For now, please guide me gently into joyful communion with you on the high planes and forgive me once again for opting out of my life, here and now.

Dearest Mother, please take care of all my loved ones and my children. I am sorry to cause them grief. Let them know as only you can, that I have loved them so deeply, but that my heart could no longer bear the pain of witnessing the denouncement of you, and that my eyes could no longer bear to see the suffering.

I am your devoted servant Knodessi.

Thus began the major leg of my adventure back in time to ancient Egypt, to unravel the mystery of that lifetime and why it was so significant to my current life's mission. From time to time, my sisters from that life, Rebel, Jean and I, uncovered more details about our collective experiences. And although occasionally a fact would surface that seemed to contradict others we had uncovered, rather than judging or attempting to research any existing historic information, I decided to simply let the story unravel in its own way. What was important to me was that I arrived at the information and truth about my own life issues and experience.

Beyond conclusively healing my relationship with my parents, I worked consistently to bring closure to all of my past relationships, intimate or otherwise. I also realized that any new people in my life were, for the most part, even more significant than in the past. Like characters molding a story in a script, they inevitably provided more clues about the role I played in my former lifetime (and other lifetimes.) It was as if the primary process being facilitated by all those in my life was to guide me back to my uncompromising power for the work lying ahead.

The next letter came through on December 2, 1994. This time it was from Knodessi to me--again an arc of energy bridging the millennia and offering support in a most fascinating way.

At the time I was ensconced in a struggle with some of the finer aspects of absolutely living by the rules and precepts I taught. I heard author Gary Zukov (Seat Of The Soul) admit to a fear he'd had to confront, that he had reached a degree of celebrity because of his exposure on the Oprah show, and therefore was faced with the question of whether he was living the standards and precepts he espoused. His days of anonymity had ended and he could no longer walk down the street without being recognized. I fully empathized with his concern and have similar thoughts every day. Am I practicing what I preach? The adage of "we teach best what we most need to learn," is foremost in my consciousness much of the time, along with the knowledge that when we have gleaned all we can from a given situation or challenge, we may move on. But the line between lovingly allowing ourselves our human foibles and staying on the straight and narrow becomes finer every day.

Knodessi's words gave me strength and courage:

I am KNODESSI, Keeper of the Truth, of the Temple of Tara and Mother Guiding Sensate

To you who am I of the future, of a time that I cannot fully comprehend, I reach forward in the Mother embrace to warn and to nurture you. You are called upon to exert your talents and truth with those who I fear cannot fully grasp the truth of what you would hold up to them--that sacred spirit and flame of the Goddess Herself. You exemplify that grace and love with a passion so loyal and beholden to the sacred texts, and your very presence holds a beacon to the people still trapped in their struggles with integrity, manipulation and materialism.

Yet your willingness prevails and I am moved to my core. Your courage I recognize so clearly. Your dedication to your purpose remains strong and clear, even as the tides of change rip and tear at your human consciousness at large, much as now, here in our beloved Egypt.

Ah, dear one, be cautious, be alert, your presence also threatens so many, as does mine, and there are those who would smite you, sneer and spit upon you, fearing that which you represent--truth, love and God consciousness.

I cannot of course tell you what to do, yet my spirit would reach from the annals of your own history to place a guiding hand upon your shoulder and whisper in your ear for you to move forward cautiously.

Now, as I extend forward across the ages, I know that I must release my own chains of despair to awaken in you the power that you so desperately desire. It is your destiny to fully stand in the power of the great and majestic love of the Mother which extends throughout the Universe, sending waves of electro-magnetic healing frequency, and which aligns with others likewise driven by the ancient calling to rise and once again hold the power, that love, so that the Earth herself may heal and survive.

And so, I say again from our soul, my blessings and my love to you dear Kay of my future. Rise and stand tall in your most worthy self. Receive, dearest one, receive now instantly the nurturance, the endowments of your time and lifestyle. Let your work now truly be of service to you, and render to you immediately all your needs and wants. Now is the time, your time is now, I know that in my heart. I can now, through the inspiration of all you represent, forgive myself for all of my choices--all those things which I had thought sinful, for which I would have damned myself for an eternity. I see now the foolishness of my resistance, and I know that to release this vice-like energy around my soul is to give you life!

I forgive myself therefore all! We align now, you and I.

I am Knodessi, Keeper of the Truth, and I am one with you.

To say that this letter warmed the cockles of my soul is an understatement. It felt like a blanket of love and compassion directly from God/Goddess him/herself, which enveloped me in comfort and encouragement, strength and reassurance.

The following year was one of truly practicing and asserting my truth in every way. The most profound thing that can be said about what I experienced is the liberation I felt, even though it still remained a challenge to stand in my convictions without closing my heart in any way and without inflicting my will on anyone. It was clear that my telepathic abilities were being stepped up and much of the time my body didn't feel like my own. It was no wonder that I felt somewhat sequestered. The exception was when Charles would make a brief visit at which time I shifted into high gear. He was recovering from a serious illness and some very intense life circumstances (a whole other book unto itself) and my energies were needed.

It was also during this time period that I began to have quite startling telepathic dreamtime experiences. Sometimes these adventures involved visits with world-class dignitaries. Later, in real time, I verified facts and information from my nighttime travels I could not otherwise have known. It was clear I was astral traveling, and that Spirit was working through me even in the wee hours.

What lay beyond this point I couldn't possibly have known; suffice it say that Knodessi's energy was coming through loud and clear, fusing with my own in wonderful synergy. Was this my manifest destiny, to reanimate her gifts and talents in my own present reality? I felt immensely grateful for the chance to know, to feel and embrace her.

I was moved to express my love and sentiments to her in one final letter:

From Kay to Knodessi – in Memorium

September 11, 1995

To my dearest Knodessi, that far-distant-past essence of myself whom I have come to understand and revere so deeply,

What a journey I have taken to meet you once again, a journey I realize now began as I concluded my career as an actress. I knew that it was time to enter more deeply into my own healing and, at the same time, into semi-seclusion. Yet simultaneously, I knew that it was a time to express your essence in me, and with that, to be able to more fully assist others in their unfoldment. In searching within myself to be with you, and to understand all that you are and have represented in me, my compassion not only for myself but also for all of my fellow humans has deepened. In remembering the challenges and tragedies of your time, six thousand years ago, the challenges in our twentieth century make sense, and I can more clearly see the purpose for being here now.

Dearest and most divine Mother--for that's what you were called in that lifetime, it is most significant that I have constantly represented the mother figure to so many, although I have not physically borne any children. Finally in 1980, the most significant role of my career, that of an incestuous mother, epitomized the embodiment of that collective sexual shame which permeates our society and for which I so passionately feel.

For all I have learned through you, with you, I know that we must now together release our futility and fear which has predominated as the Goddess energy re-emerges, and as the forces of the opposition rise up as if to defy the love which She represents. Our energies must finally fuse in one giant leap toward our destiny, the next leg of our journey, and the work we have chosen.

There must finally exist cohesion of that male and female spirit, to ground the harmony and allow us to gracefully move into the twenty-first century and embrace the new paradigm. I have taught these principles for years, and yet at my core, in that place where you resided, I have not allowed that harmony to exist in me.

In deeply remembering you and all those present in your time, many of whom of course are with me today, I have been able to forgive not only my own misnomers but assist the collective unconsciousness that perpetuated the myth that we had failed the Goddess. Now that I know it is not so and that the Prime Creator-of-all had designed the times that way for a reason, my commitment to my purpose has taken on new meaning.

So you see beloved, the seeds you planted back then did not fall on fallow ground, they have been germinating all these centuries. You did fail the Goddess as you had thought. It was all God's will. It was evolution.

And now the tides turn once again and I am ready to take my next step.

I embrace all that I am, and in that, the Father/Mother God essence. You, beloved Knodessi in me, may finally rest,

You shine through me in all that I do and all that I am. Kay

This was the last of the letters I once published as "The Knodessi Trilogy." Through these communications I had been able to stabilize my truth and power, and I felt ready to move on with whatever lay ahead with a new found inner harmony. Knodessi's essence now lived in me like a golden reservoir that I could tap into whenever I needed it. In her I had found the keys I needed to feel greater compassion for myself, as well as gaining a deeper understanding and empathy for the mission upon which I had embarked.

In late 1996 Aaron and I were sitting in my living room embarking upon one of our sessions of cosmic exploration in our usual style. I began to share with him about the Egyptian lifetime and how my writing process had helped me to release some of the pain and residual emotion from that incarnation. I admitted I didn't exactly know what had happened, although the predominant feeling I remembered above all the others had felt like a curse, and that I believed that he as high priest had somehow inflicted it upon me.

My friend listened carefully and then with great conviction offered the following,

"I did not curse you. I had to take the codes away from you. You were too vulnerable as a woman. The dark forces were close. There were men who were ready to usurp your power and use the codes for their own devious purposes, and they did not have the highest good of all in mind. I couldn't let that happen. My mission was to protect the codes at all cost, and finally to bury them, because of what was happening. That was the soul reason I incarnated. Your shield had already been weakened once when you were offered marriage to the Pharaoh. At that point you lowered your guard as you considered indulging in the games of will and ego. You had allowed a chink in your proverbial spiritual armor. I had no choice but to do what I did to protect you."

I was stunned. In a moment my friend had handed me the missing piece—the proverbial other side to the story. In my selective memory all that was clear to me was the pain of having been 'powered-down,' of my consciousness being stripped away. As Aaron shared these words with me, his eyes revealed much about his own pain at having been compelled to do what he did. He had been the one to train me and mold me into high priestess. Naturally the compulsion to reverse his actions would have also challenged him. But his ego persona then had not shown his true emotions; instead he had maintained a harsh and profoundly intimidating demeanor. He continued, and I felt his deep and unfaltering dedication to his mission, the same commitment I always witnessed in him during his life here, now.

"Time and time again, there were individuals who defiantly approached me with intent to access and abuse the codes. I repeatedly warned them, "don't cross that line," but they ignored my words, and they just keeled over and died, as if from a heart attack. I didn't want to kill them but they threatened the codes!"

As he told the story, I felt a compassion for his situation I hadn't been able to feel all those centuries ago. He had been forced, compelled by circumstance to remove the codes from me, to extract the wisdom from my consciousness with a kind of psychic surgery that left me feeling empty and a prisoner in my human shell. I was not used to feeling like a normal mortal person; my life-style as a priestess was far from three-dimensional. For a long time after his action I had felt disoriented, as I adapted to a way of life as alien to me as it was mundane. My intense grief remained with me until my death, and had bled through into many of my succeeding incarnations, finally culminating in the despair I felt in present times.

"But the seeds were sewn," I was told in numerous transmissions with the Great White Brotherhood, *"You did your work."*

To understand what that work was, The White Brotherhood assisted me in understanding the concept of the planetary ley lines, the energy grid systems of the Earth and Universe and how my mission, much like today, was simply to work energetically to prepare the Planet for the vibrational changes on the horizon. Similarly in Egypt, by the time we priestesses were forced from our temples, the work had been accomplished. But we were mortal and passionate and, like most humans, we unwittingly fell into the traps of attachment. We knew that the Earth was in for a period of devolution and, in the process, all we had physically built would be destroyed. We had known this, but once the changes began to actually manifest, our human resistance clicked into gear. We struggled and fought back. We felt defeated and many entered into deep futility. And these energies found their way deep into the recesses of our cellular memory.

Now, these eons later, many have come to continue the journey, to move into full empowerment and the fulfillment of a divine and profound destiny. In order for that destiny to manifest, deep multi-tiered healing is required to purify the many human vehicles becoming channels for Universal truth.

Channeling is simply about being an open receptor. It requires being still, listening without judgment or resistance to higher truths and information from beyond our limited third dimension frequencies (the noise of our lives and our environment,) and then delivering any messages that wish to be delivered in a way that is palatable to those participants who are listening. Like adjusting the frequency on a radio for clearer transmission, we may adjust our own antennae, our receptors, to tune in to other frequencies to receive a broader bandwidth.

I often ponder the fact of our two strands of DNA. In our most evolved state we have twelve strands! Science, in alignment with spiritual consciousness is taking us into realms where we may begin to glimpse what kind of human being with three strands would look like. Movies continue to explore this concept with countless stories of uber-beings who have such challenges fitting in "down here." It is rumored that the creator of "Star Trek" Gene Rodenberry, sat in on channeling sessions where undoubtedly many ideas were delivered to him for his amazing show. I believe that many writers and creators receive their information in this manner, where, by opening up their creativity they also become channelers, providing the general public the opportunity to allow their imagination to run wild and to dream of a broader reality.

Chapter Thirteen: Knodessi's Story: The Codes

Knodessi felt a pain in her diaphragm; a subtle terror at what she realized had happened. At the same time, her innate wisdom told her this was an omen, for the Goddess used whatever means to summon her priestesses and to awaken them to their power. Despite her young age of fifteen years, she was in line for the position of High Priestess. This was her destiny, yet a significant part of her was still at odds with the reality and yearned to bury itself in adolescence.

It was true, she had lost the artifact entrusted to her by her Mother to deliver to the High Priest Fehe, a man with whose destiny hers was intricately interwoven. To have misplaced an object of such high spiritual resonance was unthinkable. Her disbelief in the fact that, if only for a moment she had lost consciousness and allowed the object to simply disappear, was equaled only by her awe of the great responsibility to which she was heir. This indeed was a test of the deepest magnitude.

Knodessi felt paralyzed. What was she to do? Together with her Sisters, the passionate Achiheheti and stoic little Frahiti, she had searched, frantically combing every inch of every chamber, and under every rock on the temple grounds. But their combined efforts had been in vain.

Even as she came to terms with the fact that the sacred object was in fact nowhere to be found, the fledgling priestess felt invisible eyes watching her, and she sensed that there was much more to this event than was apparent.

To the unsuspecting eye, the artifact in question was a mere stone with delicately inlaid precious gems and hieroglyphic etchings that fit into the palm of an average woman's hand. It had the appearance of a personal talisman, yet in fact it was a tool of great ritualistic significance and high alchemy which Knodessi's mother, the High Priestess Knentos, had charged with a powerful frequency. Such implements played pivotal roles in the seasonal fertility rites she and Fehe together performed to bring harmony to the land and its people, and to render the crops abundant. Lengthy preparation went into the staging of the rituals over which Knodessi personally would eventually preside. For that reason, Knentos had marked in her own consciousness the event of delivering the sacred stone as the unofficial commencement of the last and most important stage of her daughter's training, which was to be conducted by the High Priest himself.

The mere mention of the name of Fehe intimidated Knodessi so much her knees trembled. This was to be her first encounter with the notorious Priest whose glance it was rumored could kill anyone who defied him or who overtly threatened the great sacred Codes of which he was the soul guardian. Regardless, Fehe was to be profoundly instrumental in Knodessi's training, for secrets to which only he held the keys were to be revealed to her at the appropriate time. These were the great keys of most powerful alchemy that were only entrusted to specific individuals from the sacred bloodline, and whose innate mystical energies were developed and honed from a very young age. For a short while longer, such chosen ones would have the capacity to access fourth and fifth dimensional reality while living on the earthly plane, to activate the Codes for divine purposes, an honor and profound responsibility to be sure.

But the tides were turning, about that there was no secret.

Knodessi wasn't sure what she feared the most, punishment for her irresponsibility, or the thought of the artifact falling into the hands of some unsuspecting individual who could unwittingly activate the energies of the stone. Horrific ramifications and chaos, not to mention infertility of the land, could result from premature activation of such frequencies. The Goddess' sacred rituals were designed and executed with meticulous timing at astronomically potent times of the year. Both High Priest and Priestess were integral parts of the rites, in body as in spirit, having purified and prepared themselves days ahead of time to receive and emit great frequencies of energy.

CHAPTER THIRTEEN: KNODESSI'S STORY: THE CODES

Awesome and terrifying thoughts passed through Knodessi's mind as she imagined the worst consequences of her careless misdeed.

However, what the young priestess had not taken into consideration was the fact that her Mother, in her infinite wisdom, had anticipated her daughter's trepidation and reluctance to face her inevitable and imminent destiny. As a precautionary measure, she had in fact only programmed the stone artifact with more subtle energies, those that could not be used in any way to the detriment of the land or people. Knentos had devised this test for her daughter to drive home the reality that it was time for her to fully accept her fate, to don her priestess mantle and begin her tutorial with Fehe. Her motherly intuition had foreseen the need for a trial run, as it were. She had felt only a slight reluctance to what was by definition, a devious action, yet her decision was based upon the memory of her own behavior little more than a few years earlier when she herself prepared for the sacred initiations. In fact, Knentos now acted more from a position of deep reverence to her daughter's process; these were the initiations to prepare Knodessi to assume what was indisputably one of the most powerful positions in the land.

Knodessi finally resigned herself to the fact that there was no other choice but to report her misfortune to her Mother. She braced herself and, anticipating some form of punishment, prepared for an audience with Knentos. By the time she stood before the elder High Priestess however, she was fully resigned to accept whatever ruling her Mother proclaimed as fair and just. This event marked a profound turning point for her, and in that, she welcomed some kind of disciplinary action. She knew that it was time to release her resistance and commit herself to her training.

Thirty days of confinement in her chamber was her Mother's decision as punishment. She was to only have contact with certain women designated as handmaidens who would assist her with her toilette and bring her food. There was to be no verbal exchange at all, since this to be a period of complete solitude, deep meditation, and the opportunity to come to terms with the reality of her manifest destiny.

Knodessi felt strangely relieved. In an instant she recognized the perfection of her situation. This would be less of a penalty, rather a perfect opportunity to prepare for the forthcoming experiences when she would be sequestered with the infamous High Priest. In this way she would begin her studies with maturity rather than as an insecure and rebellious adolescent.

During the ensuing month, the young Priestess remained diligent. With renewed passion she applied every tool and technique she had learned since she had been old enough to speak. Alone in her chamber without distraction, her relationship to the Goddess and the deep significance of her future role took root in her heart. She was at peace. Her two younger Sisters were the only diversion from her solitude. Naturally, as siblings are wont to do, they found a way to sneak sweets and gifts to their older Sister. Their actions warmed Knodessi's heart and she adored them for their gestures and even for their brazen willingness to disobey their Mother. What they didn't know was that Knodessi was actually grateful for her incarceration and for the chance to get her thoughts in alignment with her greater destiny.

At the end of thirty days, Knentos sent word that she would arrive to accompany her daughter to the sacred baths for a purification ritual to mark Knodessi's emergence from her seclusion. To the delight of her Mother, Knodessi emerged serene and confident, no longer an adolescent but a mature young woman. As they walked across the compound to the building of the sacred baths, they spoke less as mother and daughter, rather as fellow priestesses, mutually agreeing that the seclusion had been a most perfect period of preparation for the novice priestess. Knentos' intuition had paid off and she was now confident that her daughter was indeed ready for the next stage of her development.

After the bathing ritual, Knentos herself assisted her daughter, dressing her in a simple golden robe she had been saving for that day. She draped the gown on her daughter's blossoming and sensuous form, noting the significant change that had occurred in the short period of seclusion. Knodessi suddenly appeared very much a woman, not the girl who had entered into confinement. Her deep red hair fell in ringlets around her shoulders, offsetting the shimmering threads of the garment and her skin glowed in a way her Mother had never seen until that point. It seemed that the Goddess had surely been breathing her holy breath on her young novice, that she would appear so radiant.

Next, with great ceremony, Knentos produced a box from which she took three gold rings encrusted with emeralds, rubies and other precious gems. These she placed on her daughter's fingers. Around her neck she fastened a gold rope necklace into which was woven more rubies, tourmaline and malachite. On Knodessi's ears she clasped matching filigree gold earrings. The jewels were sacred to the office Knodessi would soon fulfill, to be worn on special occasions and for the rituals she would perform as High Priestess. Finally her Mother arranged her hair, twisting and interweaving garlands and other adornments in a manner befitting a priestess of her caliber.

As the two generations of High Priestesses left the bath chamber with their entourage, a procession formed behind them as the entire residents of the temple compound, abuzz with excitement over the event, drew close to catch a glimpse of Knodessi's transformation. That evening there were rituals and celebration. The following day the plan was laid out and preparations made for Knodessi's special and most intricate training with Fehe to commence.

Over the next six months Knodessi made four trips to study with the High Priest, each session lasting five days and five nights. A young priest named Taenaru would arrive to accompany her on the long trek across the city to the High Priest's enclave. He remained close at hand and at her service during her stay, following which he would escort her back to the women's sector and her beloved temple.

An apartment was provided for Knodessi during her studies, sufficient for her every need. Servants availed themselves of her at all times and every effort was made for her comfort, she was after all royalty personified. Sister Acchi' accompanied her on the first and last excursions for not only was she a formidable warrior presence to any who might have threatened the safety of her distinguished Sister, Mother Knentos wished to make sure all was in order. Acchihehiti's heightened senses rendered her most trustworthy as an assessor of protocol and order. Although she had no access to Knodessi once her training with Fehi began, she monitored all activity within close range of her, and was acutely aware of individuals making any overture to have contact with her Sister. She reported back to their Mother that everything was completely as it should be according to the highest of spiritual standards. In this way Knentos rested, assured that Knodessi was in good hands and well protected.

During the course of her studies Knodessi quickly discovered that Fehe was in fact a very gentle man, divined and dedicated to his core to guard and protect the sacred Codes. Ultimately he would be charged with transmuting them into the higher ethers for the higher good when the great changes came, and the threat of their abuse was too strong for them to remain earthbound. It would take someone with his higher dimensional background to do the job.

His Egyptian life was in fact his first Earth incarnation and he wore his human mantle somewhat reluctantly, a fact which manifested itself as a particularly gruff mannerism and impatient demeanor. The widespread mythical stories of his wrathful and fearful countenance were misguided perceptions. It was true that several persons had been struck dead upon defying him after making overtures towards gaining access to the chambers wherein objects used in the do the work together. Together we scoured our depths to understand why I/we had so obviously given up my/our power and to what end.

I also looked at the issue of why I seemed to become ill when I traveled, my relationship with money and why I still couldn't speak my truth fully, why I held back from expressing honestly. Why didn't I feel safe enough to do that? And why ultimately, did I not feel safe on this Planet?

So many patterns were still deeply embedded in my DNA from eons ago, reactivated by events and relationships early in my present life and now popping up to be healed, once and for all. The realization that despite the decades of self-examination and healing, that I was still carrying **Survivor's Remorse** from my Father, whose ship went down during WWII and who was one of only a dozen survivors, hit me like a tone of bricks. This was brought to my attention during a session of Family Constellations, a brilliant modality designed by German psychotherapist Bert Hellinger, to uncover the true source of our patterns, illness and disconnection, and to heal the ancestral "webbing" that keeps so many of us in its debilitating grips. It had become startlingly obvious that some other subconscious dynamic was still operating within me, not allowing me to receive joy in my life and causing me to have feelings of wanting to give up completely.

Why couldn't I receive the pleasure and the fulfillment I so frequently spoke of with my clients? Yes, I did feel joy when I was in my passion working with others but I couldn't sustain it for too long in my private life.

And to a large degree, this new awareness explained why I, the erstwhile porno star and "sex expert" still did not know how to fully receive from a partner, still felt unable to ask for what I honestly wanted, and still fell into certain rote behavior during sex relationships.

The truth was that for decades sex had been unsatisfying to me because I didn't believe that it was okay for me to receive pleasure. I was just going through the paces. I still hadn't found "the one" I could surrender to and with whom I could feel safe and comfortable. And, as always, I asked "who in me?"

I searched, together with fellow healers who were addressing similar, if not identical issues. Yes, I/we could find events and issues from early childhood to address. And, yes, I/we could even refer back to specific past lives and initiate more healing and balancing. But at the core, I/we knew this was ancient DNA encoding. And it was clear this was a collective undertaking, of those of us who had agreed to be here now, to help evolve this part of the ancient programming of the subjugation of the feminine principle in all of us, men and women alike. We are blessed to have the tools and the wisdom to dissolve these energies, (yes, we have the power to alter our DNA) and to restore our divine inner reservoir of unfaltering love and compassion for self and others.

So, what would it take to totally surrender and allow another person to love me exactly how I wanted to be loved? Ultimately what does it take to create a life full of joy and ease, fulfillment and pleasure?

Answer: a deep and unrelenting *self*-love!

I thought I loved myself – I *do* love myself.

My soul urges me to "Go deeper, ever deeper!"

And my guides remind me, "Your mission is to dwell in joy, for when you do, you light up the world."

And I reply, "I know, I know."

CHAPTER FOURTEEN: FULL CIRCLE

Kay lives and works in the Los Angeles area and is the subject of the documentary entitled *"A Taboo Identity"* with a projected release date in late 2016

There is also a biography in the works with a release date in 2017 Visit *www.kaytaylorparker.com* for information about Kay's counseling work, types of sessions available and to schedule a Skype or in-person session.

Visit *www.kayparker.life* for items of interest, memorabilia and other news.

CPSIA information can be obtained
at www.ICGtesting.com
Printed in the USA
FSHW011726090219
55553FS